The African-Caribbean Worldview and
the Making of Caribbean Society

The African-Caribbean Worldview and the
Making of Caribbean Society

EDITED BY **HORACE LEVY**

University of the West Indies Press
Jamaica • Barbados • Trinidad and Tobago

University of the West Indies Press
7A Gibraltar Hall Road   Mona
Kingston 7   Jamaica
www.uwipress.com

© 2009 by Horace Levy

All rights reserved. Published 2009

13 12 11 10 09   5 4 3 2 1

CATALOGUING IN PUBLICATION DATA

The African-Caribbean worldview and the making of Caribbean society /
edited by Horace Levy.

p. cm.

Includes bibliographical references.
Papers presented at a conference to celebrate the work of Professor Barry Chevannes held at the University of the West Indies, Mona campus, Jamaica, January 19–21, 2006.

ISBN: 978-976-640-210-5

1. Chevannes, Barry. 2. West Indies – Civilization – African influences. 3. Jamaica – Civilization – African influences. 4. West Indies – Religion – African influences.
5. West Indies – Social conditions. 6. Identity (Psychology) – West Indies. 7. Ethnicity – West Indies. I. Chevannes, Barry. II. Levy, Horace.

F2169. A47 2009   972.9

Cover illustration: Being in Becoming (acrylic on paper), by Clinton Hutton.
Courtesy of the artist.

Book and cover design by Robert Harris.
Set in Plantin Light 10/14.5 x 24
Printed in the United States of America.

Contents

Acknowledgements | vii

Introduction
HORACE LEVY | 1

1 Jamaica, the Caribbean, Africa: Some Oppositions and Their Politics
DIANE AUSTIN-BROOS | 10

2 Myal, Revival and Rastafari in the Making of Western Jamaica: Dialogues with Chevannes
JEAN BESSON | 26

3 Colonial Injustice: *The Crown v. the Bedwardites*, 27 April 1921
VERONT M. SATCHELL | 46

4 Education, Race and Respectability in Jamaica, circa the 1938 Labour Rebellion
KHITANYA PETGRAVE | 68

5 No Space for Race? The Bleaching of the Nation in Postcolonial Jamaica
ANNIE PAUL | 94

6 Museography and Places of Remembrance of Slavery in Martinique, or the Gaps in a Memory Difficult to Express
CHRISTINE CHIVALLON | 114

7   "Reflection" from the Margin: Jah Cure and Rastafari Celebrity in Contemporary Jamaica
    JAHLANI NIAAH and SONJAH STANLEY NIAAH | 132

8   If Yuh Iron Good You Is King: Pan in 3-D
    KIM JOHNSON | 151

9   Don Drummond: Just How Good Was He?
    HERBIE MILLER | 170

10 "Blak Up! Blak Up!": Liturgical Compositions of Barry Chevannes
    ANNA KASAFI PERKINS | 187

11 Creoles as Linguistic Markers of National Identity: Examples from Jamaica and Guyana
    BÉATRICE BOUFOY-BASTICK | 202

12 Understanding Sexual Behaviour in Jamaica
    J. PETER FIGUEROA | 210

13 The Third Crisis: Jamaica in the Neoliberal Era
    DON ROBOTHAM | 223

    An Autobiographical Note
    BARRY CHEVANNES | 241

    Contributors | 247

Acknowledgements

Acknowledgement must be made of those whose energy and commitment to acclaiming the life and work of Professor Barry Chevannes fuelled the planning and conduct of the conference in his honour from which have come the essays in this collection: Dwight Bryan, Sean Ffrench, Herbert Gayle, Sonjah Stanley-Niaah, Jahlani Niaah, Shakeisha Wilson, Lori Henry and Paul Thompson, as well as Ian Boxill, head of the Department of Sociology, Psychology and Social Work, and Mark Figueroa, dean of the Faculty of Social Sciences.

Introduction

HORACE LEVY

This book is about the identity of Caribbean people, the bold, if at times meandering, steps of its emergence and the creative breadth of its embrace across the region. It is not, however, an abstract disquisition on the subject, nor even a carefully planned and organized set of presentations. Rather, it is a collection of articles bursting spontaneously around a powerful theme: The African-Caribbean Worldview and the Making of the Caribbean. This theme generated a wealth of wide-ranging contributions from both West Indians and non-West Indians from around the world, those who have glimpsed and been struck by the worldview and the making.

So this book makes no claim to be all-inclusive and exhaustive on its subject. It is about *some* of the major expressions of identity of a small and economically weak, yet in culture – some would say – impactful civilization. It is about the birth pains of this identity, its unique creations and achievements, its historical and present-day challenges and battles, with special attention given to the Jamaican site.

The person who inspired the chapters in this collection, delivered at a conference in January 2006 in his honour, is the well loved Barry Chevannes. Professor Chevannes is a social anthropologist and former dean of the Faculty of Social Sciences at the University of the West Indies, Mona campus, Jamaica. International recognition of his work is evident in the honorary fellowship accorded him by the Royal Anthropological Institute of the United Kingdom. The depth and breadth of his perspective on the

Caribbean, emerging along the course of his life and development, elicited also from colleagues, former students and friends across the Caribbean and around the globe the quite unusual range and quality of writing represented in this collection.

The son of a shop-keeping couple in the rural village of Glengoffe in Jamaica, Chevannes knew from personal experience the life of the country poor and has used this knowledge to good advantage, for instance in his later analyses on the role of Anancy, the folk hero. He also got to know the life of the city poor – among whom he was to carry out much of his later research – when he boarded in a back street of Kingston while attending the Jesuit high school St George's College. Those school years set him on a path that was to shape his life decisively. He became a Roman Catholic and after graduation joined the Jesuits, beginning what was to be a long interest in religion. In those days, students St George's were taught by Jesuits from New England and, ironically, it was during his studies at their novitiate in the Berkshire Hills of Massachusetts that the young Chevannes, the only black among his all white fellow novices, discovered his own blackness. The occasion was a performance by a choir from Boston College, when he felt a surge of connectedness and interest upon seeing a single black face among the choristers on stage. On reflection (demanded by Jesuit daily discipline), he realized what it meant.

Roman Catholic religion and Jesuit life proved too narrow, however, for Barry's widening world; and, as he points out in his Autobiographical Note, even more compelling was the impossibility of celibacy. After the novitiate, followed by a bachelor of arts in philosophy, a master of arts in the classics from Boston College and (back in Jamaica as part of the lengthy Jesuit training) a year's teaching at Campion College, another Jesuit high school, Barry began at the University of the West Indies the study of sociology that was to lead into his life's work – social anthropology. During that year at University of the West Indies, he left the Society of Jesus and married. As Diane Austin-Broos notes in her contribution, appropriately his first quest for meaning – the quest that drives all anthropologists – was in the area of the black- and Africa-oriented Rastafari. Among them, in the mid 1970s, he began the fieldwork for what was to be his doctoral dissertation at Colombia University, published subsequently as *Rastafari: Roots and Ideology*. Chevannes's original research uncovered, within the framework of their significant difference,

Rastafari continuity with Revival. Revival was the earlier (and, he then thought, extinct) Jamaican religion that was formed out of the Myal of slavery days.

Jean Besson, in her contribution to this collection, "revises and strengthens", she asserts, Chevannes's findings. She emphasizes the continued presence in western Jamaica of female-focused, Zion-variant Revival, through its spirit beliefs, family-land cemeteries and mortuary ritual. She uncovers among the Accompong Maroons, within a continuous process of creolization, the re-emergence of Myal in the Myal play and dance, the latter even "becoming a symbol of Jamaican nationhood and a mode of participation in the island's tourist industry". "There, at the heart of Babylon or plantation/tourism society, among the descendants of plantation . . . and rebel slaves, the continuity between the religious forms of Myal, Revival and Rastafari can be clearly seen."

For her part, Australian anthropologist Diane Austin-Broos, who from her field research in Jamaica has published significant work, sees Revival, Rastafarianism and even Pentecostalism as re-inventing for Caribbean people the scheme of Christianity as a form of transcendence. Employing a series of oppositions, either analytic constructs, like Daniel Miller's (1994) transience/transcendence (wrongly applied, she feels), or folk terminologies, she catches the complexity of Jamaican culture and its links with the issues progressively tackled by Chevannes. From another opposition, Africa/Europe, Austin-Broos points out that "nurturing Africa in Jamaica is shoring up a sense of continuity and identity. It locates Jamaica as a nation", which is essential in a global marketplace.

While the continuity of Rastafari with Revival is a critical Chevannes finding, essential for perceiving the latter's roots in a centuries-old approach to reality, the difference he also spells out between them discloses the significant advance made by Rastafari. In his recent publication, *Betwixt and Between* (2006), he points out that Revival religion did not quite know how to deal with the construction of the self through a negotiation with the hegemonic order. Bedward inveighed against the social order (see below) because it denied him equal status, the right to marry people, for instance, and so to achieve respectability. Rastafari took a radical line.

Rastafari not only appropriated the spiritual power for the self that religion had always meant for Caribbeans of African descent (for from it, they drew the confidence to be defiant, to revolt and hold their own customs, though *within* the established order), but Rasta also denied *legitimacy* to that order, to the hegemon. Rasta dramatically challenged it, indeed, with innovations in beard, dreadlocks, herb, I-language, rulership and black God. Ill-clad, "mad", outcast, but with a wholeness from within, Rasta rejected European respectability. At once destructive and creative, Rasta came down decisively against the ambiguity that had marked Caribbean identity up to this point, a product of the four-hundred-year-long enslavement and subjugation of African to European. It is this racial/colour division, with its denial of black culture that was begotten in slavery and maintained to this day in education, art and monument but has been challenged in religion and other spheres, which is the theme taken up in the next set of essays.

On the Revival side, Veront Satchell, in his contribution, fills in some of the early-twentieth-century history. He retrieves from the *Daily Gleaner* and other sources a detailed account of the insult, contempt and injustice meted out by the colonial court system to Alexander Bedward and nearly seven hundred of his followers in a single day in April 1921. Revivalist Bedward, with a following at his peak of over thirty-three thousand across the island and in Panama, Costa Rica and Cuba, aroused fear among the upper classes. His crime was to have persistently summoned his black, lower-class followers to a spiritual battle with their white oppressors – the "black wall is to crush the white wall" – and, in pursuit of this goal, to have attempted a peaceful walk, clothed with all the symbols of Revival, from the (as it was then) rural village of August Town into the city of Kingston.

Colonial Office racism is further exposed in Khitanya Petgrave's account of the proposal by local British directors of education in the 1930s that black elementary school children, especially boys, were more naturally suited for practical training in agriculture than for academic subjects. This was sharply rejected by the teaching community which also, however, advocated literary education as essential for racial upliftment and social mobility. This latter position in effect legitimated the elitist tendencies of the colonial system and contrasted sharply with the viewpoint of the Rastafarians involved in the uprisings of 1938 as to what constituted black cultural autonomy and achievement.

On the contemporary scene, Annie Paul addresses the topical issue of predominantly black Jamaica having a policy of neutral and colourless "non-racialism". Adopted by the middle-class elite from after the 1938 rebellion and more formally in the independence motto of 1962 ("Out of many one people") to promote cultural assimilation, this has had the inevitable effect, in practice, of reinforcing earlier Eurocentric bias along with white and brown privilege. Blackness treated as simply biological undergoes "a kind of cultural bleaching" in order to include whites with an African ancestor. The elite then decide in their art, as in a recent emancipation monument as well as in earlier ones, what a black representative is to look like, and any protest is rejected as racist. Race and the history of slavery are neutered in the discourse of nationhood and national belonging.

This last point is further illustrated by Christine Chivallon in her piece on museums in Martinique, a contribution stemming from her acquaintance with Chevannes and his work during his four-month fellowship in 2003 in Bordeaux, a former slave port from which his own name may have originated. Martinique, in 2001, boasted forty-two museums, seven times the number in 1986, visited mostly by tourists. Taken in conjunction with numerous other memorials, they represent a "frenzy of heritage", the expression of an effort seen elsewhere to gain security through local patrimony in an era of global uncertainty. Only five, or a feeble 11 per cent, explicitly take into account, however, the experience of slavery and even these, like their parallels in the southern United States, fail to capture its true reality. Patrimonial museography continues the official silencing of collective memory. Within the republican myth of the French nation born through the double event of the French Revolution and the abolition of slavery, it maintains the racial division of the society and the dominance of the white minority, direct descendants of the slave masters.

Language and music, as is internationally recognized, offer two other critical markers of Caribbean identity. In *Betwixt and Between* (2006, 96–105), Chevannes's comments on them as channels of the creative disorder with which he characterizes the impact of Rastafari on the Jamaican scene. Celebrated in this collection are Trinidadian pan, a Jamaican trombonist, the leadership through celebrity singing given by Rastafari stars and Chevannes's own less-known songs.

Kim Johnson describes pan, in its making, as a remarkable set of skills to fashion a steel drum into a musical instrument; in its membership, as a diverse and bonded assembly of persons, extraordinarily large for a population as small as Trinidad's; in its music, as transforming rhythmic instruments into melodic; and all this in response to a hunger to reflect and creatively change the environment, to generate community. The community is party, concert, street, nation, presently the audience at Panorama fused by the sounds from battling bands, each determined on victory. There, in the words of David Rudder, "If yuh iron good, you is king."

Trombonist Don Drummond, in Herbie Miller's account, shunned commercial dance music, as well as emigration, to capture with his creative jazz sensibility and tremendous instrumentalist skill the basic communal energy and sense of life typical of Jamaica. Performing with Count Ossie and his drummers, he moved to become a leader in the 1950s and early 1960s in fashioning ska, which was to receive international recognition. Drummond was a visionary, a "conscious" innovator, engaging the aspirations of his people to produce a lasting body of African-inspired black music and a path to national identity.

Rastafari leadership through song is put forward by Jahlani Niaah and Sonjah Stanley Niaah. The impact of Rastafari leaders like Mortimo Planno on youth in the 1960s and 1970s had been noted by Chevannes. Since charisma, identified by him as foundational to leadership, passed at the same time from preaching oratory to music, to song-writing, that is, plus vocal ability, it is Rastafarian celebrities/stars such as Bob Marley, Capleton, Buju Banton, Sizzla and Garnet Silk who have come to provide a national, indeed global, leadership, even as their anti-systemic critiques of "Babylon", its politicians and "downpression" of the poor make them unacceptable to officialdom. Jah Cure, the rising Rasta star paradoxically serving time in prison for rape, is the outcast Brother Man of former times facing societal demand for the personal integrity of which Rastas have become guardians. Prison, in this scenario, represents the siege on the marginal social space from which African diasporan males operate to the frustration of emergent black leadership.

Anna Perkins writes on the pioneering liturgical music of Barry Chevannes. His songs between 1966 and 1971 reflect his criticisms of the European character of the established churches. They convey an Afro-Caribbean worldview with their use of patwa, guitar and drums, as well as in their themes such as the presence of the divine in the human person and reality, a this-world orientation, "Eena fi wi time / Gad word settle dong"; and a perspective of interdependence and community. Originally composed for Roman Catholic congregations, these songs have "become an interdenominational *lingua franca* sung by a large number of churches".

Béatrice Boufoy-Bastick highlights the increased revaluation and social acceptance of the cultural role of patwa and creolese in diglossic Jamaica and Guyana. They foster national identity and act as socio-ethnic integrators for socially segregated communities, as in Jamaica, and ethnically divided ones, as in Guyana. English is upheld for its economic function – as an international language it enables participation in a globalized economy. Contributing to these language shifts are an international regard for artfully creolized literature and a literate culture as well as, on the other hand, the search for national language identifiers within an English-speaking global context.

To his interest in religion, Chevannes added a concern with masculinity and family – on which he has done extensive research and writing – and a concern with gangs and violence. Africa, for him, Austin-Broos observes, stands for community, civil society and secure lives as well as ritually symbolic ones. "This has been anthropology's hardest brief: to link the issue of meaning and value to life's materiality. Anthropology often drops the ball. Barry's research links these domains by interpreting the lives of ordinary people – ritually, socially and also politically."

Under this rubric, then, male sexual behaviour and economy make up the last pieces in this collection. J. Peter Figueroa explores sexual behaviour in relation to the HIV/AIDS epidemic in Jamaica – the Caribbean has the second highest HIV prevalence in the world (1.6 for adults) after sub-Saharan Africa. Sexual activity begins early, ignorance on how to prevent infection is widespread; multiple sexual partnerships are common, especially among men for whom it is socially acceptable; and 60 per cent of HIV-infected persons are unaware of their infection. Over one hundred thousand new HIV infections have been averted, however, by a comprehensive control programme that increased condom sales fourfold to ten million a year. But it will be checked, as Chevannes suggests, only by structural change to end marginalization and gender inequity.

Anthropologist Don Robotham ventures into what Austin-Broos calls anthropology's "hardest brief: to link meaning and value to life's materiality". He draws a parallel between nineteenth-century global policies, *and* the global neoliberalism, of the past thirty-five years. The earlier policies, through rural immiseration, began the "colonial ghettos" and the uptown/downtown rift of Kingston, Jamaica, the "wounded city", as well as a broader Caribbean crisis. Neoliberal demands, abruptly thrust on Jamaica by Michael Manley, produced initial poverty through bank crisis and enormous debt and huge inequality; these have undermined the state and political parties, rendering them unable to deliver promised welfare. With alienation welling up have come the victory of a prime minister from the working class but also banditry and criminality, and a fractured and "wounded country". It is the economics of global neoliberalism that has created this crisis, not local politics, Robotham asserts. It can only be met, as in the early 1930s, he argues, by the inspiration, analysis and leadership of citizens' associations and the voluntary groups of civil society.

As the foregoing summaries try to indicate – doing real injustice to rich textures – the chapters in this collection touch on many of the critical facets of the Caribbean worldview and its making as it emerged from the dark days of slavery. They point to the significant meanings that Chevannes has identified in some of the most important facets; or even delved into the economic context that his activist life plunged him into. Mainly, they refer to his writings, of which the last chapters are still emerging as, on a Rastafari and masculinity foundation, he moves to grapple with the issue of the violence that has taken bloody hold on Jamaica, mirroring global imperial injustice and violence.

Chevannes's contributions have not been exclusively academic, however. From the early 1970s, after emerging from the Jesuits, he was a leading member of the communist Workers Party of Jamaica until it ceased to function in 1989. At the University of the West Indies, as dean of the Faculty of Social Sciences, he brought in Rastafarian elder Mortimo Planno and other Rasta leaders to fill positions as folk philosophers. He has served on the boards of several institutions, most prominently the Institute of Jamaica of which he is the current chairman. At the request of the Government of Jamaica, he chaired a national commission on the use of marijuana, which urged legitimization of the use of small quantities, and then the Jamaican Justice System Reform Task Force. He is an active member of the Peace Management Initiative, a state-civil society partnership set up to defuse community violence, and chairman of the Violence Prevention Alliance, a broad spectrum of some thirty agencies brought together in 2004 by two dynamic doctors in the Ministry of Health.

In short, Barry Chevannes, in his own life and active involvement – the product, he affirms in his autobiographical note, not of self-making but of "help from the Crew" to whom he "give[s] thanks" – has been an integral part of the life of his country and the region and the shaping of the worldview of the Caribbean people which still continues. Bequeathed (out of the debasing colonialism and the inhumanities of slavery) a legacy of race and class division and violence, Caribbean people have shaped distinctive forms of religion, language, family, race relations and music. They have demonstrated a remarkable creativity and carved for themselves a special place in global culture. While these domains are far from problem-free, it is in the realm of economics and, consequently, politics, subject to powerful, ongoing global pressures, that the greatest challenges and setbacks have occurred: the latter, in part, through well-meant but mistaken choices. Hopefully, this record of the thinking inspired by the conference in honour of Barry Chevannes will stimulate still further exploration of the conference theme, the Afro-Caribbean Worldview and the Making of the Caribbean, surely the chief "work in progress" for Caribbean people.

References

Chevannes, Barry. 2006. *Betwixt and between: Explorations in an African-Caribbean mindscape*. Kingston: Ian Randle.

Miller, Daniel. 1994. *Modernity: An ethnographic approach – Dualism and mass consumption in Trinidad*. Oxford: Berg.

1

Jamaica, the Caribbean, Africa
Some Oppositions and Their Politics

DIANE AUSTIN-BROOS

The great French anthropologist Claude Lévi-Strauss proposed that one of the fundamental features of human beings is the desire to classify. Wherever we are, we scan the world and seek to order it. For Lévi-Strauss, there was both a formal and historical dimension to classification. The formal part involves the fact that classification proceeds by using a series of binary oppositions – a/not a; b/not b and so on – as in a family tree, or any branch diagram. My brother and I are like and unlike; I am like and unlike my mother. We make these distinctions using oppositions – like things that have or lack a distinctive feature. This feature gives meaning to the classification and we describe the world by building up a repertoire of features. It is not surprising that early forms of information technology theory influenced Lévi-Strauss. He liked to think of the human brain as computer-like.

Yet Lévi-Strauss knew that classification is also historical. It rests on forms of society and the ways in which they shape an understanding of the world. Traditional Indigenous Australia was a clan society. People took natural species as totems for their clans. In central Australia, there were kangaroo and emu people, among many other clans. As they classified themselves, Indigenous Australians classified the natural world. In the city of Melbourne, Australian rules for football produced a like phenomenon. Hawks, Tigers and Magpies are mascots that stand for different neighbourhood teams – Hawthorn, Richmond and Collingwood.

Classification is also writ large. It is part of transnational relations and presidents of the United States are quite good at it. Witness the "Free World" as opposed to the "Iron Curtain", or as opposed to the "Evil Empire", or the "Axis of Evil". They are all variations on a basic classification of the world, using "freedom" as the distinctive feature. One think tank now conducts an annual survey, classifying nation states as "free", "part free" or "not free". Nations move up and down the scale. Freedom for the United States means democracy and the latter is supposed to produce prosperous market capitalism. Therefore, freedom = democracy = prosperity. In these classifications, freedom also implies virtue, so that virtue via democracy brings market prosperity. Various presidents of the United States have used this classification to talk about nations. Yet this is more than a classification. In the words of Max Weber, this classification also carries a "theodicy of good fortune", a theory that prosperity comes through virtue. In short, this classification has a politics.

It is here that I diverge from Lévi-Strauss. Classifications not only involve formal properties of mind and the contingencies of history, they also involve points of view. They elide some issues while foregrounding others and, in doing so, they become political. When classifications are taken for granted, they confirm a particular view of the world. The colour-shade classifications used in Jamaica over centuries present a good example of a branch diagram formed out of oppositions with distinctive features. Until they were challenged, these oppositions represented history in particular ways, some of which still skulk around in and beyond Jamaica.

Talk about the Caribbean deploys numerous oppositions: Africa/Europe, Old World/New World, black/white, north/south, haves/have nots. Anthropologist Daniel Miller (1994) argued that the Caribbean is pervaded by dualism: the propensity to classify in terms of oppositions. He proposed that societies of the Caribbean are characterized by intense struggles for autonomy, struggles to determine their own distinctive features. Miller omitted that this form of struggle grows out of a transnational economy that supports racialized relations and divides societies into classes. The worldwide and particular positioning of black people has naturalized "black/white", including its politics. In sum, classification tells us much about culture, provided that we also attend to its politics. In this chapter, I consider five oppositions that highlight features of Jamaican experience. Some of these are folk terminologies and others are analytical constructs. All reveal important dimensions of Jamaican culture.

I select this approach in order to honour Barry Chevannes. Throughout his career as an anthropologist in and of the Caribbean, Barry has focused on the issue of meaning, the classic issue in ethnography. What is the meaning and value in people's words and deeds? How do they "own" events? How are history and experience imprinted in their worldviews? Commencing with Revival and Rastafarianism, and moving on to masculinity, youth and violence, Chevannes has explored meaning and value in Jamaican life. He has sought to consider and interpret continuity, the way in which people link the present with the past. "Africa" has been a central motif in his work.

Let me state why these projects are important. Many social sciences aim to predict, to field general theories of human motivation and desire. For example, economics proposes that a micro-theory of prices can deal with most human decision-making. This is the view that cost/benefit principles apply in every decision we make. Anthropology is different. Anthropology specifies. It reveals the cumulative effort of a people to interpret their history. It studies meaning and value: the springs of various dispositions including initiative, hope and endurance. All of these need imagination, and imagination is shaped by the way we understand life and give it value. Anthropology shows that human agents are more than market individuals. It offers accounts of human projects, not just prices. At the same time, meaning and materiality go together. They inform each other. Anthropology shows that meaning and value reflect and are fed by the institutional structures of society. In the case of Jamaica, anthropology is the discipline that can and should link the practice, values and aesthetics of life – Jamaican culture – to economy, civil society and state.

In my view, this has been the agenda that underlies Barry's work – to reveal the manner in which human culture must inform civil society and productive life; to find the potential in Jamaican meanings to inflect and reinvent the crucial institutions of society. I propose to honour Barry Chevannes by bringing my own approach to this task. Finding out what oppositions reveal, as well as hide, extends our insight into a culture.

First Opposition: Transience/Transcendence

I begin with an example from popular culture, North American rather than Caribbean, but definitely transatlantic. It involves the Quentin Tarantino film *Pulp Fiction*, and a particular scene with Samuel Jackson. It helps me to make some connections in Jamaica and to introduce the first opposition. For brevity's sake, I will use the actors' rather than their characters' names.

Pulp Fiction centres on the lives of two West Coast criminals. At one point in the film the two are sent to confront a group who have tried to cheat on a drug deal. The youths are quite inexperienced, almost comical in the face of the professionalism of Samuel Jackson and John Travolta. In a panic, one youth opens fire. Bullets whistle past Samuel Jackson's head, missing him by a "hair's breath". Later, he examines the wall and wonders how fate could have saved him. Those of you who know the film will know that, following this incident, Samuel Jackson gives up crime and becomes something of a preacher. Samuel Jackson makes the event entirely real – possibly because he has a sense of it. Many Jamaicans also have this sense.

In his book on modernity in Trinidad, Miller observes that much of life is ordered around an opposition between transience and transcendence (Miller 1994). He notes that writing about modernity emphasizes the experience of change, of transience in life. He also observes that the New World experience of the middle passage and slavery was, perhaps, the first experience of change on a scale that marks modernity. Miller proposes that most writing on modernity fails to mention that human beings struggle to balance transience with transcendence. The constant experience of change or danger leads people to search for an anchor whereby they can transcend the present. This can come through burying a navel cord on family land, through badging national heroes, or embracing a religion. Each act casts events in terms of a cosmology, a larger logic. For Miller, the important point is that, in modernity, transience and transcendence go hand in hand. Nowhere, Miller argues, is this more apparent than in the Caribbean. All of this resonates, with Jamaica. Ironically, transcendence can also mean rootedness, and many Jamaicans have sought such rootedness either in attachments to God, antecedents or the land: anchors that withstand the hurricanes of transience.

Miller's own example is more problematic. He suggests that carnival in Trinidad is transience whereas Christmas is transcendence. He contrasts the secular, rude bacchanal of carnival with the moral, cosmological spread of Christian celebration and its related institutions – family, church, school and the like. Yet, Miller has made a switch with this example. Europe brought Christianity to the Caribbean along with the rest of its cultural repertoire. It was the forces of *discontinuity* that brought Christian ideas to the Caribbean. Europeans wished to change New World Africans. Moreover, Christianity asked them to find their own transcendence in the very complex of thought and ritual that helped create the transience of slavery and the middle passage. Part of the history of Jamaican culture, of Revival, Rastafarianism and even Pentecostalism, is taking the scheme of Christianity and reinventing it as a form of transcendence for a Caribbean people. In his discussion, Miller suppresses the very contradiction that has been an engine of Caribbean and Jamaican culture: seeing through impositions from Europe to reinterpret and turn them back.

In addition, Miller separates the moment of bacchanal and the moral in a very British way. As I have argued in my book *Jamaica Genesis*, folk practice brings these moments together (Austin-Broos 1997). In a world that is hard to control, transcendence comes through the beautiful moment, in all types of ritual, dance and performance. Creativity in art and religion confirms the humanness challenged by events. This was true of Revival's beginnings that came as emancipated slaves confronted scarce land and the prospect of migration. Rastafarianism and Jamaica's own Pentecostalism were also forged in the midst of different types of labour migration. All involve the creation of ritual to sustain hope and courage through hard times (Austin-Broos 1992, 1997, 17–33).

Flying bullets and casual death are the transience of downtown Kingston today, and clearly many youth, female as well as male, are unimpressed by the forms of transcendence that organized religion brings. Its promise of coherence for an older generation has been thwarted by inequity and the gross, felt deprivation that transnational media bring. Dancehall and sport provide other moments, fleeting relief from the terrible transience of structural adjustment. Others, again, pursue a transcendence in the moment of power that pulling the trigger brings. Yet the illusion of *these* resorts is revealed in the fact that they cannot provide an anchor that endures. Later I will say more about transcendence, religion and society. For the moment, Samuel Jackson in *Pulp Fiction* made me think of Jamaica.

Second Opposition: Respectability and Reputation

In his study of Providencia, a small island in the western Caribbean, Peter Wilson (1973) remarked that life in a fishing village there was ranged between the poles of respectability and reputation. He gendered this opposition, proposing that the respectable is female, associated with the domestic domain and the church. It is also, in Wilson's eyes, irretrievably colonial. Wilson modelled his account of reputation on a tradition of "street corner society" studies that invariably involve men. Reputation is on the street, not in the house or yard. It is amoral, rebellious, performative and ephemeral. In Jamaica, we would associate it with earlier days of Rasta's display. I recall in the 1970s an elderly friend in Rollington Town remarking of a Rastafarian – "there he goes, his hair jus lookin like a mattress". Shoes with the backs turned down and open, flapping shirts were further signs of the revolt against respectability (see Austin 1984, 169–71).

When Yellowman posed the fateful question, "Wha yu want, consciousness or slackness?", he was working the poles of this same opposition (Stanley Niaah 2005, 50).[1] Yellowman's remark, which refers quite centrally to female sexuality, puts the lie to Wilson's claim that reputation is solely male. Dancehall in particular makes the claim outmoded. It was always outmoded though, as critics including Constance Sutton (1974), Jean Besson (1993), Christine Barrow (1998) and Rhoda Reddock (2003), among others, have made clear. Women higglers, with their toughness and turn of phrase, have always embodied reputation. Moreover, even among the religious, Revivalists and Pentecostal saints embrace ecstatic states that exclude them from respectability in the eyes of other Christians.

Still, this opposition has many dimensions and its allure lives on. Recently, Carla Freeman (2005) of Emory University linked Val Carnegie's concept of "strategic flexibility" (Carnegie 2002, 106ff) to Wilson's notion of reputation. Street life means "occupational multiplicity", flexibility in terms of employment.[2] People fish and farm and higgle, or work two domestic jobs and produce sewn goods for sale. The central role of remittances for many is another dimension of strategic flexibility. Even as the economy struggles, these inputs manage to reduce poverty. Crime, both domestic and transnational, is another strategic flexibility.

Carla Freeman argues that in Barbados this strategy, previously identified as working class, has been adopted by the middle class. Middle-class Barbadians have become entrepreneurs trading from home, moving between occupations and juggling multiple interests. We all know of more than one Jamaican professional who has turned to commerce in the hard times and found that "business" becomes the first, not the second choice. Freeman reports that in Barbados, like the United States, the term "flexibility" is now a catchword among the middle class.

These renderings of reputation and respectability invite two comments. First, it is important to note that the roots of Wilson's opposition are in accounts of domestic life – the street/yard dichotomy. Wilson extends this when he attaches to the yard a repertoire of institutions that includes not only family but also education and religion. He struggles with education, at the outset assigning it to respectability and later admitting it to reputation (cf. Wilson 1973, 103–4 and 160, 173). There is little mention, in his discussion, of local and national governance. By implication, all of these are mere colonial legacies, so that autonomy and critique are located on the street, in performance (Wilson 1973, 24–25). There is nothing wrong with performance, and Wilson's opposition underlines a dramatic and creative part of Caribbean life. However, by making the institutions of civil society all part of respectability – derivative, colonial and inert – Wilson's opposition denies the struggle for society and the state, which is a central part of Caribbean politics (see also Sutton 1974).

Freeman's position on economy compounds Wilson's weakness. In her view, the middle class, like the masses, now have the flexibility associated with "reputation". In one way she is right. Risk, uncertainty and occupational multiplicity are now more prominent among the middle class. People need to diversify, and fortunes can wax and wane. Yet Freeman wants to say more: that to leave the respectability of the professions and public service for market trading or small business is a superior path. We are all so flexible now, so market-oriented. Her romanticizing of working life *and* finance capitalism is very Barbadian,[3] and problematical. It is important to remember that in Jamaica, as elsewhere, "flexibility" has also seen significant deterioration in education and other types of social service, resulting in a weakening of the nation state. In addition, a small but significant part of Jamaica's population has been drawn into the transnational drug trade. Is this another example of entrepreneurship "out-sourced" for the sake of American economy?[4] Dons, after all, have reputation and strategic flexibility.

Miller's transience/transcendence distils a significant part of New World experience, and yet it fails to reflect enough on Caribbean religion. Wilson's respectability/reputation centres performance as a critical practice. At the same time, the discussions of Wilson and Freeman mask the politics of Caribbean life and, in Freeman's case, romanticize economy. Linking cultural and institutional analysis has never been easy.

Third Opposition: Inside/Outside

Inside/outside was a Jamaican idiom that I discussed in my early ethnographic work (Austin 1978, 1984). I reintroduce it here because it gives a class/race connotation to some of the issues that Peter Wilson raised. I also introduce it because this opposition, unlike the first two, was not a mere analytical device. It was also grounded in the idiom of downtown Kingston.

In the 1970s, I recorded and transcribed a large number of life histories among various residents in Rollington Town and Harbour View. Our interviews were relatively unstructured and I encouraged people to speak in their own terms. On reviewing my transcripts, I found that people used the classification inside/outside in three spheres of life. Children born in and out of wedlock were referred to as inside and outside children. White-collar and manual work were described as inside and outside work. In addition, people often established a positive status for a mother by remarking that she did not "work out". Finally, people stipulated whether or not bathroom and cooking facilities were inside a house or out in the yard when they described a childhood home. This seemed to be a taken-for-granted way of stipulating class environment, *their* idea of how to convey to me where a household stood in status terms. In sum, though people distinguished a range of classes, this inside/outside classification seemed fundamental. It evoked two basic models of how to live: born inside, to work and live inside, or born outside, to work and live outside – a rough scheme to conceptualize haves/have-nots, brown/black and uptown/downtown.

Since I did that research, much has changed to modify this classification – not least, the 1970s Manley government's legislation revoking the legal implications of birth out of wedlock. One might say that, in Jamaica, the outside has come in – at least in some degree. Beginning in the 1970s, as many of the middle class left the society, there has been social mobility in which children of the black working class have become middle class. A new form of nationalism has increased the prominence of black business and a black financial class (see Robotham 2000). This is not to deny that conditions remain "flexible". The hold of the recently mobile on their new positions can be tenuous. Moreover, Jamaica's masses still remain a central feature of society. I remember a man in Rollington Town remarking to me that progressives had proposed that there should be "just upper and middle class in Jamaica, no lower class". He paused and said, "It'll take some time to get that in working order." Inside/outside is evocative not only of how things have changed but also of the ways they remain the same. There are still ways to be "outside", especially where work is concerned: being unable to get continuous work, a green card or even bank loans for small businesses. Trading drugs and guns in a criminalized economy is also being "outside", surplus to requirement in the normative economy of transnational capitalism.

The links between this opposition and reputation/respectability are fairly clear. They overlap. There are two important differences though. The first is that inside/outside does not trifle with the advantages of being middle class. The clear implication of the opposition is that insiders win. It is hard being outside. The second difference is equally significant. Being outside connotes acknowledged subordination. When I did the research, this position was often associated with not being "recognized" by "uptown". This idiom has changed now. Demands for "respect" have taken its place. The terminological shift reflects a change in values brought by black mobility and state endorsement. The masses have more confidence and a larger portion of the middle class is prepared to acknowledge their achievements and human worth. Patois, the language that children of the middle class once reputedly learned from helpers, has become an overt lingua franca. Where "outside" is negative, respect sits happily with reputation. All manner of heroes now have reputation that deserves respect.

Fourth Opposition: Fame/Abjection

To continue this theme, I want to distil something useful in Peter Wilson's work. What he means by "reputation" is a set of values, an orientation that extends throughout institutional life, at least in Jamaica. It is not simply a street-corner style or even a black working-class style. It is certainly not just male. The value I am looking for might be described as "the refusal of abjection". No matter how bad things are, people fight on with flair. The French theorist Julia Kristeva (1982) provides an account of abjection. She proposes that being abject is being unable to defend one's boundaries; not being in charge of one's self. Jamaicans have used a history of suffering and progress in order to refuse abjection. In so doing, people I know develop a "double consciousness", a sense of the world as it is structured *and* a sense of who they are. Strictly speaking, this definition does not conform to that of Dubois, who described double consciousness as "always looking at oneself through the eyes of others" (Du Bois 1989, 3). However, with a little help from Marcus Garvey and a release from "mental slavery", double consciousness can become *the made self protected from unwanted invasion* and thereby refusing abjection. Rastafarian use of the first person pronoun "I" and the refusal of plurals or other personal pronouns is an example of focus on the bounded and unsubjected self.[5] It goes hand in hand with acknowledging God in the image of an African (see Nettleford 1970).

Refusing abjection and seeking fame tend to go together. From anthropologist Nancy Munn (1992), I take the view that fame involves the ability to have an impact even in one's absence. It is not simply to be known but also to have influence in a way that travels. Jamaicans seek fame in particular spheres – politics, entertainment, sport and crime. People who have embodied this fame include Marcus Garvey, Alexander Bustamante, Michael Manley, Merlene Ottey, Bob Marley, Dancehall Queen Carlene, the Reggae Boyz collectively and the Donald "Zeeks" Phipps. These Jamaicans shine in a world made dim by inequity. Recently, Barry Chevannes observed to me that Jamaicans can be very, very good at being good *and* bad. Refusing abjection and seeking fame seems to capture something of this, the social psychology and the art of personal transcendence.

I now propose to turn to Africa, transcendence and the work of Barry Chevannes.

Fifth Opposition: Africa/Europe

Why African Nationalism? Why would the study of culture in Jamaica, or popular culture, focus on Africa? Chevannes provides an answer when he speaks of the role of the middle class in "nurturing the creative impulses of the African majority" (Chevannes 2005, 197). Embedded in this is the fact that "blackness" is now a contested category. As a colonial classification, black was a sign of social-moral worth, negative worth, on the body's surface. Today, modern blackness can mean black entrepreneurship or the global reach of rap and dancehall (see Thomas 2004). Nurturing Jamaica's African majority is claiming blackness back both from colonialism and from the commodification of global markets. Nurturing Africa in Jamaica is shoring up a sense of continuity and identity. It locates Jamaica as a nation.

Let me explain what I mean by posing a question: What is "Africa", in Jamaica? There is more to this concept than merely the notion of cultural survivals. The Africa in Zion Revival and Kumina is different from the Africa in Rastafarianism. True, both these cultural genres in Jamaica deploy the drum and forms of dance: embodied performance that clearly connects with an African rather than a European past. However, the forms of possession common in Revival and the ancestral links that Kumina invokes are different from Rastafarianism's modernist aim to reunite with Africa through political critique. Both these cosmologies, their trance states and performances involve pursuit of transcendence from everyday transience. However, their fashioning of these forms of transcendence are different – one forged before the advent of a modern nation state, the other forged in the midst of it. Yet they are both "African", and none of us, I suspect, would have it otherwise. This is so because both are part of a folk tradition that refuses abjection. They use imagination manifest as rhythm and language, colour and garb to maintain autonomous cultural domains. "Africa" names these domains and locates them in a specifically Jamaican history. When some call dancehall or Pentecostal trance "African", they seek to include them in Jamaica's history. This particular version of nationhood, of intimate shared experience, allows people to hope and plan for each other. It is integral to governance.

Notwithstanding the opportunities that transnational relations bring, it remains important to nurture this history. Before we go transnational, all of us are subjects first, wrought in communities. We are all particular subjects before we are market individuals. Moreover, although markets act to weaken geographic boundaries, they also use them for their own ends to regulate the flow of labour between more and less prosperous sites. Correlatively, market participants need state boundaries supported by a people who share a history in order to protect themselves, to clothe themselves in enduring communities. This is why Jamaica needs to nurture its African majority and this brings me to Barry Chevannes and his lifelong research.

Over time, Barry has brought to his interest in Jamaican religion a growing concern with masculinity, the gangs and violence of downtown Kingston, and attaining peace. I want to propose that this particular passage should be seen as claiming civil society back from Europe in the name of people of African descent. In a fashion that moves beyond the equivocation of Peter Wilson, Chevannes's research has claimed institutional life as well as "reputation" for Jamaicans. People need religion and performance. They also need a coherent and viable civil society. Barry's focus on masculinity has been a route into this domain. This is reflected in his remarks on the tenuous link between masculinity and education among lower-class youth (Chevannes 2001). In parts of Kingston, the gun and the gang are more closely connected with manhood. Chevannes canvases new ideas about education and the role of teachers in supporting youth. He observes that educational pursuits must become an integral part of Jamaican manhood (Chevannes 1999). Another route into civil society came with a study for the World Bank directed by Barry Chevannes and compiled by Horace Levy (Levy 2001). This study, on "urban violence and poverty", documents the experience of area stigma in ghetto neighbourhoods. It also documents popular disillusion with organizations, including churches, the law and politics, along with an intense desire for peace, employment and communities that work – aspirations clearly enunciated by both women and men, old and young, in the five communities.

Areas like these are wellsprings of religion and yet transcendence from their strife needs more than ritual performance. It also requires residents with training that can help them find work, and legal local organizations that, crucially, link with the state. In his studies of masculinity and neighbourhoods, Barry has begun to compile a critical folk analysis of these issues just as previously he pursued folk philosophies of religion (Chevannes 1994). His work makes *each* an integral part of understanding popular culture in Jamaica today. I trust I will be forgiven for noting that his trajectory also follows a central course in the history of social science. The path I am referring to concerns the grounding of transcendence in the everyday conditions of life. It is the one travelled by Hegel and Marx, who sought to find in histories of the state and class, respectively, the means to transcend inequity. Today we cannot endorse numerous aspects of their work, and yet the overall sentiment was right: that transcendence requires more than the act of creating imaginative worlds. (It is well to reflect on where we would be without the humanizing art of religion, its aesthetic in the broadest sense. These are real effects in the world, and here Barry Chevannes and I both diverge from Marx.) Yet, the anchoring that religion foreshadows also requires work on society, and this is the good sense that we derive from Barry's research: if "Africa" stands for the creativity and continuity in Jamaican history, then it stands for community and civil society as well as ritual life. Nurturing the African majority in Jamaica involves the cultivation of secure lives as well as richly symbolic ones.

This has been anthropology's hardest brief: to link the issue of meaning and value to life's materiality. Anthropology often drops the ball, and the oppositions reflect this, even as they offer us insights on Jamaica. Miller's transience/transcendence implies that an uninterpreted Christianity can provide an anchor for people whose lives were disrupted by this very force. Wilson's reputation/respectability corrals civil society and state in a colonial heritage that cannot be transformed. Both ignore the global economy that is the ultimate source of all these dualisms. Inside/outside places beyond society the masses who have done so much to shape it. Fame/abjection makes the work of transcendence personal and thereby ephemeral unless it becomes a symbol for community effort.

The "Africa" in Africa/Europe risks embracing art and religion while alienating community, the force of civil society. Like Wilson's opposition, Africa/Europe can dislocate the social, assigning it only to external domination. Yet Jamaican society is just that, a complex of cultural heritage and social organization. Like Rex Nettleford before him, Barry's research links these domains by interpreting the lives of ordinary people – ritually, socially and also politically. And through the dialogue that he and others foster, almost every Jamaican knows that it takes more than "flexibility" and "democracy" to find prosperity in freedom. Hearken, presidents of wealthy states.

Coda

We are all aware that Jamaica faces a monumental task wherein many of the parameters are controlled externally. Part of the issue is defining how to shape and use the resources of a small-scale economy; part of the issue involves understanding the state's capacities in such an economy, a painful but central task. As Don Robotham (2005) argues, these types of deliberation require a clear and steady grasp of finance capitalism.

Yet all of this also involves mobilizing people, a nationalism that shifts the emphasis from colour classification to cultural heritage and then to social innovation in that heritage – from black to Africa and back to blackness working in and on Jamaica. Thinking more than ever before about small-scale society in the midst of finance capitalism needs to be partnered by appropriate education and effective communication to dignify and motivate ordinary people – to learn from and enrich their own unique ideas. Throughout his career, Barry Chevannes has devoted his anthropology to this task. He continues to do so. I am confident that other Jamaicans will follow him.

Notes

1. DJ Yellowman was at the height of his popularity on the Jamaican dancehall scene in the 1980s. He became notorious for his lurid lyrics, often aimed against women.
2. Carnegie is referencing Lambros Comitas (1973), who discussed occupational multiplicity within the Caribbean.
3. See Robotham (2000) for remarks on the relative success of the relations between a white private sector and politics in Barbados.
4. Freeman (2005) describes a new focus on the market in the Caribbean middle-class as responding to the challenge of the United States "out-sourcing entrepreneurship".
5. These issues link with the classic philosophical theme of master/slave discussed by Hegel and taken up in different ways by Marx and Sartre in modern existentialism.

References

Austin, Diane. 1978. History and symbols in ideology: A Jamaican example. *Man* 14, n.s.: 497–514.

———. 1984. *Urban life in Kingston, Jamaica: The culture and class ideology of two neighborhoods.* New York: Gordon and Breach.

Austin-Broos, Diane. 1992. Redefining the moral order: Reinterpretations of post-emancipation Christianity in Jamaica. In *The meaning of freedom,* ed. Frank McGlynn and Seymour Drescher, 221–43. Pittsburgh: University of Pittsburgh Press.

———. 1997. *Jamaica genesis: Religion and the politics of moral order.* Chicago: University of Chicago Press.

Barrow, Christine. 1998. Caribbean masculinity and family: Revisiting "marginality" and "reputation". In *Caribbean portraits: Essays on gender ideologies and identities,* ed. Christine Barrow, 339–58. Kingston: Ian Randle.

Besson, Jean. 1993. Reputation and respectability reconsidered: A new perspective on Afro-Caribbean peasant women. In *Women and change in the Caribbean,* ed. Janet Momsen, 15–37. Kingston, Ian Randle.

Carnegie, Charles V. 2002. *Postnationalism prefigured: Caribbean borderlands.* New Brunswick, NJ: Rutgers University Press.

Chevannes, Barry. 1994. *Rastafari: Roots and ideology.* Syracuse: Syracuse University Press.

———. 1999. *What we sow is what we reap: Problems in the cultivation of male identity in Jamaica.* Grace, Kennedy Foundation Lecture Series. Kingston: Grace, Kennedy Foundation.

———. 2001. *Learning to be a man: Culture, socialization and gender identity in five Caribbean communities.* Kingston: University of the West Indies Press.

———. 2005. Globalisation and culture in Jamaica. In *Jamaica human development report.* Kingston: Planning Institute of Jamaica.

Comitas, Lambros. 1973. Occupational multiplicity in rural Jamaica. In *Work and family life: West Indian perspectives,* ed. Lambros Comitas and David Lowenthal, 157–73. New York: Anchor.

Du Bois, W.E.B. 1989. *The souls of black folk.* Introduction by Henry Louis Gates. New York: Bantam Classics. (Orig. pub. 1903.)

Freeman, Carla. 2005. "Exporting America?" Out-sourcing entrepreneurism, and the crisis of the middle class. Paper presented at the Meetings of the American Anthropological Society, Washington, DC.

Kristeva, Julia. 1982. *The powers of horror: An essay on abjection*. New York: Columbia University Press.
Levy, Horace, comp. 2001. *They cry "Respect!" Urban violence and poverty in Jamaica*. Kingston: Centre for Population, Community and Social Change, University of the West Indies.
Miller, Daniel. 1994. *Modernity: An ethnographic approach – Dualism and mass consumption in Trinidad*. Oxford: Berg.
Munn, Nancy. 1992. *The fame of Gawa*. Durham: Duke University Press.
Nettleford, Rex. 1970. *Mirror, mirror: Identity, race and protest in Jamaica*. Kingston: William Collins and Sangster.
Reddock, Rhoda. 2003. Men as gendered beings: The emergence of masculinity studies in the anglophone Caribbean. *Social and Economic Studies* 52, no. 3: 89–117.
Robotham, Don. 2000. Blackening the Jamaican nation: The travails of a black bourgeoisie in a globalized world. *Identities* 7, no. 1: 1–37.
———. 2005. *Culture, society and economy: Bringing production back in*. London: Sage.
Stanley Niaah, Sonjah. 2005. Kingston's dancehall: A story of space and celebration. PhD diss., University of the West Indies, Mona.
Sutton, Constance. 1974. Cultural duality in the Caribbean. A review of Peter Wilson's Crab Antics. *Caribbean Studies* 14, no. 2: 96–101.
Thomas, Deborah. 2004. *Modern blackness: Nationalism, globalization and the politics of culture in Jamaica*. Durham: Duke University Press.
Wilson, Peter. 1973. *Crab antics: The social anthropology of the English-speaking Negro societies of the Caribbean*. New Haven: Yale University Press.

2

Myal, Revival and Rastafari in the Making of Western Jamaica
Dialogues with Chevannes

JEAN BESSON

This chapter highlights the ground-breaking work of Barry Chevannes on African-Caribbean worldviews and the making of Caribbean society through a focus on the significance of the Myal, Revival and Rastafarian religions in western Jamaica. The analysis is based on my fieldwork in ten communities, in three parishes (Trelawny, St Elizabeth and St James), over thirty-eight years from 1968 to 2006.[1] These three adjoining rural parishes were at the heart of Jamaican plantation-slave society, the Caribbean region and African America in the context of early globalization following the European Conquest of 1492. In the twenty-first century, these parishes remain embedded in the global economy through the agricultural, bauxite and tourist industries of Jamaican postcolonial society and through overseas migration.

Within these global, regional and national contexts, the ten communities that I studied are rooted in the dynamics of colonial plantation slavery and surrounded by plantations, bauxite mines and tourist hotels. These communities include former slave-trading planter towns, post-slavery villages and a plantation squatter settlement in Trelawny; a free village and a maroon polity in St Elizabeth; and a non-maroon community established on the site of a former maroon village in St James (Besson 1995a, 1997, 2001, 2002, 2005, forthcoming).

In these communities, colonially derived Christianity (the established Anglican Church of the slave masters and the nonconformist Baptist,

Methodist, Moravian and Presbyterian churches of the slave missionaries) coexists with North American Pentecostal and Seventh-Day Adventist sects and African-Jamaican Myal-Revival-Rastafarian worldviews. These African-Jamaican religions are variants of African-American Protestantism (cf. Frey and Wood 1998; Miller 1999; Besson 2002, 244).

Within such rich contexts of African-Protestant culture building in Jamaica, Chevannes has greatly illuminated the Myal-Revival-Rastafarian worldviews, arguing that Rastafari has both continuities and discontinuities with Revival which evolved from the Myal slave religion (Chevannes 1994, 1995d). But in the context of his path-breaking research on the burgeoning male-oriented Rastafarian movement in Jamaica, Chevannes initially concluded that female-focused Revival was "a disappearing religion" in the island that was "virtually dead" and "buried under the forces of change" (1978, 16) and that "as far as the peasantry is concerned, it is no longer a force" (ibid., 15). Yet, even at that time, this conclusion did not apply to so-called Baptist villages in my native Trelawny, where I was doing fieldwork. There, I found that Revival was a vibrant force in the oppositional peasant culture in which women play a central role (Besson 1974, 1987, 1993, 1995a). In the 1990s, following a stimulating dialogue with Chevannes (Besson 1995b; Chevannes 1995a, 1995b, 1995c, 9), my conclusion was reinforced by his own research on the resurgence of Revivalism in urban Kingston (Besson and Chevannes 1996).

The first part of this chapter takes our analysis further, showing the endurance of Revival into the twenty-first century. The second section reinforces Chevannes's illuminating research on the significance of Myal in the making of the Revival and Rastafarian worldviews, but revises his conclusion that "there is no religion in Jamaica today to which the name Myal applies" (Chevannes 1995c, 7) by examining the Myal worldview of the Accompong Maroons in St Elizabeth (Besson 1995a, 1997, 2005 and forthcoming). The third part shows how Chevannes's pioneering work on Rastafari is reinforced by my research in Trelawny, St Elizabeth and St James, but underlines my conclusion that, rather than replacing Revivalism, Rastafari coexists with both Myal and Revival.

These conclusions further show that Myal, Revival and Rastafari in western Jamaica are variations on the theme of gendered African-Jamaican culture building in the face of globalization and related land monopolization.

I show that, within these contexts, Rastafari, Myal and Revival all relate to peasantization – rooted in the Caribbean tenures of family land, common land and "captured" land. Such peasantization is a creative oppositional process of creolization among free villagers, squatters and maroons, originating in the "proto-peasant", "squatter peasant" and "runaway peasant" adaptations of the slavery past (see Mintz 1989, 146–56; Besson 1995b, 1997, 2002). These dialogues with Chevannes's research in Jamaica (especially in urban Kingston), based on my fieldwork in the rural western part of the island, reinforce and expand the significance of his pioneering studies on the African-Jamaican worldview.

Revival in Western Jamaica

Revival and the Obeah-Myal Worldview

The roots of Revivalism in western Jamaica, as throughout the island, were forged in the Obeah-Myal worldview of the enslaved population that was consolidated by the mid eighteenth century. "Obeah" originally referred most often to morally neutral magical/spiritual power that could be accessed through spirit possession, or "Myal", and used for protection and healing (Schuler 1979a, 1979b; Handler and Bilby 2001; Besson 2002, 30–32). With Baptist missionizing in the later slavery period (which was the most successful proselytizing among the enslaved), the slaves of Trelawny and St James (who were at the centre of both the Obeah-Myal complex and Baptist missionizing) attended the Baptist chapels, while on the slave plantations, Obeah and Myal controlled Baptist Christianity in the Native Baptist variant.

Integral to the Obeah-Myal complex, which was both a belief system and a religious organization similar to West African secret societies, was the belief in a dual spirit or soul. One spirit, the *duppy*, was believed to leave the body at death and, after remaining for a few days at the place of death or burial, to journey to join the ancestors. Elaborate funeral ritual was practised to mark and effect this transition. Another spirit was thought to be the *shadow* of the living person (buried with the corpse at death) that could be caught, harmed and restored by Obeah/Myal-men and -women (Besson and Chevannes 1996; Besson 2002, 30).

On the Jamaican slave plantations, Obeah-Myal ideology, with its elaborate mortuary ritual reflecting the perception of an active spirit world including ancestral kin, reinforced the customary land-transmission system in slave-village house-yards and on plantation provision-grounds traced through both males and females. These landholdings (which reflected the slaves' re-creation of identity, kinship and community) included kin-based cemeteries incorporating both women and men. This non-unilineal or cognatic system of descent, land-transmission and burial would provide the basis for family land in post-emancipation communities. This interrelation of magico-religious beliefs and ritual with customary land tenure was especially marked in Trelawny and St James, which had pronounced proto-peasant adaptations and were the stronghold of the Obeah-Myal complex (Besson 2002, 26–32). Obeah-Myal also reinforced marronage, such as escape into the Cockpit Country mountains straddling the interior of the parishes of Trelawny, St James and St Elizabeth, and fuelled slave revolt, as in the great slave rebellion that swept through western Jamaica in 1831 (and started on the Kensington plantation near Maroon Town in St James).

In "Baptist" free villages, after emancipation in 1838, Orthodox Baptist faith provided the formal religious focus and a means for acquiring land. At the same time the Native Baptist variant, reinforced by a "Myalist Revival" from the 1820s to the 1850s (when Trelawny, with St James, was the vanguard of the "Myal movement"), formed "the core of a strong, self-confident counter-culture" against the persisting plantation system (Schuler 1980, 44). In 1860, this Myalist Revival combined with an intense Euro-Christian evangelical revival, known as the Great Revival, and generated a new Afro-Protestant religion, "Revival", which continued both to control the Baptist faith and to incorporate more elements of Baptist Christianity in opposition to Obeah as sorcery (Chevannes 1994, 20; Besson and Chevannes 1996).

However, in 1861, the Great Revival "turned African" (Curtin 1970, 171); that is, it was appropriated by the original Obeah-Myal ideology. In this way, two variants of Revival were distinguished, Revival-Zion (seen as nearer to Baptist Christianity and as opposing Obeah) and Pukumina (closer to the original Obeah-Myal complex and regarded as practising Obeah). These two variants, also known respectively as "the '60" and "the '61", persisted in the twentieth century. However, since the 1990s, Revival-Zion has become ascendant, with Pukumina being attributed by rural and urban folk to either other practitioners or to another time and place (Besson and Chevannes 1996). Yet, despite the distinction between the two versions of Revival and the apparent disappearance of Pukumina, the belief in the morally neutral magical/spiritual power of Obeah is retained and cocooned at the heart of Revival-Zion ideology; it is not only hidden behind the symbol of the Baptist church, but also kept from view even at some Revival-Zion meetings (Besson 2002, 243–44).

Revival in Trelawny, St James and St Elizabeth

In Trelawny, I undertook fieldwork in five "Baptist" free villages (The Alps, Refuge, Kettering, Granville and the former slave-trading port of Martha Brae) established by emancipated Myalist plantation slaves in association with Baptist anti-slavery missionaries; in Martha Brae's satellite squatter settlement of Zion, consolidated on a former slave plantation; and in the parochial capital and former planter town of Falmouth, where the peasant market originated in the small-scale trading of proto-peasant plantation slaves (Besson 2002, 2003).

All the Trelawny peasant communities that I studied are hemmed in by persisting plantations and the world-famous North Coast tourist industry. The core of the free-village populations are the Old Families, traced from male and female slaves through both women and men. These Old Families hold small plots of family land, created from purchased land by their ex-slave ancestors. Such family lands, which include Revival cemeteries, exist together with bought and rented land. In these free villages, Revival ideology coexists with the Baptist church[2] (and with the Rastafarian movement) and the Zion squatter settlement was established by Revivalists and Rastafarians from Martha Brae. There are links between these Revivalists and those in Falmouth and in the western parishes of St Ann, Westmoreland and St James. For example, Revivalists at Zion have links with a Revival Bishop in the Maldon area of Maroon Town, St James, where I also conducted fieldwork.

Maroon Town is a non-maroon community, in the Cockpit Country mountains, that was established in the context of Jamaican post-slavery peasantization on the site of the former maroon village of Cudjoe's Town. This was the primary settlement of the historic Leeward Maroon polity (and was renamed Trelawny Town following the colonial treaty of March 1739 with Governor Trelawny), until the deportation of the Trelawny Maroons to Nova Scotia after the Second Maroon War of 1795–96. In the twenty-first century, most Old Families in Maroon Town (renamed in memory of the deported maroons) claim "slave master pickni" descent from slave masters and slaves (Besson 2005 and forthcoming). Maroon Town now includes Flagstaff (a site of the Second Maroon War) and Maldon, which was the first Baptist free village in St James – established around the Maldon Baptist Church founded by the Reverend Walter Dendy (Sibley 1978, 101). Today, many villagers in Maldon are Baptist-Revivalists. Other Maroon Town villagers are Seventh-Day Adventists and Methodists, but family-land Revival cemeteries are evident throughout the entire community.

From the viewpoint of the Baptist churches in Trelawny and St James, Revivalism and Baptist Christianity are still "competing faiths", as they were in Sturge Town, in the parish of St Ann (neighbouring Trelawny), in the aftermath of emancipation as described by Sidney Mintz (1989, 168). However, from the perspective of the free villagers themselves, Baptist Christianity and Revival have long been complementary – the Baptist church providing a formal framework for religious life and Revival negotiating with, appropriating and transforming Baptist Christianity (Besson 2002).

In St Elizabeth, I studied the Accompong Maroon society descended from rebel slaves (who had an Obeah-Myal worldview) and the neighbouring free village of Aberdeen, both in the Cockpit Country (Besson 1995a, 1997, 2001, 2005, and forthcoming). Accompong Town was the secondary village of the Leeward Maroon polity, which defeated the Anglican plantation regime in the First Maroon War of 1725–38; the primary Leeward village is Cudjoe's Town/Trelawny Town in St James. Following the colonial deportation of the Trelawny Maroons in 1796 after the Second Maroon War, Accompong became the sole surviving village of the Leeward polity.

In the late nineteenth century, the Accompong Maroons invited Presbyterian missionaries to establish a church in the community and today many Accompong Maroons attend the United Church (Kopytoff 1987; Besson 1997, 2001).[3] Others are Pentecostalists, Rastafarians and Revivalists. There is a Revival tabernacle and three "Seal Grounds"[4] in Accompong and family-land cemeteries (similar to Revival burial grounds in non-maroon free villages) are emerging in house-yards within the wider framework of the common treaty land and its ancestral Myal cemeteries. However, at the heart of the maroon polity is the annual Myal Dance or Play (discussed later);[5] for though the maroons say they "practise" Christianity, they explain that "Myal is a gift from the spirits" of the First-Time Maroons who fought the war and won the peace.

Aberdeen was established as a free village by Myalist emancipated slaves from the Aberdeen plantation, bordering the maroon commons, in association with the Moravian church which missionized the slaves on Aberdeen Estate. However, some Aberdonians have ties of kinship and/or conjugality with Accompong Maroons and also assert maroon descent, as well as claim Afro-Scots ancestry from slave masters and slaves. Aberdonians of maroon descent have land and voting rights in the Leeward polity and participate in its Myal Play. However, in Aberdeen, where Revivalism coexists with Moravian and Pentecostal Christianity, the Revival worldview is widely manifested in family-land burial grounds that symbolize both the continuity of kin groups descended from slaves and maroons and the perceived links between these kin groups and the Revival spirit pantheon.

REVIVAL IDEOLOGY AND MORTUARY RITUAL

Revival ideology in Trelawny, St Elizabeth and St James closely resembles that outlined by Seaga (1982, 10) and Chevannes (1978, 5) for elsewhere in Jamaica. Revival is based on the perception of an integrated world of living persons and spiritual beings that include God (especially the Holy Spirit) and the dead. While the unseen portion of this world includes the Christian Trinity, the total spirit pantheon is Africa-derived. As Seaga noted, this Revival spirit pantheon has three dimensions: "Heavenly" spirits, "Earthbound" spirits and "Ground" spirits. "The first category consists of the Triune Christian God, Archangels, Angels, and Saints. In the category of 'Earthbound' spirits, are the satanic powers (Fallen Angels), Biblical Prophets and Apostles. The third group consists of all the human dead except those mentioned in the Bible" (Seaga 1982, 10). Variations on this theme differentiate Revival-Zion and Pukumina, each of which focus to some extent on different categories of spirits (ibid., 10–11).

In addition to tabernacles, seal grounds, ritual symbols and meetings, in which Revival leaders, healers and evangelists play a central role (Besson 2002, 244–56), Revival ideology in western Jamaica is reflected in elaborate mortuary ritual (originating in the African past and Jamaican slave society) in which Revival and nonconformist Christianity are complementary. For example, in the Trelawny villages and in the Maldon area of Maroon Town, while funerals are often conducted in Baptist churches, Revivalism is manifested in wakes or "set-ups" whereby members of the community visit the household of the deceased. During my fieldwork, such ritual reflected both continuity and change and by the turn of the millennium had become intensely transnational. The traditional Nine Night and Forty Night wakes are dying out, and there is an increasing emphasis on the lyke-wake the night before the burial, now known as "Singing Night". Escalating urbanization and overseas migration are contributing to such transformation, as migrants return from urban areas and abroad to attend mortuary rituals (Besson and Chevannes 1996; Besson 2002, 235–36, 256–60; Besson forthcoming).[6]

In the communities that I studied, it is believed that tombing, traditionally undertaken a year after interment, completes the placing of the dead. The new fashion throughout the island of the earlier, final, sealing of the grave through concrete vaulting, completed at the burial, may be transforming the perception of the *duppy*'s journey to the spirit world – hastening this transit. Such a transformation may also be contributing to the decline of Nine Night and to the increasing emphasis on Singing Night, as migrant kin and friends gather for the funeral. Annual transnational memorials in free-village and family-land cemeteries have also become a prominent feature of Revival mortuary ritual. However, the continued use of such burial grounds reflects continuity, as in the Trelawny villages, Maroon Town and Aberdeen, as do the emergent house-yard cemeteries in Accompong.

MYAL IN THE ACCOMPONG MAROON SOCIETY

This second section reinforces Chevannes's research on the significance of Myal in the making of the Revival worldview, but revises his conclusion that "There is no religion in Jamaica today to which the name Myal applies" (Chevannes 1995c, 7) by outlining the Myal worldview and Myal Dance or Play of the Accompong Maroons in St Elizabeth today. This revision not only strengthens the significance of Chevannes's research on the place of Myal in the African-Jamaican worldview but also revises some of the conclusions of Kopytoff's (1987) and Campbell's (1990) classic studies on the Jamaican maroons.

Accompong's annual Myal Play, held on or around the sixth of January, derives from the Obeah-Myal slave religion (which as Chevannes [1995d] and Schuler [1980] showed was the first creolized religion in Jamaica, being a transformation of African religions), in which a neutral magical/spiritual power was believed to be accessed from the ancestors through spirit-possession and dance (Besson 2002; Handler and Bilby 2001). Myalism was transformed in marronage, through further creolization, to focus on the ancestral spirits of the First-Time Maroons (Kopytoff 1987; Besson 1995a, 1997, 2005).

My research reveals a continuing process of creolization in the maroon Myal Play, when compared with Barbara Kopytoff's earlier ethnohistorical study. Kopytoff described the ascendance of the Christian God over the "Town Massa" in Accompong Town's traditional cosmology, from the 1930s to the 1970s (1987, 463–84). At that time, the town master was Captain Accompong and the annual ritual in early January celebrated his birthday. This celebration included (Myal) dancing in front of a sacred hut built over his reputed grave at Old Town, which Kopytoff described as "the site of the original settlement" of Accompong Town (ibid., 476). Kopytoff explored the confrontation of the maroon ancestral spirit beliefs with Christianity, crystallized in the burning of the hut at Old Town in the mid 1930s, the related decline of the traditional dancing and beliefs, and the simultaneous ascendancy of the Christian God over the ancestors into the 1970s.

However, my subsequent research reveals the re-emergence, strengthening and further creolization of Myalism in Accompong from the 1980s into the twenty-first century – including its embedding in the common treaty land. During the period of my fieldwork in Accompong (1979–2006), Colonel Cudjoe (whose status is superior to that of Captain Accompong) has become the main focus of the Myal Play, which since the 1980s is said to commemorate both the signing of Cudjoe's Leeward treaty and his birthday. Another change is that the Myal Dance is now held at the Kindah grove, at the edge of the residential zone, rather than at the Old Town grove, which is about a mile beyond the village in the area of provision grounds and pasture. Kindah represents a microcosm of the Cockpit Country landscape of the maroon commons, being a hillside of grassland and limestone outcrops surrounded by bush and stones that are said to be the "tribal" burial grounds of the early African maroons (Besson 1997). At the centre of the Kindah grove is the sacred Kindah Tree, a fruitful mango tree with a sign "Kindah: One Family" (replacing previous signs "Kindah: We Are Family" and "The Family Tree"), symbolizing the kin-based African-Jamaican maroon community (ibid.).

In addition, with the ascendancy of Colonel Cudjoe in Accompong Town's Myalist cosmology, Captain Accompong's reputed grave has been shifted (and demoted) from Old Town to a grove between Kindah and Old Town, where Cudjoe's other captains or "brothers" (Quaco, Cuffee and Johnny) are said to be buried (Besson 1997). Moreover, the Old Town grove, where Cudjoe and his "sister" Nanny are reputedly interred, is now said to be the site of Cudjoe's Old Town. However, the actual site of Cudjoe's Old Town (renamed Trelawny Town and now Maroon Town) is fourteen miles away in the parish of St James. As I discuss later, this symbolic relocation of Old Town from St James to St Elizabeth encapsulates the continuities and discontinuities in Leeward Maroon history.

On the day of the Myal Play, the maroons make a pilgrimage from Kindah, through the grove of the captains' graves, to Old Town, where a sacrificial meal is offered on an altar to Colonel Cudjoe. The Myal pilgrims continue on to the Peace Cave, deep in the forest, where a bottle of rum for Cudjoe is placed inside the cave. The whole sequence of sacred groves and graves traversed by the pilgrimage (or marked by other Myal rituals) reflects a continuing process of creolization from African enslavement to Caribbean freedom. This sequence of sacred sites includes the African cairns at Kindah; the graves of the Afro-Creoles Cudjoe and Nanny at Old Town and those of the other First-Time African-Jamaican maroon leaders between Old Town and Kindah; the cemetery of colonial and maroon warriors at the Peace Cave; the tombs of more recent generations of maroons in the United Church cemetery; and the vaults of cognatic lineages in house-yards. This sacred landscape and its Myal rituals, commemorating the ancestor-heroes of the First Maroon War and their descendants, also reinforces the identity of the Leeward Maroon polity and symbolizes its historical resistance to, and subsequent ambiguous alliance with, the Jamaican colonial/postcolonial state (Besson 1997, 2005).

As well as revising Kopytoff's (1987) conclusion on Myal's demise in Accompong, and Chevannes's (1995c) observation that Myal does not exist in Jamaica today, my research clarifies the so-called confusion regarding the maroon ancestress Nanny raised by Mavis Campbell (1990) in her history of the Jamaican maroons. Campbell notes that both the Windward community of Moore Town and the Leeward Maroons of Accompong "have claimed Nanny, some holding that she was the 'sister', others the 'wife', of Cudjoe – which would shatter the generally held view that she was of the windward's" (ibid., 178). Campbell states that "Equally confusing is the fact that both these communities have burial places for Nanny", and adds that, in Accompong, Nanny's reputed burial place "is so sacred, that, ironically, the author was not permitted a visit, on the grounds that no woman is allowed there" (ibid.).

My analysis revises Campbell's interpretation of confusion regarding Nanny's role and burial place by highlighting symbolic meanings in the sacred sites and shifting histories of the Leeward Maroon polity, portrayed through the continued creolization of Myalism in Accompong. As with other non-maroons, I was not allowed beyond the Kindah grove at the Myal Dances that I attended in 1991 and 2002. However, I have twice been taken by maroons on the route of the Myal pilgrimage, including to Nanny's reputed grave, during the preparations for the Myal Play in 1989 and in the immediate aftermath of the ritual in 1991. This enriched my understanding of the sacred maroon landscape and its enduring Myal rituals, which I attended again at Kindah in 2006.[7]

My research reveals that the ritual relocation of Cudjoe's Old Town to Accompong and the symbolic shifting of both Cudjoe's and Nanny's graves to Accompong's Old Town grove reinforce the continuity and identity of the enduring but shrunken Leeward Maroon polity. Since the deportation of the Trelawny Maroons by the colonial state in 1796, Leeward Maroon identity and land have continued to be threatened by globalization. The ritual relocation of Cudjoe's Old Town to Accompong, and the symbolic shifting of Cudjoe's grave to Accompong's Old Town grove, symbolically redraw and tighten the boundary of the Leeward Maroon polity around the Accompong community. Simultaneously, the claim in Accompong that Nanny is buried there at Old Town symbolically expands the Leeward Maroon boundary to include the Windward Maroons, who attend Accompong's Myal Dance and participate in the Old Town pilgrimage. This inclusion of the Windward Maroons in the Leeward Myal Play strengthens Jamaican maroon ethnicity.

My revision of Campbell's view of maroon confusion may be taken further still. The ritual relocation of the burial place of Nanny (as either Cudjoe's "wife" or "sister"), from the Windward polity to Accompong's Old Town grove, and the related Myal pilgrimage, also highlight the complementary male and female principles at the heart of Leeward Maroon society that have reinforced the endurance of the polity through gendered land transmission, work and ritual, marriage and descent. These gender relations are likewise symbolized by the perceived possession of maroon women by the spirits of the male ancestor-heroes, as the women dance and trance to the music of male maroons under the Kindah Family Tree at the Myal Dance. Throughout my research, Accompong Maroons stressed Nanny's role to be that of Cudjoe's sister. This reputed sister-brother sibling bond represents the sacred origin of the cognatic system of descent and land transmission, traced through both women and men, perpetuating the Leeward Maroon community and its common land (Besson 1997, 2001, 2005).

Since the turn of the millennium, Accompong's Myal Dance has been further creolized, becoming a symbol of Jamaican nationhood and a mode of participation in the island's tourist industry.[8] For example, the Myal Plays that I attended in 2002 and 2006 drew crowds of around six thousand, including Rastafarians, Jamaican government officials, market vendors, tourists, non-maroon Jamaicans, and maroons from elsewhere in the island and overseas. Myal is therefore very much alive in Jamaica today.

Rastafari in Trelawny, St James and St Elizabeth

This third section shows how Chevannes's pioneering work on Rastafari is validated by my research in Trelawny, St James and St Elizabeth – except for his initial conclusion that male-oriented Rastafari was eclipsing female-focused Revival, which was thought to have replaced the Myal slave religion (Chevannes 1978, 1995d). I also highlight the interrelationship of Rastafarians (whose ideology is a critique of colonial plantation slavery and postcolonial race-class stratification) with peasantization and land, and I explore the coexistence of Rastafari, Myal and Revival in western Jamaica today.

Rastafari and its coexistence with Revival in Trelawny

In the Trelawny communities that I studied, male Rastafarians were prominent in some family-land house-yards in the Baptist-Revivalist free villages of the Alps, Granville, Kettering and Martha Brae; on "captured" land in the Revivalist-Rastafarian squatter settlement of Zion; and in the Falmouth marketplace. They are part of a parish-wide and island-wide network of Rastafarians that includes other Trelawny villages, St James, St Elizabeth, Kingston and the commune founded by the late Prince Emmanuel in the eastern parish of St Thomas (Besson 2002 and forthcoming).

The origins of the Rastafarian movement in Trelawny (as throughout Jamaica), like those of the Revival cult and the Baptist church, reach back to the proto-peasant past. The roots of Rastafari lie partly in eighteenth-century Jamaican slave religion, with the emergence of the ideology of Ethiopianism (symbolizing the homeland of Africa or "Zion") among the Baptist-Myalist plantation slaves (Barrett 1988, 68, 75–76). The link between Ethiopianism and the Baptist church during slavery can be clearly seen for Trelawny. There, in the William Knibb Memorial Baptist Church in Falmouth, a plaque commemorating emancipation erected by "The Sons of Africa" includes an Ethiopian theme (Besson 2002, 265).

In the early twentieth century, Ethiopian ideology was reinforced by the teachings of Marcus Garvey (born in 1887 in St Ann, bordering Trelawny, and known to the author's father) in Jamaica from 1914 to 1916 and 1927 to 1935.[9] The Rastafarian movement itself crystallized with the crowning of Ras Tafari as Haile Selassie, emperor of Ethiopia, in 1930; the preaching of the Howellites from the 1930s to the 1950s; and the innovations of the Youth Black Faith, founded in 1949. These innovations by young activists included the introduction in the 1950s of the dreadlocks or matted hair complex, which symbolized both the construction of a greater social distance from Jamaican colonial society and the perception of Rastafari by that society as derelicts and outcasts. It also symbolized the male focus of the movement (Chevannes 1995e, 1995f). The destruction of Pinnacle, the first Rastafarian commune in the hills of the parish of St Catherine, by the colonial-state police in 1954 dispersed the Howellites to Kingston and other parts of Jamaica, and the movement grew in the rural parishes including Trelawny where it has taken root in post-slavery peasant adaptations on family land

and captured land. The coexistence of the male-oriented Rastafarian movement with female-focused Revival in these communities elaborates the gendered African-Jamaican culture building that is opposed to Euro-American styles of life and related land monopoly.

Dreadlocked Trelawny Rastafarians meet to "reason" at village crossroads, house-yards and tabernacles. They are cultivators, wood-carvers for the tourist industry and craft-traders in the Falmouth market. Like Rastafarians elsewhere in Jamaica, Trelawny Rastas do not acknowledge death, which they either deny or suffocate with taboo. They also reject the elaborate mortuary rituals of Baptists and Revivalists, looking instead to a symbolic return from "Babylon" (exile in Jamaica) to "Ethiopia" (Africa or "Zion"). Nevertheless, Rastafarians in Trelawny do sometimes participate in Revival rituals. The coexistence of Rastafarians and Revivalists in these communities, sometimes in the same house-yard and/or household, along with the now early removal of corpses from house-yards by Revivalists, may account for this.

RASTAFARI, REVIVAL, AND MYAL IN ST JAMES AND ST ELIZABETH

Male Rastafarians were prominent in the Flagstaff area of Maroon Town at the Emancipation Day commemorations that I attended on the first of August at the turn of the millennium and into the twenty-first century. Flagstaff is a highly symbolic part of the Maroon Town landscape (being associated with the Second Maroon War) and has been the site of the post-slavery village's emancipation commemorations since the national and regional revival of these rituals in 1997 (Besson forthcoming). For example, on 1 August 2000, the crowd that gathered at Flagstaff included several dreadlocked Rastafarians, and reggae music (such as "Goin' to Burn Babylon") blasted through the Cockpits, highlighting resistance to slavery and opposition to postcolonial oppression. Several of these Rastas whom I reasoned with highlighted the significance of emancipation and underlined their role in the culture building of the nation, reinforcing the emancipation commemorations. These celebrations included a Jonkonnu masquerade deriving from the Obeah-Myal slave religion, whose continuity is also reflected in Revival family-land cemeteries and mortuary rituals throughout

Maroon Town. On 1 August 2002, the Rastafarian presence at Flagstaff was even more pronounced, with Rastafarian T-shirts on sale.

In Accompong, St Elizabeth, a network of male dreadlocked Rastafarians has been established. They participate in the maroon economy, consolidated on common treaty land, through farming, raising livestock and making crafts such as Gumbay Drums for the tourist industry. As in the other communities that I studied, their Rastafarian identity is reinforced by networking with Rasta organizations elsewhere in the island such as the Twelve Tribes in Kingston.

This island-wide network of Rastafarians was highly visible at the Myal Plays in Accompong that I attended in 2002 and 2006. In 2002, in addition to Rastafarian craft vendors and many other Rastas in the crowds, there were Rastafarians from Nine Miles in St Thomas, the late Prince Emmanuel's camp (cf. Chevannes 1994), who had travelled across the island to attend the Myal Dance. One of them told me that he had been the Prince's "Deputy". In 2006, the street stalls included Rastafarian flags, crafts and I-tal food.

Conclusion

In his ground-breaking work on Rastafari, Chevannes (1994, 1995d) argued that the Rastafarian movement must be seen as both a new departure from and a continuity with the traditional Afro-Jamaican peasant worldview, Revival (that appeared to have replaced Myal), which he initially concluded was disappearing in Jamaica due to the growth of Rastafari and "American-derived evangelical sects" (1978, 1). Chevannes identified continuities and transformations of Revival in Rastafari and drew four related conclusions (1995d, 31–39). First, that Rastafari is an African-derived religion with direct continuity from Myal,[10] Native Baptism and Revival. Here Chevannes went beyond Alleyne who, in the search for African continuities in Jamaican religion, found such continuities in Myal,[11] Native Baptism and Revival, but argued that "whereas Africa remains very high among Rastafarians at the level of ideological consciousness, there isn't very much of African continuity in the system of religious belief and religious behaviour" (Alleyne 1996, 103). Second, Rastafari may be regarded as the fulfilment of Revival, though this was seen as fulfilment through rejection, Rastafari being anti-Revival and patriarchal. Third, Rastafari represents a worldview movement rooted in Myal and Revival. Fourth, Rastafari is a cultural movement constructing a new reality rather than being political and millenarian.

Chevannes (1995e) also established, through new evidence based on oral sources, that the Rastafari matted hair complex was the innovation of the Youth Black Faith in the 1950s, rather than originating earlier in Howell's Rastafarian camp at Pinnacle (Smith, Augier and Nettleford 1961). He also concluded that the Youth Black Faith "represented a reform trend of younger converts bent on purging the movement of Revivalist beliefs and practices" (Chevannes 1995e, 77). He further argued "that the dreadlocks phenomenon symbolized both a rejection of social control . . . [and] a triumph of male power over the female" (Chevannes 1995f, 97). In this process, "the Dreadlocks sought to overthrow the religion of the peasant, Revival" and "attempted to . . . isolate the negative ideas about women, which were abroad in the culture, ritualize them, and by so doing establish ritual distance from the contaminating source of their confinement in Jamaican society, in Babylon" (ibid., 104, 120).

Much support for Chevannes's new approach to Rastafari can be found in the cultural history of the communities that I studied in Trelawny, St Elizabeth and St James. There, at the heart of "Babylon", or Jamaican plantation/tourism society, among the descendants of plantation slaves and rebel slaves, the continuity between the religious forms of Myal,[12] Revival and Rastafari can be clearly seen. However, I have suggested a revaluation of Revival, within the context of Revival-Rastafari continuity, that highlights the persistence of Revival itself as oppositional to Euro-American hegemony (Besson 1987, 1993, 1995b); a revision that was reinforced by Chevannes's subsequent research (Besson and Chevannes 1996). This chapter takes our conclusions further, revealing the endurance of Revival into the new millennium. I have also shown that Myal is very much alive in Jamaica today. In addition, I have highlighted the continued significance of women in such African-Protestant culture building, from the maroon and proto-peasant slavery past into the twenty-first century (see also Besson 2001, 2002, 2005).

The Rastafarian movement has only made an impact in western Jamaica since the 1950s, while enduring Myal and Revival have been modes of cultural opposition there to globalization and related land monopoly for three centuries of African-Jamaican life. Moreover, this chapter suggests that the future of male-focused Rastafari in Trelawny, St Elizabeth and St James lies partly in gendered post-slavery peasant adaptations, based on the Caribbean tenures of family land, common land and captured land (held and transmitted by both women and men), where Myal and Revival have long had a central place.

Notes

1. I conducted fieldwork in Trelawny during the period 1968 to 2006, in St Elizabeth from 1979 to 2006 and in St James from 1999 to 2006. My research was partly funded by the British Academy, the Carnegie Trust for the Universities of Scotland, the Nuffield Foundation, the Ministry of Education in Jamaica, the Social Science Research Council, the University of Aberdeen and Goldsmiths College, University of London. I thank these institutions for their support. I am also grateful to the many Jamaicans in the communities that I studied for their help in my research.
2. The Alps, Refuge, Kettering and Granville each have their own Baptist church. The Martha Brae Prayer House is "Class 5" of the Falmouth Baptist circuit focused on the William Knibb Memorial Baptist Church.
3. A sign outside the church in Accompong states that in 1965 "the Presbyterian Church in Jamaica and the Cayman Islands combined with the Congregational Union to form the United Church of Jamaica and the Cayman Islands".
4. Seal Grounds are sacred sites, where Revival meetings may be held, perceived to be associated with Revival spirits and with spiritual protection and healing. The three Seal Grounds in Accompong are believed to protect various areas of the village.
5. The concept of play derives from the dances and rituals of the enslaved, which formed "the spiritual heart of Jamaican slave culture" (Burton 1997, 18). Schuler (1979b, 67) notes that Edward Long referred to the Jamaican slaves' "myal dance" in the 1760s. Accompong Maroons use both the concepts of "Myal" and "play" to refer to their annual Sixth of January celebrations and dancing remains a central part of these rituals.
6. I am grateful to Dr Hermione McKenzie for highlighting the significance of this point in my analysis.
7. In 2006, there seemed to be a breach, through tourist tours, of the taboo on non-maroons visiting Old Town; this incensed some older maroons.

8. The Accompong Maroons have been involved with heritage tourism on a limited scale throughout the period of my fieldwork. However, since 2002, the Tourism Product Development Company Limited, an agency of the Ministry of Tourism and Sport of the Jamaican government, has been formally developing tourism in the community.
9. Garvey portrayed blackness and African culture as a symbol of greatness and promised repatriation of African-Americans to Africa.
10. But Myal interpreted as anti-Obeah from the mid eighteenth century (Chevannes 1995c, 6–7).
11. Alleyne (1996, 83–84) interpreted Myal as overlapping with Obeah.
12. Both the Obeah-Myal worldview and the later "Myal movement".

References

Alleyne, Mervyn. 1996. *Africa: Roots of Jamaican culture*. Chicago: Research Associates School Times Publications. (Orig. pub. 1988.)

Barrett, Leonard E. 1988. *The Rastafarians: Sounds of cultural dissonance*. Boston: Beacon Press.

Besson, Jean. 1974. Land tenure and kinship in a Jamaican Village. 2 vols. PhD diss., University of Edinburgh.

———. 1987. Family land as a model for Martha Brae's new history. In *Afro-Caribbean villages in historical perspective*, ed. C.V. Carnegie, 100–132. Kingston: African-Caribbean Institute of Jamaica.

———. 1993. Reputation and respectability reconsidered: A new perspective on Afro-Caribbean peasant women. In *Women and change in the Caribbean*, ed. Janet H. Momsen, 15–37. London: James Currey.

———. 1995a. Free villagers, Rastafarians and modern maroons: From resistance to identity. In *Born out of resistance*, ed. Wim Hoogbergen, 301–14. Utrecht: ISOR Press.

———. 1995b. Religion as resistance in Jamaican peasant life. In *Rastafari and other African-Caribbean worldviews*, ed. Barry Chevannes, 43–76. The Hague and London: Institute of Social Studies and Macmillan.

———. 1997. Caribbean common tenures and capitalism: The Accompong Maroons of Jamaica. *Plantation Society in the Americas* 4, nos. 2 and 3: 201–32.

———. 2001. Empowering and engendering hidden histories in Caribbean peasant communities. In *History and histories in the Caribbean*, ed. Thomas Bremer and

Ulrich Fleischmann, 69–113. Madrid and Frankfurt am Main: Iberoamericana and Vervuert.

———. 2002. *Martha Brae's two histories: European expansion and Caribbean culture-building in Jamaica*. Chapel Hill: University of North Carolina Press.

———. 2003. Gender and development in the Jamaican small-scale marketing system: From the 1660s to the millennium and beyond. In *Resources, planning and environmental management in a changing Caribbean*, ed. David Barker and Duncan McGregor, 11–35. Kingston: University of the West Indies Press.

———. 2005. Sacred sites, shifting histories: Narratives of belonging, land and globalisation in the Cockpit Country, Jamaica. In *Caribbean narratives of belonging: Fields of relations, sites of identity*, ed. Jean Besson and Karen Fog Olwig 17–43. Oxford: Macmillan.

———. Forthcoming. *Transformations of freedom in the land of the maroons: Globalisation and creolisation in the Cockpit Country, Jamaica*. Kingston: Ian Randle.

Besson, Jean, and Barry Chevannes. 1996. The continuity-creativity debate: The case of Revival. *New West Indian Guide/Nieuwe West-Indische Gids* 70, nos. 3 and 4: 209–28.

Burton, Richard D.E. 1997. *Afro-Creole: Power, opposition, and play in the Caribbean*. Ithaca: Cornell University Press.

Campbell, Mavis C. 1990. *The maroons of Jamaica 1655–1796: A history of resistance, collaboration and betrayal*. Trenton, NJ: Africa World Press.

Chevannes, Barry. 1978. Revivalism: A disappearing religion. *Caribbean Quarterly* 24, nos. 3 and 4: 1–17.

———. 1994. *Rastafari: Roots and ideology*. Syracuse: Syracuse University Press.

———. 1995a. Afterword. In *Rastafari and other African-Caribbean worldviews*, ed. Barry Chevannes, 253–56. London: Macmillan.

———. 1995b. Introduction. In *Rastafari and other African- Caribbean worldviews*, ed. Barry Chevannes, xv–xxv. London: Macmillan.

———. 1995c. Introducing the native religions of Jamaica. In *Rastafari and other African-Caribbean worldviews*, ed. Barry Chevannes, 1–19. London: Macmillan.

———. 1995d. New approach to Rastafari. In *Rastafari and other African-Caribbean Worldviews*, ed. Barry Chevannes, 20–42. London: Macmillan.

———. 1995e. The origin of the dreadlocks. In *Rastafari and other African-Caribbean worldviews*, ed. Barry Chevannes, 77–96. London: Macmillan.

———. 1995f. The phallus and the outcast: the symbolism of the dreadlocks in Jamaica. In *Rastafari and other African-Caribbean worldviews*, ed. Barry Chevannes, 97–126. London: Macmillan.

Curtin, Philip. 1970. *Two Jamaicas: The role of ideas in a tropical colony, 1830–1865*. New York: Atheneum. (Orig. pub. 1955.)

Frey, Sylvia R., and Betty Wood. 1998. *Come shouting to Zion: African-American protestantism in the American south and British Caribbean to 1830*. Chapel Hill: University of North Carolina Press.

Handler, Jerome S., and Kenneth M. Bilby. 2001. On the early use and origin of the term "obeah" in Barbados and the anglophone Caribbean. *Slavery and Abolition* 22, no. 2: 87–100.

Kopytoff, Barbara Klamon. 1987. Religious change among the Jamaican maroons: The ascendance of the Christian God within a traditional cosmology. *Journal of Social History* 20, no. 3: 463–84.

Miller, Randall M. 1999. Review essay. The making of African- American protestantism. *Slavery and Abolition* 20, no. 3: 127–35.

Mintz, Sidney W. 1989. *Caribbean transformations*. New York: Columbia University Press.

Schuler, Monica. 1979a. Afro-American slave culture. In *Roots and branches: Current directions in slave studies*, ed. Michael Craton, 121–55. Toronto: Pergamon Press.

———. 1979b. Myalism and the African religious tradition in Jamaica. In *Africa and the Caribbean: The legacies of a link*, ed. Margaret E. Crahan and Franklin Knight, 65–79. Baltimore: Johns Hopkins University Press.

———. 1980. *"Alas, alas, Kongo": A social history of indentured African immigration into Jamaica, 1841–1865*. Baltimore: Johns Hopkins University Press.

Seaga, Edward. 1982. Revival cults in Jamaica: notes towards a sociology of religion. *Jamaica Journal* 3, no. 2: 3–20. (Orig. pub. 1969.)

Sibley, Inez Knibb. 1978. *Dictionary of place-names in Jamaica*. Kingston: Institute of Jamaica.

Smith, M.G., Roy Augier and Rex Nettleford. 1961. *Report on the Rastafari movement in Kingston, Jamaica*. Kingston: Institute of Social and Economic Research, University of the West Indies, Mona.

3

Colonial Injustice
The Crown v. the Bedwardites, 27 April 1921

VERONT M. SATCHELL

INTRODUCTION

The Jamaica Native Baptist Free Church founded in August Town, St Andrew in 1889, led by Alexander Bedward between 1891 and 1921, developed to become one of the largest and most significant lower-class religious movements in Jamaica. Administered from its headquarters at Union Camp in August Town, the movement, during its heyday, had over thirty-three thousand adherents situated in mission stations or camps all over Jamaica, from St Thomas to Westmoreland, from St Ann to Clarendon. Membership also spread overseas to places such as Colón (Panama) and Port Limon (Costa Rica) in Central America, and Cuba. Wherever black lower-class Jamaicans emigrated during this period, Bedwardism followed (Satchell 2004).

Entrenched racism, discrimination, poor social services, low wages, oppressive taxation and little or no political representation led to a situation in which the lower classes saw no redemption in their own country. Many sought to escape by emigrating overseas. The thousands who remained found solace in religion, through which political protests came to be disguised. The society, at this time, was one in which the lower classes had little political voice and in which outright protests were constrained by the presence of a strong paramilitary police force established by Sir John Peter Grant in 1867. Any form of dissension, riot and protest was met with the extreme force of the law.[1]

Bedward emerged to challenge the status quo and so became the voice of the poor and oppressed lower classes. To them, he was prophet, shepherd, healer and deliverer from racial injustice, inequality and oppression; in short, he was Jesus Christ who had returned to earth in the flesh to end white oppression. Bedward himself declared that he was the reincarnation of Jesus dwelling among the Jamaican lower-class black population with a mission to liberate oppressed lower-class Jamaicans (*Daily Gleaner*, 28 April 1921, 3).

Bedward's strong message of hope and deliverance from what the lower classes considered a tyrannical and oppressive government, along with his ministry of healing, greatly appealed to the people. Consequently, he developed a most significant politico-religious mass movement in Jamaica during the late nineteenth and early twentieth centuries. His overwhelming influence over the black lower classes, coupled with his rhetoric against the white upper class and his pro-nationalist sentiments, characteristic of his sermons, posed a serious threat to the colonial government and to the political stability of the colony. His activities could not have gone unnoticed by the political authorities. The result was a protracted conflict between Bedward and the Bedward movement, on the one hand, and the government, on the other. His activities were to come under close surveillance by the government. Strong police presence was common at Bedward's healing and church services. After preaching one of his most politically charged sermons on Wednesday 16 January 1895, Bedward was arrested and taken before the court and tried

> for wickedly, maliciously and seditiously contriving and intending the peace of Our Lady the Queen and of this island to disquiet and disturb, and the liege subjects of Our Lady the Queen to incite and move to hatred and dislike of Our Lady the Queen of the government established by law in this island and to move and persuade the liege subjects of Our Lady the Queen to insurrections, riots, tumults and breach of the peace and to prevent by force of arms the execution of the laws of this land. (*Daily Gleaner*, 22 January 1895, 3)

In this sermon, he declared to his followers that the time had come for the black majority to end white oppression by rising up and crushing the white minority and taking control of their destiny. If this was not done, he exclaimed, "[H]ell will be your portion" (*Daily Gleaner*, 24 January 1895, 2). This message could only be interpreted by the government and the upper classes as a call to arms, a rallying call for the lower classes to revolt against the government. The editor of the *Colonial Standard* newspaper (23 January 1895, 4) described Bedward's utterances as "blasphemous and wicked . . . inflammatory incitement to sedition, insurrection and rebellion". It was his hope that Bedward's "mischievous career . . . be brought to a close".

At his trial, which took place three months after his arrest, the jury found him not guilty on the grounds of insanity. But, rather than setting him free, the judge ordered that he be placed in the lunatic asylum. His lawyer, however, was able to get him released on a writ of habeas corpus (*Colonial Standard and Jamaica Despatch*, 28 May 1895, 2). On his return to Union Camp, he continued his politico-religious activities, though in a somewhat subdued manner. But his arrest, detention and incarceration rather than reducing his influence among the lower classes served only to bolster it. He was virtually canonized by his followers. The potential threat to the status quo, to the "peace and tranquillity of the society" remained as long as Bedward and the movement continued to exist. Consequently the authorities became even more vigilant in their surveillance of this movement. Indeed, most members of the upper classes as well as the government opined that Bedward and the Jamaica Native Baptist Free Church had to be crushed if a mass uprising of the type experienced at Morant Bay in 1865 led by Deacon Paul Bogle of the Native Baptist Church was to be prevented.

THE MARCH

This continued conflict and tension between Bedward and the government came to a head in December 1920 when Bedward declared that he was Jesus Christ; that, like Elijah, he would ascend to heaven in a flaming chariot on the last day of that year; and that he would return three days later to take his faithful followers to glory. He would then rain down fire upon those who were not among the elect and destroy the whites. He instructed his followers to gather at Union Camp to witness this ascension. Thousands of those residing throughout the island and abroad gathered at the camp in obedience to him. The governor, in response to this mass gathering and in anticipation of a widespread revolt against the constituted authority, dispatched a strong police contingent to ensure that no civil disturbance took place (*Daily Gleaner*, 3 January 1921, 3). Neither of the anticipated events occurred. There was no physical ascension, neither was there any civil disturbance.

Although somewhat disappointed that nothing spectacular had happened, the Bedwardites returned home, unwavering in their belief in Bedward, their prophet (*Daily Gleaner*, 3 January 1921, 3).

On 26 April 1921, Bedward announced that the following day, 27 April, he and his followers would march into the city of Kingston, about eight miles away, for a manifestation. He summoned his followers to August Town to prepare for this momentous march to "do battle with the enemies", presumably the whites. He also sent a messenger to the city to obtain permission from the authorities to use the park for this public meeting. But given his history, given the strained and, indeed, outright hostile and antagonistic relationship existing between himself and the state, given his known strong nationalist sentiments, and given the volatility of the situation with the potential for social unrest or even outright revolt, it is obvious that the government would not have granted his request. Neither would it tolerate or permit any march by Bedward and the Bedwardites. The request for the park was thus flatly refused. The government, however, sent a senior police officer to August Town to meet with Bedward to dissuade him from proceeding with his intended march. Bedward, however, was obdurate. In defiance, he retorted: "I must go, I must go to deliver my people. Do you know who I am? I am the Lord Jesus Christ. Must I obey you and disobey my father?" At which time the elders of the church began singing: "We nuh care what Satan a grumble, we are all going to glory" (*Daily Gleaner*, 28 April 1921, 3).

Ninety-three year old Esther Grant, one of the few surviving Bedwardites who, as a child of about eight years old, was part of the marching band, recalled the confrontation between Bedward and the police officers:

> Well him [Bedward] seh him going to have a march, him mek di, him mek di bigger man dem know, di bigger people dem know seh him gwine to have a march, an when dem come police come, an so on an so on an come on and visit, him [Bedward] seh what yu come about? Him [the police officer] seh a hear that yu gwine to have a march, but if yu love your people, if yu love yourself and love your people, yu don't have that march, yu hear what a say? If you love yourself and love your people don't have a march. Him [Bedward] seh, must I obey you and your colleagues and mustn't have a march and disobey my father? Must I obey you and your colleagues an wah? And not to have a march? I want to have a march and am going to have it! . . . Come out of my house! Clear out a my house! And the police man better tek up im foot an walk out a him house, yeah,

him pick up him stick wah him have like [dis one] yah, a did have one a him stick a don't even see it yah, have a bump pan di top . . . if yuh [hear] him come tell you seh (inaudible mumble) . . . him seh cum out! Alright that done. Policeman run gone, another one might a come an him tek up him stick fi, fi run after him, an him [the police] hat drop a groun, ah don't know if him weh tek him foot an kick di hat, anyway, leave out that. (Grant 2004)[2]

Sir Leslie Probyn (1862–1938), governor of Jamaica (1918–24), an experienced statesman, having served as governor of Sierra Leone (1904–10) and Barbados (1911–18), after assessing the situation as most dangerous, immediately convened an emergency meeting at King's House with the attorney general and the inspector general of police, during the night of 26 April, to decide on how best the situation, and especially Bedward, should be handled. At the meeting, it was agreed that any possible disturbance of the peace should be averted and that no march should take place. However, if Bedward decided to proceed with the march, he should be met with the strongest joint police-military force available and he should be arrested on two trumped-up charges: first, for assaulting a constable while the latter was acting in the execution of his duties, also for common assault on a district constable; and second, threatening to commit a breach of the peace in Kingston and inciting others to do so. The first charge was for an alleged offence committed some long time ago and the second was anticipatory; the event had not yet occurred.

Immediately after the meeting, at around midnight, Sir Leslie dispatched an urgent telegram to resident magistrate Sam Burke, instructing him to immediately go to August Town with the necessary force and fire power to stop the march. Burke was also instructed to read the riot act and fire directly into the crowd if Bedward insisted on proceeding with his march.

The telegram from Governor Probyn to Burke reads as follows (Bedward File, National Library of Jamaica):

Kings House
Jamaica
26. 4. 21

Dear Mr. Burke,
    I am very sorry to give you the trouble, but I am convinced that it is essential for you to accompany the Police when they go to August Town to-morrow morn-

ing. My chief reason is that you will possibly have to read the Riot Act. Another reason is that your presence will have a valuable effect.

Yours sincerely,
(Sgd) L. Probyn

The Riot Act reads as follows (Bedward File, National Library of Jamaica):

> Our Sovereign Lord the King chargeth and commandeth all persons being assembled immediately to disperse and peaceably to depart to their habitation, or their lawful business, upon the pains contained in this Act made in the Twenty-First year of Queen Victoria for preventing tumults and riotous assemblies. God save the King.

The governor then dispatched the following orders and instructions to the police and to Burke (Bedward File, National Library of Jamaica):

H.E. the Governor's Orders

a) Get a warrant to arrest Bedward, the warrant to be for Assaulting a Constable whilst the latter was acting in the execution of his duty; also for a Common Assault on a D.C. [District Constable]

b) Get a warrant to arrest Bedward for threatening to commit a breach of the Peace in Kingston and for inciting others to do the same.

c) These warrants are not to be executed unless and until Bedward has started with his followers to go to Kingston. By his starting, he will give evidence in support of (b) Supra: This is why he shall not be arrested until after he has started.

d) An ample force must be employed – by ample force, I mean that the force must be so great that it will over-awe and therefore make resistance seem to be hopeless.

On account of the foregoing, the Military should be asked to supply a company so that the latter may be in the vicinity of August Town and thus be ready to act in aid of civil Power.

(Sgd) L. Probyn
26.4.21

This course was settled after consultation with H.E. the Governor. Please see to drawing up necessary information.

> (Sgd) F.C. Well
> Durrant,
> Attorney General,
> 26.4.21

The inspector general of police then gave the following orders to the deputy inspector general (Bedward File, National Library of Jamaica):

> D.I.G.,
> You will proceed and take charge of a party of sixty S.O. and men from Sutton Street, and proceed to the top gate of Mona Common, to await the arrival of a procession from Bedward's camp, which he has stated is his intention to head and to march to Kingston. The party should be at the Mona iron gate at six a.m., 27th instant.
> Inspector Wright will join you at the iron gate with a party of S.O. and men from the St Andrew Division. Inspector Wright will bring with him warrants for the arrest of Bedward, if he persists in marching his procession to Kingston.
> Bedward must on no account be permitted to carry out his intention, and if necessary such force as the Magistrate who will be in attendance may direct, must be used to defeat the carrying out his object of marching on Kingston. If Bedward's procession is met on the road, Bedward must be arrested and taken to Half-Way-Tree and also any of his followers who may resist the Police. Thirty of the party of S.O. and men must be armed with carbine and ten rounds of ammunition each, the rest of the party to carry batons.
>
> (Sgd) W.E. Clarke,
> Inspector General,
> 27.4.21

The Arrest

Preparations to intercept and prevent the march into Kingston began from the wee hours of the morning. From as early as 3:30 a.m., sixty well-armed police officers drawn from the Sutton Street, Half Way Tree and Matilda's Corner police stations, were brought up to Mona estate old works, about a mile and three-quarters from Gordon Town, where they were camped. At about four o'clock, a larger force of armed police from Kingston came up. Acting Inspector General O'Sullivan, "the 'handy man' of the force, who is brought forward when the police mean business – when they are up against trouble", took charge of the operations. At about five o' clock, two platoons of the Sussex Regiment, numbering sixty men, armed with rifles and ammunition and under the command of Lieutenants C.R. Fry and H. Kirby, augmented the police detachments. This joint military police detachment, along with Sam Burke, waited in ambush inside the Mona Estate old works compound for Bedward and the Bedwardites (*Daily Gleaner*, 28 April 1921, 3).

Around the same time, Bedward and approximately eight hundred of his followers, men and women from all walks of life – bakers, butlers, carpenters, dock workers, domestics, dressmakers, wage labourers, peasants, shoemakers, tailors and unemployed persons – and children, all dressed in white clothing and armed with small wooden crosses and palm leaves, started their march to Kingston, singing the hymn "Onward Christian Soldiers".

The *Gleaner* reported the proceedings thus:

> [At the head of] a column of white stockinged, white robed, white turbaned figures with banners held aloft at their head, dressed the same as his followers, strode Bedward, . . . his flock singing vigorously "Onward Christian Soldiers", as they trudged slowly along. The largest banner which was of white cloth stretched on poles carried by two men bore this inscription in part: "Jamaica Native Baptist Free Church: A. Bedward, Shepherd. J.S. Francis, leader". A verse from the scriptures followed. Bedward's chief lieutenants carried white wooden swords – there were six of these men altogether – and nearly every man and woman in the crowd had a small wooden cross, while practically all the women also carried pieces of palm leaves. (*Daily Gleaner*, 28 April 1921, 3)

On reaching Mona Estate old works yard gate at around quarter past six in the morning, the marchers were accosted by Burke with the joint police-military force. Bedward was arrested immediately and taken in a motor car to the Half Way Tree Police Station lock-up, while the Bedwardites followed on foot, under police escort, to the same destination. The *Daily Gleaner* (ibid.) graphically reported the proceedings thus:

> At 6:15 a.m. they had reached up to the Government forces and then the dragnet closed in on the marchers . . . . [A]s the procession neared the iron gate on Mona, the police and soldiers marched out into the roadway. But the white robed

host kept steadily and slowly onward. The police motor lorry with fifteen armed men in it was driven right through the procession, stopped on the far side and the armed party jumped out and formed up. Simultaneously Inspector Wright stepped up to Bedward and read the warrants for his arrest while the remainder of the police and soldiers closed around the party.

Bedward made no overt act to resist neither did any of his followers. He was quickly placed in a motor car with an armed escort and rapidly driven to the Half Way Tree Police Station where he was locked in a cell. His lieutenants, Roman Henry – Bedward's private secretary, N. Steele, Isaac Gooden, Levi McKenzie and George Burke (son-in-law), were paired off and sent ahead under escort to the same destination as their leader. Behind them the Bedwardites, minus their "Lord" and minor leaders, with armed men before them, beside them and behind them, started again on their interrupted march also for the Half Way Tree Police Station.

Esther Grant vividly remembers:

The day when we going to have di march now. A Tuesday or Wednesday, musi Wednesday morning, we all get ready in wi white, an so on, an get wi banner an flag, an all march from here the morning, who was on fasting, who couldn't go on fasting drink dem tea who could go on fasting go on fasting an then, we get out, all get out, an when on the parade ground [the church yard] . . . yu cah see parade ground now because dem tek it mek emmm garage, motor garage. A motor garage dem put it deh fah now. [Pause]. So dem an di motor gwine go, weh dem fi go when it ready, when him [Bedward] ready, him nuh deh ya now, but anytime him ready an fi him business ready [laughs] . . . mi wont seh mi sorry fi mi self, mi sorry fi dem . . . Anyway, we march on an we go to, when we go to Edy hill, you know Edy hill? [Hill just below Mona gate] You know Bryce Hill?

After yu pass Bryce Hill an go up, to the other high hill, we reach up there . . . an after we reach up there, police and soldiers was on two side in di bush. August Town didn't have no road yu know, likkle bit a road, a Mr Bedward mek road deh yah an car, when yu walk pan di road yu cah go, if yu nuh mine sharp car mash yu up, but a him cause road to build inna August Town here, that gentleman, cause road to build inna August town, because it didn't have a road, it was pure bush, an through him . . . a don't seh it wouldn't happen, a don't seh it clean up, a can't tell, but, through him, it start. An dem have big road that two car can run two side a road now and if yu nuh mine sharp, car mash yu down, because mi deh go up pan deh bicycle deh [pointing to her wheelchair] an mercy save mi an di bicycle. Alright, when we reach a Edy Hill deh now di whole a dem [police and soldiers] Whoooooooooo! . . . Like dem come like a hooligan pan we, but we neva stop we sing, we was singing, an marching an dem come and take up Mr Bedward an put him into a car, don't remember the road, before we reach out Mona road yu know, clear out, an dem put him inna di car, when him drive inna car an we walk, an march. A nuff a we yu know, thousand a we, on the road. We was going to Parade go keep a meeting, but instead of going to Kingston to the parade to the meeting, dem carry wi right down to Half-Way-Tree [police station]. Dem don't mek wi turn so, dem mek wi go straight down and wi go right down to Half-Way-Tree. An him [Bedward] was in di car whe go right down, an we was behind di car. When we go in [Half Way Tree Police Station], dem carry we inna di . . . dem seh a jail yard nuh? (laughs) From dat mi nuh see it again, inna those days mi nuh see it again. Dem seh alright, dem lock up di gate deh now, an all of us was in there, children an everybody who march, inna di jail yard. Well when dem deh come, mi nuh hear yu nuh, mi a pickney mi nuh inn a mi, mi nuh tink mi when a ten [years old] yet, not even nine, bout eight, musi bout eight. But mi like inna, mi like inna good tings yu know, mi like fi inna good tings. Anyting a go, marching, yu know dem way, likkle yu know but when dem carry mi inna lock up, mi a go dance same way inna di lock up, because mi like it good. (Grant 2004)

The over eight hundred Bedwardites were locked up in the compound of the Half Way Tree Police station, where they were lined out in a rough semi-circle made up about equally of men and women. The police and soldiers remained outside guarding the approaches of the jail. The Bedwardites remained patiently and silently in line, with their banners bravely held aloft, with the palm leaves in their hands and their wooden crosses prominently displayed. The police soon took away the banners, and began taking the names of their "great catch of prisoners". Information charging vagrancy under the Vagrancy Act of 1902 – "being able to work and habitually abstaining from labour"[3] was laid against 685 of them. The Bedwardites were then grouped in batches of between eight and twelve ready for trial. Sam Burke, supernumerary resident magistrate, who had been through all the operations at Mona, dressed in military attire, visited the police station, "preparatory to [the Bedwardites] being brought before him in his court, for sentence to be meted out to them" (*Daily Gleaner*, 28 April 1921, 3). There is no doubt that the fate of these Bedwardites were already decided as excerpts from the court procedures will indicate. They were all going to prison.

The Trial[4]

At about ten minutes to twelve, the acting inspector general and Inspector Wright along with two armed policemen escorted Bedward from the station to the courthouse, a short walk away. A party of over two hundred Bedwardites were, soon after, escorted across to the courthouse, where they were placed in an open space to the west of the courthouse building. There, they were kept under guard until they were taken for trial. At about noon, Bedward's case was called.

"Bring up Alexander Bedward," called the deputy clerk of the courts, Mr Aubrey De Leon. According to the *Daily Gleaner* report, there was breathless silence as Bedward entered the court room escorted by Corporal Eddie and Sergeant Park, both armed with rifles. Mr Burke, before proceeding with the case, ordered that the armed policemen be removed from the court. Bedward, in the meantime, removed his white cap and stood at the side bar. The trial then began:

> His Honour: What is this man charged with?
>
> Mr De Leon: Assaulting a constable in the execution of his duty.
>
> His Honour: Are you pleading guilty or not guilty?
>
> (*Bedward made no answer.*)
>
> Mr De Leon: Under such circumstances won't your honour remand him for medical observations?
>
> His Honour: I am going to remand you for medical observation for a week.
>
> (*Bedward made no reply. Not even the slightest gesture.*)
>
> His Honour: Remand him in custody until next week Wednesday.

Bedward was thereupon removed from the sidebar without any noise or interruptions and escorted back to jail to await trial after a medical assessment.

The magistrate then turned his attention to the rank and file Bedwardites who were lined up, in batches, for trial. The first set – Francis Burrell, James French, David Lewis, Francis Rutherford, Charles Bell, Caleb Da Costa, Rainford Allen, Alfred Dennis and Naboth Stewart – was called. They pleaded not guilty to the charge of vagrancy and, in a chorus, exclaimed that they all laboured hard. One was a barber in August Town, two worked at

Caymanas sugar estate, while the others who had jobs were only recently visiting Union Camp, August Town for the pilgrimage (that is, the march to Kingston). One said that he had been a rogue, but had since been changed after he became a Bedwardite. On hearing this testimony, Mr Burke remarked that there was a quicker change in store for him.

Witness for the Crown, Corporal Sutton, stated that he knew all the defendants, that they all lived in August Town and that they did no work. "They yelled, shouted, sung, made noise from 4 a.m. until all hours of the night. This morning over 200 men and women were marching to Kingston." Inspector Wright was then called. He testified that there were over eight hundred people marching that morning. Burke, feeling that he had heard enough to indict the defendants declared, "I am going to show you what a little labour will do for you people. Fourteen days hard labour in the St Catherine District Prison." Inspector Wright then commanded the orderlies to take the convicted men away.

The acting deputy inspector then ordered the second batch to be brought in. This batch included Gerald Ballantine, James Myres, Charles Hyatt, Adolphus Ranger – who worked with Mr Gerald Abrahams, Samuel Henry, George Jones, Edward Edmondson – who came from St Thomas, Thomas Britton, Newton [?] Dennis, Samuel Fisher. In this batch were labourers, cultivators, carpenters and so on, all working people. Some were from the country and had come into Kingston for the pilgrimage at the request of their leader. The first witness for the Crown, Sergeant James Edwards, was then called. He stated that he knew all the defendants, that they habitually abstained from work and that they were all at August Town and "did no work except to make a noise since December".

Edmondson, in his defence, stated that he was a Bedwardite and was in Kingston in response to a telegram he had received from "Our Lord" to come to Union Camp for a pilgrimage into Kingston. Mr Burke then asked, "He sent for you eh?" To this Edmondson replied, "Yes Sir."

Mr Burke then asked "You didn't know what he was bringing you to? Better you had stayed there!"

Edmondson replied, "We were going on a pilgrimage sir!"

"Well it is ended here," responded Mr Burke stoutly.

Adolphus Ranger stated that he hailed from Clarendon where he received the advice of the Holy Spirit to cut out what he was doing and proceed to

August Town. Since he had been there he had been working with Mr Gerald Abrahams. On hearing this, Mr Burke then asked, "What were you doing in the crowd this morning?" "I was called out on a pilgrimage," Ranger replied.

Samuel Fisher stated that he owned his own dray, which was at August Town. The clerk of the courts then asked him, "When Mr Bedward was to ascend you did not sell the dray?"

"No sir," replied [Fisher].

Mr Burke then asked, "What did you give him?"

"What money I could," was the reply.

Mr Burke then asked, "Where were you going this morning?"

"To Kingston on a pilgrimage," [Fisher] replied.

"Pilferage did you say?" asked Mr Burke sardonically.

"No sir, pilgrimage. I got a message from the lord and master and as a soldier of the cross I had to obey."

Mr Burke, on hearing the defendant refer to Bedward as "Lord and Master", shouted "I remand you, Fisher, for medical observation."

All, with the exception of Fisher, were sentenced to fourteen days hard labour in the St Catherine District Prison.

In like manner, Magistrate Sam Burke summarily tried the rank and file men assembled in the yard of the courthouse. After sentencing the men, labelling them "all lazy, worthless scoundrels only disturbing the peace in the parish", Burke declared that they were "jolly lucky in getting only fourteen days", as he could have sent them away for twelve months.

Then came the officers and the elders of the church – Levi Steele, Benjamin Steele, Isaiah Gooden, Roman Henry, Levi McKenzie, George Burke and Christian Duke, who was a revivalist from Franklyn Town – for trial. Witnesses for the Crown were Inspector Wright and Corporal Sutton. Inspector Wright was called as the first witness. He stated:

> [He] had August Town under observation for nine months and the defendants were ringleaders of the business. There was nothing but roguery about it. Steele was the leader in the ascension movement and Gooden was one of the worst of the lot. He would not listen to reason. Roman Henry was next to the "Lord". Wright continued that he had spoken to them the Tuesday night and advised them not to come to Kingston. They had simply banded themselves together to take people's money at a meeting they had on Tuesday night [where] it was stated that they were going to beat their enemies and that they were not afraid to

come out. It was not religion at all. It was nothing but a lazy, good for nothing people. It was a big band of roguery that had been going on for many years.

Isaiah Gooden, on hearing Wright's testimony, shouted out, "I am a most industrious man; I am a cook and pastry man. I kept an ice cream place in Kingston."

Wright retorted, "He does nothing. Roman Henry is the arch leader. There is another charge against him. Burke is married to Bedward's daughter. These are the people who trade the poor fools, sir. I warned them last night."

Magistrate Burke, on hearing that they could be charged for another crime, ecstatically remarked, "They can be charged for another offence? This sort of nonsense must be stopped."

Corporal Sutton was then called to the stand. He testified that he knew the defendants. He claimed to have "had the encampment under supervision for some time, that they did no work, but robbed the poor unfortunate people. They used bad language and did all sorts of things". He, however, confirmed that, up until November the previous year, Gooden had kept an ice cream parlour in Kingston. Gooden retorted, "I am a chief cook sir." To which Mr Burke replied, "That is no recommendation."

A Mr Davis, overseer on Mona Estate, was the next witness. He stated that he knew the defendants, that they organized gangs and cut the fences, stole anything they could get, even the barbed wire. He further stated that they claimed "a piece of the Commissioner's land as having been given to them by the Lord. Roman Henry was the secretary of the Society and keeper of the money bag". The final witness for the Crown, Corporal Warden of Franklyn Town, was then called to the stands. He stated in his testimony that he knew Duke, who used to hold Revival meetings in Franklyn Town, but he had to chase him out. Mr Burke then asked, "So he came to August Town?" Then, addressing the seven he said:

> I look upon you fellows in a different light to the others. You are all ring leaders and if the Inspector chooses he might have charged you with inciting these unfortunate people. You are very leniently dealt with when you are brought under the Vagrancy Law. You are all idlers and vagabonds and I am going to deal with you differently. I am going to give you the limit. You must be imprisoned and kept at hard labour for two months. Thus the leaders were severely dealt.

By this time, the trial of 212 males was disposed of and almost all were sent to prison. In fact, a batch of 130 of those sentenced was able to be sent over to the St Catherine District Prison in Spanish Town by the 4:15 train from downtown Kingston to start their fourteen days hard labour prison sentence. These men were imprisoned despite evidence indicating that they worked at various jobs. They were labourers, cultivators, carpenters, wharf labourers, tailors, butlers, bakers. One declared that he was a contractor who had taken "a little contract at August Town" to which Burke replied, "You have taken too big a contract this time. Since you choose to follow the multitude you are in for it. Fourteen days!" Several of the brethren, cognisant of the futility in their pleading not guilty, and hoping for mercy, pleaded guilty to the charge. One Joseph Dixon, for example assuming that by making a guilty plea he would be fined rather than jailed, proceeded to ask the court for time to pay the costs. Burke retorted sardonically, "You are jumping before you reach the stye. I am going to lock you up." True to his word, Mr Burke sent him to prison for fourteen days hard labour.

Not all were sent off to prison immediately; four were remanded in custody pending medical assessment. This, in essence, meant being locked up in jail until seen by a doctor. Samuel Fisher, whose trial has been alluded to above; Richard Ferguson, who declared that his presence in August Town was in obedience to the Holy Spirit; and Ezikiah Martin and old Asher Brooks, who both affirmed that Bedward was the Lord and saviour Jesus Christ, made up this group.

With the men duly tried and sentenced, Burke now turned his attention to the four hundred and sixty women who were yet to be tried. These women, like their male counterparts, were grouped in batches for trial. Since it was nearly five o'clock in the evening, the court could only take one batch of twenty-five. This group included Elvira Beckford, Roslyn Taylor, Naomi Wilson, Adina Salmon, Catherine Bill, Elizabeth Foster, Jane Johnson, Bernice Clayto [sic], Henrietta Dixon, Margaret Dunn, Helen Campbell, Iris Gooden, Agnes Boyd, Elizabeth Small, Sarah Thomas, Mabel Sinclair, Eliza Edie, Cecelia Lewis, Clarice Grant, Helen Melvin, Ann McKenzie, Maria Goldson, Jemima Paterson, Charlotte French and Annie Scott. As in the case of their male counterparts, their cases were expeditiously dealt with, that is, without them being given a chance to prove their innocence. The *Daily Gleaner*, in its report on the proceedings, confirmed that the police knew of the careers of twenty-three of these women. The police, however, chose not to testify to this, so, with the exception of Cecelia Lewis and Iris Gooden, who were discharged with a warning, they were all sentenced to seven days hard labour in the General Penitentiary in Kingston. Their only reaction to the sentence meted out to them was a simple response: "Thank you sir." They were then escorted from the courthouse to the prison to serve their sentence. The court was then adjourned.

There were still, however, 445 women and children awaiting trial. To expedite matters, Burke, accompanied by Acting Inspector General O'Sullivan and Inspector Wright, went across to the police station to "deal with" the remaining prisoners. After soundly lecturing these women and children "on the evil of their ways and to what goal Bedwardism was leading them", he told them that he was giving them a chance, that they should "go home quietly and don't let him catch them again or it would be serious, that he hoped it would be a lesson to them and that they would stop the foolishness".

The *Daily Gleaner* (29 April 1921, 1) commented:

> The hours of detention in the station yard had a peculiar effect on some of the ladies of the cult, many of whom manifested anything but eagerness to get outside the gates when they were free to go. They frankly confessed that with their men folk on the way to prison they were afraid to go back to August Town . . . But the Law's fiat was inexorable, and through the gates they went . . . . [F]or a little while they congregated in the vicinity of the jail, taking counsel among themselves as to how best to proceed[,] then in one and two's [*sic*] and in small batches they headed up the Hope Road on the five mile tramp back to their camp at the August Town hamlet. A non-singing, sobered lot they were of a truth. On the way they were molested by non-followers for a good distance. Their pretty white turbans were torn from their heads and they were subjected to considerable ridicule on the part of the people who looked on them as fools or scapegoats.

Esther Grant (2004) confirmed this:

> So, after wi in there about between four o' clock to five mi hear dem come seh some fi go home, but unno must go a unno home, unno right home, not go back to August Town. Mi hear dem seh, August Town everybody to August Town. Mi seh alright . . . some fi . . . emmm . . . di higher one dem now fi go a jail, some fi two month, some three month.

The higher ones, the ministers, the ministers, and deacons and elders and the elders dem. Dem fi go a jail go lock up. My good gentlemen seh jail? Mr Bedward man. Him seh, one days one days, one days, one day a seh no more than one days. Dem come home back, dem let them out, dem cah lock dem up.

A total of 237 defendants out of the 685 Bedwardites charged were tried in five hours. Of those convicted, 130 men were sent to Spanish Town by rail that Wednesday afternoon and the women went by special car to the penitentiary the morning of the following day. The final batch of 55 male prisoners was sent over to Spanish Town where, according to the *Gleaner* reporter (28 April 1921, 8), "It is hoped they will with their other followers meditate at nights for it is presumed that they will work hard by day, over the folly of Bedwardism and the futility of the claims made to omnipotence by their self declared 'Lord and Master' Alexander Bedward." Indeed, the *Gleaner* reporter was in high praise of the police and court officials for expeditiously putting away these Bedwardites, and possibly bringing to an end Bedward and this menacing movement. The *Gleaner* reported (ibid.), "all together 685 persons were arrested by the police and everything went through without a hitch, reflecting the highest credit of the Police as well as the Court Staff".

Conclusion

The arrest and trial of the Bedwardites forcefully demonstrates the contempt, disregard and disdain the upper and official classes held for the lower classes. The gross denial of basic civil and human rights by colonial authorities, as manifested in this trial, were indeed typical of Crown Colony government. It is also indicative of the fear authorities had of Bedward and the Bedwardites. The following question may be asked: Why were the marching Bedwardites arrested although the order specifically stated that only Bedward should be arrested and that others should be arrested only if they attempted any resistance? The evidence shows that the marchers put up absolutely no resistance, even with the arrest of their revered leader, yet the entire bunch was marched off to the Half Way Tree Police Station where they were charged for vagrancy under the Vagrancy Act.

One possible explanation is that the police took pre-emptive measures. If Bedward alone had been arrested and his followers were left free, there was no telling what would be the result. The awe and respect the Bedwardites had for their esteemed leader was well known in the society and could not be underestimated. It would appear that the authorities assumed that the Bedwardites would not take lightly their leader being disgraced before their eyes. There was indeed a strong possibility that serious civil disturbance could have resulted. It thus seemed expedient to the police to arrest both Bedward and his fellow marchers to prevent any ensuing disturbance. A much stronger explanation, however, seems to lie in the grudge the authorities held against Bedward and their anxiety to quell the Bedward movement. Bedward and his movement had long been a problem to the authorities and there was a strong desire to crush it. Arresting Bedward and the entire lot of marchers presented a golden opportunity to "teach them all a lesson" by a show of force and so suppress the movement. The Vagrancy Act was indeed a most convenient law under which to charge these Bedwardites and so achieve the desired aim. Sections 1, 2 and 4 of this law are instructive as they indicate the effectiveness of this law as a most useful means of social control.

> Section 1: The term *vagrant* shall be taken to mean any person who has no visible lawful means of subsistence, and who, being able to labour, habitually abstains from working at any trade, profession or calling.
>
> Section 2: All prosecutions for vagrancy shall be begun by an information upon oath or solemn affirmation in the form provided in schedule "B" and in addition to swearing or affirming such information *the prosecutor shall not be bound to prove that the accused person has no visible lawful means of subsistence and does not habitually work, but it shall be for such person to prove that he has lawful means of subsistence, or that he does habitually work at a trade, profession or calling* [emphasis added] . . .
>
> Section 4: On conviction a vagrant shall be liable to imprisonment with or without hard labour for any period not exceeding two months. (A Law to Consolidate and Amend Laws Relating to Vagrancy, Jamaica Law no. 12, 1902)

The very important section 2 placed the onus of proof, *onus probandi*, on the defendant. Essentially, the defendant was deemed guilty until proven innocent. The defendant had to prove to the court that he or she was gainfully employed. The evidence in this trial clearly showed that these Bedwardites were not vagrants as defined by the law. They had "visible lawful means of subsistence". They were labourers and other wage earners, such as artisans, peasants. Most importantly, the occupation of many of those charged were known by witnesses for the Crown. But in their anxiety to "put the Bedwardites away", they had no desire or inclination to testify to this fact in the court. In the rare cases in which they did, Burke made light of it and found the defendants guilty anyway.

The Bedwardites were summoned by their religious leader to gather at their headquarters at Union Camp to participate in a pilgrimage to downtown Kingston. These persons, in obedience to their leader, took a few days leave from their employment for religious purposes. This is an accepted norm and is done often by all classes, and it in no way indicates vagrancy. Yet they were indicted as vagrants by Burke. Burke, from his upper-class position, interpreted this action of these lower-class Jamaicans – and worse, Bedwardites – as idleness and an aversion to work. Consequently, he classified them as vagrants and proceeded to send them to prison with hard labour. It is plain that Burke had already decided on the fate of these defendants; hence no evidence to the contrary would be admitted. And the law enabled him to do so. Undoubtedly, he operated within the ambit of the law. Under these circumstances, it is obvious that the Bedwardites would and could never have had a fair trial. This becomes even more evident when the swiftness with which "justice" was executed is considered. Between twelve thirty and five o'clock in the afternoon – just over four hours – 237 persons were tried, convicted and sentenced by one magistrate. Indeed, the accused persons had absolutely no time to seek legal representation, neither were they given a chance to prove their innocence, for when they attempted to do so, Burke responded in the most condescending and contemptuous manner.

The court proceedings, the gross injustice meted out to the Bedwardites, were much too blatant to be ignored by well-thinking Jamaicans. While not having any sympathy for Bedward, many considered the trial and conviction of the Bedwardites a travesty of justice and took measures to have it redressed. Indeed, Dr Oswald Anderson, Mr R.E.H. Nelson and Mr Caleb Campbell, three prominent gentlemen from St Andrew, led a deputation to the governor at Headquarters House the following afternoon to protest the manner in which the trial was conducted. They made it clear to the governor that the defendants had not been given a trial in accordance with the strict and true principle of British justice and impressed on him the necessity of having a full enquiry into the whole matter which, to them, was a blatant travesty of justice.

While these gentlemen were meeting with the governor, the matter was being hotly discussed in the Legislative Council, which was in session (*Daily Gleaner*, 29 April 1921, 1). Two black members, the Hon. Reverend George Leslie Young, elected member for St Catherine, and the Hon. Mr Dunbar Theophilus Wint, elected member for the parish of St Ann,[5] brought the matter of the trial to the attention of the council. This resulted in a lengthy debate between them and the attorney general. Both gentlemen argued that the exhibition in court did not savour British justice, because the people were not given an opportunity to defend themselves. The whole thing, they contended, looked like lynch law, and they concluded with the hope that the matter would be thoroughly investigated and that fair play would be given to those people who were tried in court so that every opportunity would be given to have justice in a British colony.

In response to the deputation and the debate in the legislative council, the attorney general recommended the granting of a free pardon to all the Bedwardites who were imprisoned. On the afternoon of Friday 29 April, the governor signed the "free pardons" and, on Saturday, the prisoners were liberated. The *Gleaner*, in its report on the "free pardons" stated: "The 208 [*sic*] Bedwardites who were convicted in the Resident Magistrate's Court at Half-Way-Tree on Wednesday of last week by His Honour Mr S.C. Burke and sentenced to terms of imprisonment from seven days to two months, *are again at large*" (emphasis added). It is obvious from the language used by the *Gleaner* reporter that he was dissatisfied and disappointed with the freeing of the Bedwardites, despite the overwhelming evidence that their imprisonment was an act of injustice that did not "savour British justice". The term "at large", as used by the reporter, suggests that these persons were chronic wrongdoers, or criminals, whose rightful place was in prison, and it implies that they were now let loose to continue terrorizing decent law abiding citizens. Such emotionally charged language undoubtedly shows forcefully the contempt the upper classes had for Bedward and the Bedwardites and, indeed, lower-class Jamaicans who tended to deviate from "British or

European" norms and culture and leaned towards a culture that they were better able to identify with.

Right, however, finally overcame might and justice won the day. The Bedwardites were exonerated and went home to August Town to await the return of their "Lord and Master". An event that never happened.

Notes

1. See "A Law to Organize a Constabulary Force". The preamble to this law states the paramilitary structure clearly: "Whereas it is expedient to constitute an improved police force, to be called 'The Jamaica Constabulary Force' which shall be under partially military organization and discipline. It is enacted by the governor of Jamaica, with the advice of the Legislative council thereof" (Jamaica Law no. 8, 1867).
2. Excerpts from the interview have been reproduced courtesy of Jodi Ann Johnson, then a graduate student at the University of the West Indies, Mona.
3. It is not clear from the literature whether or not the children were charged as vagrants; what is clear is that they were incarcerated with the adults on the compound of the police station.
4. The details of the trial, as set forth here, were taken from " 'Lord' Bedward, his chief lieuts", *Daily Gleaner*, 28 April 1921, 3.
5. Reverend Young was a trained teacher and minister of the United Methodist Free Church in Jamaica, a religious denomination formed in England in 1857 and established in Jamaica in 1898 by Reverend Francis Bavin. Young, elected in 1920, was one of five black Jamaican middle-class politicians elected to the Legislative Council. He was born in Mile Gully, Manchester, Jamaica. He was educated at St Georges Elementary Day School, Mile Gully; the Government Training College, Spanish Town; and Mico [Teachers'] College. He taught for several years until 1906. He was assistant secretary of the United Methodist Free Church in Jamaica for some years before becoming its secretary in 1906. He became superintendent minister of the Brown's Hall Circuit, consisting of eight churches from 1906 to 1920. He was once acting president and twice president of the Jamaica Union of Teachers and, for fourteen years, sat on its executive. He also served as member of the Parochial Board of St Catherine and chairman of the St John's District Committee of the Board; member of the

parish school boards of St Catherine and St Andrew; vice chairman of the district school boards of St Joseph's and Dallas; secretary of the district school boards of St Dorothy and St John; president of the Brown's Hall branch of the Jamaica Agricultural Society; and member of the Committee of Management of the Linstead People's Cooperative Bank Limited.

Dunbar Theophilus Wint was a teacher, planter and journalist. He was born in Snowden, Manchester, on 28 January 1879. He entered the teaching profession in 1897, and was a member and, for years, a director of the Jamaica Union of Teachers' Mutual Aid Society. He was the editor of the *Jamaica Tribune* (1908–19); secretary of the Alexandria branch of the Jamaica Agricultural Society; secretary manager of the Alexandria People's Cooperative Bank; secretary of the Alexandria Recruiting Committee; a leading preacher of the Wesleyan church; owner of properties in St Ann and Clarendon, and a planter of bananas and coffee; and a member of several secret societies. He travelled extensively through Central and South America between 1899 and 1901 (*Who's who in Jamaica*, 1916).

References

Grant, Esther. 2004. Interview by Jodi Ann Johnson. 16 March. Union Camp, August Town, Jamaica.

Satchell, Veront M. 2004. Early stirrings of black nationalism in colonial Jamaica. *Journal of Caribbean History* 38, no. 1: 83–84.

Who's who in Jamaica. 1916. Comp. Stephen Hill. Kingston: Gleaner Company Ltd.

4

Education, Race and Respectability in Jamaica, circa the 1938 Labour Rebellion

KHITANYA PETGRAVE

Over thirty years ago when anthropologist Peter Wilson (1973) suggested his "respectability and reputation" theory as a paradigm for understanding the Anglo-Caribbean society, his was one of various incipient analytical models[1] used to explain the region's social structures and *attitudes* emanating from the colonial period. Based on field research conducted in Providencia (an island off the coast of Colombia) during the 1960s, Wilson's dialectical concept of respectability and reputation describes what he saw as two interlocking value systems upheld by local peoples of the region, generated in response to European hegemony.

"Respectable" values generally refer to those associated with European-imported institutional structures which have stratified society into social classes based on privilege (Green 1986, 151); whereas an ethos of reputation describes an alternative system developed initially as a default by marginalized lower-class groups but which came to represent ideals antithetical to "metropolitan values" (ibid.).

The theory's binaries of respectability/middle-class/white/women and reputation/lower-class/black/men, though seen by some academics as useful for describing the tensions between social groups seeking upward mobility in colonial/neo-colonial society, have been challenged by others (Besson 1993, 15–37; Burton 1997) not least because of its oversight of gender and class nuances.

One of the least explored aspects of Wilson's arguments, however, concerns the issue of education. According to Wilson, "Euro . . . ideas and ideals enter the [Anglo-Caribbean] society most pervasively and influentially through the [school] system" (Wilson 1973, 231); "brown" and black peoples sought social status through education. In other words, education was one of two bastions of respectability in the British West Indies, the church being the other. Those who subscribed to values of reputation, on the other hand, were often uneducated and illiterate, states the theory.

Though significant works have dealt with education as cultural imperialism in the region[2] and (the focus of my doctoral research) Jamaica[3] regarding the motives of British authorities/Jamaican social elites in maintaining status quo, very little is understood about the attitudes of the island's lower classes towards education in relation to this situation.

Few studies have focused on the meaning of education to black lower-middle-class Jamaicans of the colonial period, who occupied the interstitial spaces between the island's lower and established middle classes, that is, those who do not seem to be accounted for in Wilson's theory (for they did not associate with so-called values of reputation, and they could not, for mainly reasons of race and class, readily access respectability).[4] In particular, no work has looked at educational discourses of this group near the turn of the twentieth century, when they increasingly saw themselves as ideological representatives and role models for the peasant labouring class.

This chapter looks at how elements within the black Jamaican lower middle class viewed education in itself and vis-à-vis the "masses" circa the 1938 labour rebellions, in which elements within the latter initiated a series of uprisings against colonial subjugation, and explores the educational attitudes of the petty bourgeoisie and elementary school teachers who saw education as a means of improving blacks' status. It suggests that, although the groups' educational impulses were politically anti-racist, their focus on education as a symbol of respectability legitimated the elitist tendencies of the colonial system. Moreover, it shows that their approach to education, which distinguished them from "reputational" groups shaping the uprisings (such as Rastafarians), lay in the differing definitions of what constituted black cultural autonomy.

The chapter focuses first on the state education policy's conceptions of Jamaican blacks in the period leading up to 1938 and then the educational attitudes of the black lower middle-class elements during the uprisings and after, when the West India Royal Commission conducted investigations.

British Education Policy in 1930s Jamaica

When Stanley Hammond, the director of education in Jamaica,[5] suggested in 1930 that "the fostering of an interest in the soil and of skill in practical cultivation should play a . . . larger part . . . in education" (Education Department 1930, 44), he was expressing what the Colonial Office saw as a solution to the economic depression then gripping the colony. At the time, the main tiers of the island's school system were literary in orientation: the curriculum of the primary system, which had enrolled about 40 per cent[6] of the island's child population,[7] was heavily centred on the basic skills of reading, writing and arithmetic; the secondary system, which catered to the island's elites, was shaped by the academic Cambridge examination syllabus (Whyte 1977, 48). Of the existing vocational schools, only one, the Government Farm School for Boys, founded in 1909 (Cover 1939, 261), focused on agricultural education.

During the first decades of the twentieth century, the economy of Jamaica was in a moribund state. The sugar industry, which had been the mainstay of the British-run, export-oriented economy since its inception (Eisner 1961), and whose plantation ethos informed the tenets upon which the society had been organized, was increasingly unable to match international competition.[8] Even with the institution of British imperial preference in 1932, from which "West Indian sugar companies benefited more than most" (Whitman 2002, 2), plantations of the region, crippled by inefficient infrastructures, succumbed to the effects of the Great Depression (Rampersad 1979, 82). Moreover, the banana trade which, by the 1930s, eclipsed sugar as the staple of the Jamaican economy, accounting for 55.2 per cent of exports against 21.07 per cent for sugar between 1934 and 1937 (Davis 1942, 24), also faced a collapsing world market towards the end of that decade (Sunshine 1985, 37). The resultant unemployment problems, emanating from monocultural dependence, were exacerbated by a growing trend of rural to urban migration and the influx of returning expatriates from Latin America and the United States, who had increasingly, after 1929, been excluded from host societies.[9] Between 1921 and 1943, St Andrew (a largely urban parish) experienced "a phenomenal 134.7 percent increase of population" (Jamaica Central Bureau of Statistics 1945, xxx); meanwhile, most of the 28,000 returning emigrants, between 1928 and 1934, resettled in Kingston – the island's capital (Cumper 1956, 272). Interwar officials, therefore, even while supporting multinational corporations in Jamaican agriculture,[10] increasingly saw the development of agriculture – through the growth of rural peasant holdings – as a panacea to its problems.[11]

Education was identified as a key component of economic resuscitation efforts.[12] British officials in the island's Education Department reasoned that, if pupils were to have a "fuller and richer understanding of their immediate economic environment" (Howe and Easter 1934, 1) and if pride in the land were fostered, then the result would be resourceful, intelligent workers. The idea was not only for education to bond students with the land via agrarian pedagogy but, generally, to direct pupils to occupations that were potentially productive of wealth, preferably within a rural context.

This was a race-, class- and gender-biased policy. *Practical* education, which emphasized the creativity of the brain and the dexterity of the hands, was directed towards state-controlled schools which, not fortuitously, accommodated the progeny of the Jamaican working classes. Labouring-class Jamaicans of largely African and, to a certain extent, East Indian descent,[13] who were settled in the countryside (Clarke 1975), were assumed fit for agricultural work.

Boys in particular were singled out.[14] The desire to enforce the idea of the male as family breadwinner, which had heretofore been inoperative among the majority (French 1988, 45), was central to the thinking of education administrators in the 1930s (Shepherd 1995). This new policy was one which did not match the reality of the extant socio-economic milieu: peasant-class Jamaican women, to whom vocational education was directed, operated in both public and private domains. Lower-class Jamaican women had been a critical part of the island's agrarian labour force since the period of slavery when European capitalist impulses allowed for a relative lack of gender discrimination amongst workers (Shepherd 1995, 236). Nonetheless, a practical education policy of this kind was increasingly promoted by the interwar Colonial Office throughout the British West Indies and certain other depressed areas of the Empire, notably those with significant non-white populations.[15]

In Jamaica, the free tuition elementary system and its fee-paying extension, the post-primary "continuation" system, were natural targets of British reformers and their allies. Grant-aided secondary schools, which by definition were financially linked to the state, were under the jurisdiction of autonomous governing bodies and not subject to Education Department policy per se. The island's elementary system, on the other hand, germinated from a religious missionary movement in the mid nineteenth century, which coordinated with the government to educate the children of ex-slaves (Gordon 1963, 15). Throughout the post-emancipation era, Jamaican elementary and secondary education evolved separately, as both systems, following the pluralistic tendencies of society,[16] were oriented to groups on the opposing ends of the social scale: the agro-proletariat class (generally black) and the upper/middle classes (mostly white/"brown") respectively (Turner 1987, 54–87).

Centring on the concept of the "school garden", calls in education reports between 1929 and 1938 seemingly challenged the premise of the original elementary system which, according to some historians, sought to "reinforce [black] dependence on a plantation system" (Moore and Johnson 2004, 205) but still assumed that agricultural work was appropriate for blacks. The Elementary Education Scheme enacted in January 1938 was the culmination of official efforts to channel pupils onto a vocational track. The scheme, evolving from a 1937 Board of Education inquiry, allowed for a new syllabus of instruction in schools which was hoped to "break from the old tradition" (Education Department 1939) of the three Rs and to provide a "well-balanced education" (*Daily Gleaner*, 31 January 1938, 21) incorporating vocational subjects with literary ones. Overall, the scheme was seen by its authors, the supervisors of the elementary system,[17] as necessary "measures . . . adopted in the nature of economic investment" (Education Department 1940).

HEALTH AND MORALITY

Other evidence points to anxieties about economic decline being closely linked to fears of sociocultural degeneration. In the eyes of authorities, part and parcel of producing a resourceful workforce in response to the Depression needed to be the cultivation of wholesome subjects.

Public health was a foremost concern. Consistently low attendance rates in the elementary schools, which averaged nearly half of the enrolment figures during the period, highlighted the poor health and living standards of pupils.[18] The problem manifested not only in country areas where, in 1934 "yaws and worms were . . . important causes of illhealth" among school children, but also within the Kingston metropolitan region where 74 per cent of 2,475 pupils medically examined that year showed "defects" (Colonial Office 1934, 8). The malnourishment rate among elementary school students in one year was estimated at between 50 per cent and 60 per cent.[19] For British observers of the post-depression society, the "best hope" for "civilizing" islanders lay in promoting "a *healthier*, educated and economically fitter black population" [my emphasis] (Macmillan 1936, 19).

Thus, the teaching of human biology was increasingly seen as significant by the colonial administration. The "scientific" enlightenment of pupils at state elementary schools could, after all, help counteract their physical deficiencies, an ostensible product of their parents' "immorality". The escalating illegitimacy rates of the "masses" during the 1930s were seen as anathema to "family life", upon which "racial progress depends" (Mayhew 1938, 281). Education was viewed as a necessary forum to counter the problem as, according to the European orthodoxy, "darker colour, woolly hair and other conspicuous physical Negro characteristics" were "associated with servile status, backward culture, *low intelligence* performance and lack of morals" [my emphasis] (Myrdal 1944, 98). In British-controlled Kenya, white eugenicists, who were influential in education, believed that the "average adult native was incapable of achieving a standard of intelligence higher than an eight to ten year old European schoolboy", and among the "causes of this deficiency" was the tendency of "natives" to "reproduce abundantly" (Campbell 2001, 2). In Jamaica, while such beliefs were not so grotesquely enunciated, the philosophies underpinning elementary education were motivated by similar impulses.

For example, in 1935, B.H. Easter recommended that moral hygiene be taught in the schools (*Daily Gleaner*, 3 April 1935, 18); two years later, representatives from the British Social Hygiene Council, who were invited by the state, "provoked keen interest in the biological approach to sex education" (Education Department 1939) and by 1938, the newly enacted Education Scheme, whose religious and secular proponents were concerned about "child motherhood and lack of parental control", claimed to feature "radical changes" in science (Education Department 1940).

THE 1938 REBELLIONS

Referring to the first of major labour riots to impact Jamaica in 1938, a local newspaper article in that year, ominously titled, "A Warning from St Thomas", stated that "there is little hope for the much oppressed labourers if conditions remained unchanged. They cannot hope to rise far by education, as there are but few elementary and no secondary schools [in the parish of St Thomas], and by reason of their low economic standard, they cannot go elsewhere to seek knowledge" (*Public Opinion*, 15 January 1938, 6).

The series of working-class protests which punctuated the Jamaican landscape in that year were an expression of socio-economic grievances against their employers fermenting in the aftermath of the Great Depression (St Pierre 1978).

Explicitly, the cause of the riots, which marked the climax of other British West Indian protests,[20] was economic: demonstrations by largely unskilled labourers, dockworkers and the unemployed revolved around "bread and butter" issues of land and employment. Implicitly, the "disturbances", which involved both male and female participants (Reddock 1989, 86–96), many of whom were just past the school age,[21] were a symptom of frustration induced by lack of opportunity for the island's labouring classes. Race was a major factor precluding their advance: the riots of the region took place in an environment "where people of one colour are predominant among employers and the workers are found almost wholly from those of another colour" (WIRC 1945, 59).

According to Trevor Munroe, the crisis in the world capitalist system after 1929 combined with the Italian invasion of Ethiopia in 1935, which Britain appeared to sanction, had increasingly heightened feelings of class exploitation and racial discrimination among black Jamaicans (Munroe 1974, 2). The Rastafarian/Ethiopianist movement, whose African-centred worldview had informed its formation as an anti-colonial protest group in Jamaica after 1930,[22] was a major influence among segments of the urban poor in 1938

(Post 1978, 205; Bolland 1995, 135). Thus, an embryonic racial consciousness whose seeds blossomed in reaction to the above (Carnegie 1973, 38), but which were being intermittently sown from the post-emancipation period (Bolland 2001, 166–67), was critical to the self-assertion of poor blacks in 1938.

In 1930s Jamaica, education was a facilitator of upward social mobility; at the same time, that society "owed its form to self-perpetuating distributions of political, civil, economic and educational inequality" (Smith 1958, 42). Few scholarships were available for fee-paying post-primary and elite secondary schools; moreover, there was a growing feeling among certain blacks[23] that scholarship requirements were either skewed in favour of non-black Jamaicans or deliberately appropriated to them. The above case of the St Thomas parish riots, ostensibly about labourers' protests for better wages (Hart 2002, 16), suggests that workers' grievances, in part, stemmed from inequitable distribution of educational facilities in the colony. Yet, lower-class demonstrators did not explicitly articulate education as an issue of concern.[24] The 40 per cent to 60 per cent illiteracy rate of the Jamaican population in 1938, itself evidence of widespread lack of education, perhaps reflected a universal characteristic of the oppressed who are "unaware of the causes of their condition" (Freire 2003, 30, 64).

Rather, education was a key discourse raised by local "spokespersons" for the labouring class emerging amidst the uprisings. During the course of 1938, elements from the island's black, lower-middling strata and the petty bourgeoisie, who had increasingly related to the racial plight of the disenfranchised (Post 1978, 205), seized the initiative from the peasant-wage labourers to agitate for improved conditions of the "masses". In spite of their relatively better social positions, a significant number of spokespersons were descendants from the peasantry class who were able to ascend the colonial hierarchy only after returning to the island from overseas (Thomas-Hope 2002, 167). Only few had had the opportunity of accessing the Jamaican education system. Thus, the consciousness of these persons bore the stamp of their mixed reality: they saw themselves as natural leaders of the oppressed, with whom they largely shared a common racial ground, but at the same time they had no plans for overturning the status quo as such. Much of their energies was directed towards demanding from the establishment, however subtly, the amelioration of working conditions.[25] But for several of these self-appointed "labour" leaders, the social plight of their protégés was significant to, and interlinked with, their economic status. Education of the working classes was seen as key to both concerns.

THE MEANING OF EDUCATION: RACE AND RESPECTABILITY

The idea of education, in their minds, was equated with the concept of racial upliftment. Inspired by certain doctrines of the Universal Negro Improvement Association (UNIA), founded by Jamaican Marcus Garvey in 1914 to empower blacks (Hart 2001), emerging mediators of 1938 raised education in their interactions with both labourers and authorities. Though Garveyism had appealed to poor Jamaicans, after the onset of the depression its principal objectives, which were "to encourage material success through individual effort, encourage educational attainment, race consciousness and racial pride" (Sherlock and Bennett 1998, 299), increasingly resonated with "professional middle-class, artisans and self-employed working-class people" (Hill 1990, xxxix) of the colony.[26] The Anti-Oppression Social Reconstruction League of Jamaica was a strong voice emerging during the riots which leaned on UNIA philosophy (Williams 1959, 8) – the Garveyite movement in Jamaica had, by this time, become more or less dormant.[27] The Social Reconstruction League, founded in early 1938 by Barrington Williams, an ex-constable, was comprised of "approximately 2,500 members . . . belong[ing] to the peasantry" ("Notes of a deputation from the 'Social Reconstruction League' received by the colonial secretary at Headquarters House on the 2nd April 1938"), whose executive was concerned with "social and economic questions" (Williams 1959, 8) of the poor. In the minds of Williams and his "better off" black peers, acquisition of knowledge by poorer classes would not only improve that subset of the race but would be an improvement for all within the race.

Intrinsic to these desires to use education as a mode of racial upliftment, however, was the incentive of education's symbolism as respectability. The following excerpt of Williams's speech at a 5 March 1938 meeting of the Social Reconstruction League suggests the meaning that spokespersons invested in education: "All you people do in Jamaica is to play Peeka Peow,[28] dance Pocomania,[29] and belong to Rastafari[30] cults. Look first at the *education* of your children, you the majority have no respect for your mother"

("Minutes of a meeting of the anti-oppression and social reconstruction league held on the 5.3.38 at Beeston Street and Spanish Town Road [as recorded by officers of the Criminal Investigation Department in letter sent to Inspector, 6.3.38]"; emphasis added). In Williams's mind, the apparent relegation of education by certain of the oppressed was equated with subscription to values of reputation – the antithesis of respectability. Men who originated from the lower class were just as likely as their female counterparts and upper-class compatriots to value and uphold respectability. For the black lower middle class of the colonial Anglo-Caribbean, of which Williams was a part, "respectability was not an ideal, it was an armour" (James 1963, 18); it was the route to their definition of "whiteness" and status.

Thus, amidst the tensions of the uprisings, one's position on the social scale and one's relation to modes of production were critical to concern or non-concern about education. Among a certain contingent of the Jamaican lower classes, who bore the brunt of the economic decline, ideas of empowerment were constructed on their own terms (Gray 2004, 14–15). In contrast, for the petty bourgeoisie and lower-middle-strata "labour" leaders, the anxieties of their social class, which aspired for respectability, both fed and competed with those of race: education promised both continued social ascent and racial redemption.

That education stood at the heart of the divide between certain segments of the aggrieved and their "better off" leaders is suggested in the following 1938 article from an establishment newspaper concerning other black activist forces:[31] "At present there is a movement on foot in Jamaica to make the masses more race conscious and teach them to avoid servility . . . [I]n their effort to avoid servility the masses are indulging in downright disrespect for everything that time has sanctioned worthy of respect. It is a source of regret to notice . . . the lack of respect of youth for age, of the vulgar for the cultured, of the *ignorant* for the *educated*" (Isaacs 1938, 23; emphasis added).

THE WEST INDIES ROYAL COMMISSION: "PRACTICAL" VERSUS "CULTURAL" EDUCATION

In the aftermath of the 1938 "disturbances", British authorities desired a stronger implementation of agricultural education as a means to restore order to the West Indian economy and society. Literary subjects ought not to be the focus in elementary schools, they argued. The West India Royal Commission (WIRC), appointed by the British Parliament in the summer of 1938 to investigate conditions in the affected colonies, supported and perpetuated this ideal (WIRC 1945, xiii).

Their message was clear: the children of the Jamaican/West Indian lower class, who were mostly black, should be trained in agriculture because they were naturally suited to it rather than intellectual work. The pupils of the elite secondary system, who were largely white and "brown", should not engage in agriculture, as they were naturally fitted for academic training (WIRC 1945, 120). The following excerpt of a commentary made by an American from the southern states in 1934 sheds insight into possible motives behind British indifference towards literary education for lower-class blacks in the period: "The belief that education spoiled the slave carried over with but little modification for many years into the belief that education spoils a field-hand . . . Reading and figuring carry elements of danger to established relations" (Myrdal 1944, 894).

It was not that black Jamaicans and West Indians should not have "cultural" academic education: they definitely needed it. Certainly British officials could not justify mitigation of European-content education to the black West Indian, unlike the case of the black African who had his "own native institutions and native customs" (Macmillan 1936, 143–44). The contemporary European orthodoxy, according to W.M. Macmillan, was that western institutions were unsuited for the African mentality. By the British definition, black Caribbean people of the early twentieth century were neither "pure" African nor European; they were considered "in-between" and almost "touching elbow[s] with modern civilization" (March 1940 memorandum on recommendations of report of West India Royal Commission Jamaica from B.H. Easter, CO/318/444/14 cited in WIRC 1945, 216).

At the same time, those Jamaicans who opposed practical education, largely blacks, were derided as "backward" and uncivilized. According to the WIRC report, an educational system's sole focus on book learning exemplified "tribal simplicity" which "Western society [had] long since outgrown" (WIRC 1945, 118). In March 1940, B.H. Easter proclaimed that to not support an agricultural education policy in certain areas of Jamaican schooling "would be contrary to educated opinion in every civilized country of the world" (*Hansard*, 12 March 1940, 73). The ability of an education system to adapt itself to "changing needs" (WIRC 1945, 119) was argued by the British colonials as a sign of modernity. Rather than indicting the system of Crown Colony rule in Jamaica, as some scholars such as Philip Sherlock (Sherlock and Bennett 1998) contend, the WIRC report, in terms of its ideas on practical education, validated the assumptions made by Crown Colony administrators in Jamaica during the 1930s.

The Jamaica Union of Teachers: A Voice for the "Masses"?

Opposed to the British policy of agricultural education, particularly for the island's elementary school children, were the teachers of that system. Key executives of the Jamaica Union of Teachers (JUT), the main elementary teachers' guild of the period, saw the platform of the Moyne Commission investigations as critical for vocalizing remonstrations.

Economic Pragmatism or a Matter of "Respectability"?

Economic reasons alone should militate against an agricultural-biased curriculum, as far as influential members of the JUT were concerned. When local agrarian schemes were untenable and little opportunity for socio-economic progress existed for blacks in agriculture,[32] how could the island's working classes be expected to pursue agricultural vocations? The apathy of these classes towards agriculture, brought about by economic conditions, underlay their indifference towards an agrarian-based elementary curriculum, and this, in the minds of teachers, was justified. The JUT pointed out to the WIRC that "such neglect of Agriculture [in education] where it exists, is caused almost entirely by the ruinous system of land tenure, whereby tens of thousands of would-be cultivators are unable to cultivate. This has been the condition for generations, so, naturally the masses have been forced to look elsewhere" (JUT 1938a).

Remuneration in agriculture was also significantly less than in other occupations, particularly for the majority of labourers who owned neither the land nor the means of production. A British metropolitan official visiting

West Indian society in the 1930s conceded that "agricultural work must have presented an unattractive prospect to thoughtful young people; in most cases they have seen their parents engaged in long hours [of] hard work for meagre pay. The prospect in itself must be unattractive, and there is little to which the aspirant can look forward" (Orde-Brown 1939, 38).

According to elementary teachers, indifference to an agricultural syllabus was not a matter of snobbery, as was implied by Director Easter (in a memorandum to the WIRC in 1938), it was a matter of survival. When asked by Lord Moyne, during the oral testimony, whether the former was a factor, J.J. Mills, then president of the JUT (Who's Who 1945, 407) replied: "I do not think so. I think that has been rather over-stated in this country. My experience, and the experience of a good many of us, is that the majority of the educated or semi-educated boys from the peasantry . . . have no land on which to work . . . they will not work for other people who have land at salaries which cannot feed them" (JUT 1938b, 62).

The agrarian wages, which provided "only for bare maintenance" (WIRC 1945, 215), compounded by asymmetrical relations between workers and employers/landlords, only reinforced the perception, among certain local peoples, of farming as an occupation of low socio-economic status. Even the visiting investigators conceded, albeit with a mindset confirming the suspicions of teachers, that "if education is to fit the West Indian to make the most of the opportunities afforded by his own country, those [agricultural] opportunities in their turn must be sufficient to attract those who have had a *good* education" (ibid., 108).

The underlying *raison d'être* for the JUT's prioritization of literary education, however, centred on the issue of respectability. In the minds of elementary teachers, blacks' access to academic, non-manual education would help qualify pupils for training leading to so-called dignified jobs, carried out by, and seemingly limited to, those with higher social status. In 1930s Jamaica, the secondary school certificate, awarded after completion of the Cambridge-influenced syllabus, was practically the sole gateway to the island's civil service and professional sectors (Johnson 2002, 28).

The message which the JUT executive presented to the Moyne Commission was that agricultural labour in Jamaican society was as much socially as it was economically disrespected, and poor blacks, already labelled as inferior, should not be limited to that. One's ascent up the island's colonial ladder was contingent on the attainment of an intricate mix of social and economic status, which were interlinked and mutually dependent phenomena. As one teacher testified, "the difficulty has been that while you induce a man to have ambition and to rise, he does not want to rise to the state where he is called a 'common labourer'. If he goes to the Court to give evidence, for instance, he is paid perhaps 1s 6d a day as a 'common labourer', whereas a doctor gets two guineas. It does not give a man any aspiration to educate himself up to the point of being called a 'common labourer' " (JUT 1938b, 63).

Academic-oriented education, through its material association with "black-coated" jobs (Orde-Brown 1939, 38), was therefore seen by the island's working classes, through the eyes of the lower middle class, as crucial to mitigating feelings of inferiority. Elementary school teachers, themselves, as offspring of peasant-labourers, had pursued their quasi-professional occupations as they "saw no prospect of a satisfying future on the land" (Goulbourne 1988, 73). Theirs symbolized a movement of black Jamaicans to wrest social prestige through educational means available; according to Claude McKay's epic *Banana Bottom,* set in 1930s Jamaica, "so many black boys had pushed up out of the canefields from under the fat spreading bananas and forced their way into clerical and scholastic places" (McKay 1961, 9). Harry Goulbourne argues that attempts by the British to incorporate agriculture into the island's state curriculum since the turn of the century had been interpreted by teachers as a threat to their "social and professional" status (Goulbourne 1988, 140).

In the JUT's official mind, elementary graduates, equipped with "cultural" education, could potentially progress onto the elite secondary track or the clerical vocational track in the post-primary system. Even those not fortunate in terms of scholarships would be armed with the knowledge to compete, not realistically for professional occupations, for at least low-end clerical jobs. Clerical employment in the early twentieth century was increasingly associated with middle-class ambition (Rury 1991, 147). Despite the fact that most clerical wages in Jamaica were only marginally better than those offered for agricultural work,[33] a corollary of the overcrowded industry to which the island's schools contributed no small part,[34] the position of clerk was seen as psychologically superior.

The social distance between clerks, described by a visiting British official as "the most depressed class" (Orde-Brown 1939, 39), and the lower classes from which most had originated was considerable. As Jamaican labour activist Richard Hart expressed in his 1938 diary documenting the workers' uprisings that year, "the shops on King Street were . . . closed, but by dockmen and their sympathizers, not by the shop assistants working for 9/- and 8/- (per week). These were to be observed clapping their hands from the top of buildings, as police drove a small band of strikers from lower King Street . . . They are . . . too snobbish to sympathize with ordinary labour" (Hart 1989, 48). It was, nonetheless, imperative to the JUT that, within the island's elementary schools "so-called 'literary' subjects . . . be retained and emphasized . . . [and] the so-called 'practical' (particularly agricultural) subjects . . . be introduced, but not overemphasized" (JUT 1938a).

Race and "Cultural" Education: The Case for Black Intellectual Ability

Additionally, these teachers' convictions were aimed at projecting the message that blacks were intellectually capable of cerebral work and thus deserved educational opportunities to gain social status. The target of the island's interwar practical education policy had not eased their anxieties concerning the perception by European authorities and their collaborators of lower-class blacks as non-intellectual beings. In 1937, the Western Federation of Teachers vehemently opposed the concept of the school garden on the grounds that elementary school pupils would be pigeonholed as "hewers of wood and drawers of water" (Carnegie 1973, 30).

The paradoxical nature of pro-agrarian arguments would only have served to reinforce the anxieties of elementary school teachers. For, on the one hand, practical education was promoted by the Education Department as an embodiment of modern civilized education, yet on the other hand, vocational education was sometimes recommended by department officials for children who were perceived as developmentally slow. For example, in a report to the WIRC (26 October 1938, 5), the Select Committee of the Board of Education, headed by B.H. Easter, claimed that "the problem of dealing with backward children (of elementary school background) . . . might be solved by providing Special Classes in the Senior Schools in which

Manual Occupations and Handicraft should play an important part" (emphasis added). The JUT's advocacy of literary education for blacks was, therefore, directly linked to challenging the racial criterion of the imperial status quo – the idea that poor blacks were unintelligent and should, therefore, naturally occupy subordinate positions.

Debates concerning "practical" versus "cultural" education vis-à-vis blacks would characterize societies in which white-controlled power rested on black subjugation. In the American South, "almost as soon as the movement for the education of Negro youth began, the quarrel started as to whether Negro education should be 'classical' or 'industrial'. If the white Southerners had to permit the Negroes to get any education at all, they wanted it to be of the sort which would make the Negro a better servant and labourer, not that which would teach him to rise out of his 'place'" (Myrdal 1944, 889).

According to Gunnar Myrdal (ibid.), a Swede who conducted a study of American "Negroes" in the late 1930s, the push for agricultural education for blacks in the late nineteenth century by a white union officer of the Civil War had been "extremely timely in the actual power situation of the Restoration". In British colonial Africa, a 1925 edict which would influence imperial education policy, enacted by the Advisory Committee on Education in British Tropical Africa (Whitehead 2003, ix), called for the adoption of mass education more closely related to the local environment and rural lifestyles – essentially an agricultural education (Whitehead 1988, 211).

In all aforementioned societies, factions of local blacks contested the idea of a non-literary schooling for their racial compatriots. Although each polity was distinct in its customs and social configurations, blacks within Africa and across the African diaspora shared an underlying mindset. Their position can be gauged from the missives of Ethelred Brown, a Jamaican expatriate residing in Harlem during the 1930s, in response to a proposal from the New York Department of Education to institute a vocationally inclined "Negro Curriculum": "We must see to it that all Negroes, as all whites, receive that type of education which will send them from school fully prepared not only to be what others decided beforehand they should be, but to fill any position to which they may rightly aspire, and to which they may respectively be called" (*New Amsterdam News*, 27 October 1934). Brown's 1934 letter to the district superintendent of the department said, "I do not object to differentiated courses as such but I do object to differentiation [the italicized words were struck out] *aimed at race or a class on the presumption that* which aims to limit the . . . activities of a group because of preconceived notions as to the inherent ability and aptitude of that group" (draft of Brown's reply to Oswald Schlockow's letter sent on 29 October 1934).

It was not simply, as asserted by scholars such as Clive Whitehead (1988) that colonized blacks against practical education were subversives motivated by elitist desires. Rather, working within hegemonic power structures, these blacks, as exemplified by the Jamaican elementary school teachers, believed that they could "win the respect of the whites and take their place as equal[s] . . . only if they [were] educated in non-vocational cultural values" (Myrdal 1944, 900). Moreover, Jamaican teachers, particularly in the absence of practical policy criticism by the elected members,[35] the official representatives of the people, saw it their duty to communicate to the WIRC the desires of the majority. The "brown" proxies could not be relied on for support in this instance.

At the same time, a less noble motive underlay the JUT's pro-literary education position. Far from being against the principle of "civilizing" blacks through education, teachers believed that those of the lower class were "backward", albeit not naturally but due to environmental factors. These persons, at impressionable ages, could therefore be reformed through "cultural"/ academic-oriented education. At a January 1938 JUT conference, the union's retiring president, J.H. Loftman, pronounced:

> [W]e, as teachers, must realize that the masses, on the whole, are lacking in many of those elements which contribute to self-respect and recognition. They lack culture definitely, they act objectionably, on the whole . . . and they seem to perpetuate too many of the features usually associated with servitude . . . Here, then is a clear path along which useful and reformative work can be undertaken by the JUT. (*Daily Gleaner*, 4 January 1938, 14)

Amy Bailey claimed that a more soundly educated population would, therefore, mean that "Pocomania and street corner meetings would have few followers" (*Jamaica Times*, 18 June 1938, 20).

The union's push for non-vocational education, made clear to the WIRC by the end of that year, was to protect and legitimize elementary school teachers' tenuous positions in Jamaica's social hierarchy. As Nigel Bolland articulates, British West Indian teachers of the late colonial period "struggled above all to maintain their social status on the basis of a respectability that kept them socially distinguishable and apart from those whom they considered to be below them" (Bolland 2001 165). As persons with largely dark-coloured skin, who were, for all intents and purposes, "Negroes", elementary school teachers suspected that very little distinguished them from the "masses" in the eyes of Europeans. They believed, therefore, that all must be done to convince the colonial authorities that they were different from poor blacks and were "improving" these poor people, even if this meant opposing official policy.

Conclusion

In 1938, while one kind of rebellion was being waged on the Jamaican streets, a more subtle, though no less genuine, protest was being carried out by two separate branches of the lower middle class seeking status and dignity for blacks through education.

This chapter has explored the educational attitudes of the aspiring "respectable" in colonial Jamaica. It has suggested that, although the groups' educational impulses were politically anti-racist, their focus on education as a symbol of respectability legitimated the elitist tendencies of the colonial system. Moreover, it has shown that their approach to education, which distinguished them from "reputational" groups shaping the uprisings (such as Rastafarians), lay in the differing definitions of what constituted black cultural autonomy.

Notes

1. "Functionalism", which refers to "white bias" as a unifying factor of the Anglo-Caribbean colour-classes, and "pluralism", which seeks to portray culturally distinctive value systems in the region, constitute the main theories.
2. There is considerable literature on the sociocultural effects of British schooling in various territories of the "British Empire". Carl Campbell's (1996) ground-

breaking research on British education policy in Trinidad between 1834 and 1939 warrants honourable mention.

3. Ruby King has pioneered research in British education policy in nineteenth-century Jamaica. Notable works which have examined Jamaican colonial education within a wider framework of cultural imperialist projects include Patrick Bryan (1991) and Brian Moore and Michelle Johnson (2004). A valuable quantitative study has been done by Errol Miller (1990).

4. A notable exception is Harry Goulbourne (1988).

5. The post of director of education in Jamaica involved heading the island's Department of Education during the colonial period; the person was typically a Briton appointed by the Colonial Office.

6. This figure may be an overestimate as it is based on the percentage of children *enrolled* in the interwar Jamaican elementary schools (128,154 in 1930) divided by the total Jamaican child population (aged fifteen and under) in the period (337,669 in 1921). The number of enrolled children who actually *attended* elementary school typically stood at 50 per cent of the enrolment figure.

7. The total population in the island was just over 1 million; The total population rose from 936,927 in 1926 to 1,138,558 in 1936 according to the *Parliamentary Debates*, Official Report, 5th ser., Commons, vol. 336 (16 May to 3 June 1937: 26 May 1938), columns 1423–24. There are no official statistics for the Jamaican population of the 1930s, as economic conditions precluded a census from being taken.

8. During the mid nineteenth century, Jamaica's once pre-eminent position in the *entrepôt* sugar trade was challenged largely due to the growing dominance of independent republics in Latin America (which, after their revolt against Spain, were able to trade directly with Britain) and Cuba (which was still a colony at the time). Moreover, the conditions of the global economy were increasingly unfavourable to Jamaica's planter class, many of whom abandoned the island after continuously low crop returns and increasing overhead costs (Eisner 1961, 312).

9. See "Manley Committee's Plan", *Jamaica Standard*, 10 June 1938, page number unknown. For general discussion of the socio-economic impact of returning Anglo-Caribbean migrants, see Mary Chamberlain (2004) and Elizabeth Thomas-Hope (2002, 61).

10. According to Thomas Holt (1992, 359), the Jamaican colonial government of the mid 1930s endorsed the monopolistic policies of the Boston-based United Fruit Company to the detriment of the island's small-scale cultivators.

11. Both the governor and elected members of the legislature regarded land settle-

ment policies as the solution to curbing urban migration and liquidating unemployment problems during much of the 1930s. See Post (1978, 40) and Rampersad (1979, 96).
12. The Colonial Office executives encouraged the poorer colonies of the empire to amalgamate their educational, agricultural and social service departments, as this was seen as a cost-effective measure to help counter the effects of the depression (Watson 1938, 5).
13. According to the 1921 census of Jamaica (Jamaica 1922, 7), the number of Jamaicans classified as "black" (not including "coloured") was 660,420 out of 858,118 (77 per cent), and the number of "East Indian" Jamaicans was 18,610 (2.2 per cent).
14. It was widely believed during the post-Depression period in Jamaica that the lack of skilled workers, which contributed to unemployment problems, was due to the reluctance of boys to remain in the upper forms of elementary schools. See the *Annual Report by the Director of Education* (Education Department 1930, 449).
15. A key recommendation of the Colonial Office's Marriot-Mayhew Report of 1933, which dealt with education systems in Trinidad, Barbados, St Vincent, Grenada, St Lucia and the Leeward Islands was the establishment of schools with vocational biases. See WIRC (1945, 105). For a discussion on the case in Trinidad, see Campbell (1996, 281). See also circular despatch from J.H. Thomas, secretary of state for the colonies, 18 April 1936.
16. See Smith (1958). Smith's thesis argues that in Jamaican/West Indian society, there were no compulsory institutions to hold races/cultures together.
17. The Jamaican Board of Education, during the 1930s, included top officials in the recognized Christian religions, a representative from the island's Legislative Council (which after 1935 had increasingly more black and "coloured" members) and the director of education. See "Board of Education report for the year ended 31 December 1938" (1939).
18. School attendance rates were often higher in compulsory areas, sometimes reaching the 60 per cent range. However, these areas, which numbered fourteen during the period, encompassed only a negligible portion of the total elementary student population.
19. See "Oral evidence from the director of education to the West Indies Royal Commission, 1938".
20. Labour riots occurred in British Honduras, St Kitts, St Vincent, St Lucia, Barbados, and Trinidad and Tobago during the mid to late 1930s. See Hart (1989, 14).

21. See "Jamaica Welfare Ltd. oral evidence to the West Indies Royal Commission, 1938", CO 950/110.
22. In that year, Prince Tafari Makonnen, the supposed divine leader of blacks, according to the central basis of the Rastafari belief system, was crowned emperor of Ethiopia. See Chevannes (1998).
23. Particularly those who formed "private" secondary schools for poor blacks such as A. Wesley Powell, the founder of the Excelsior schools.
24. The evidence from the research showing a possible connection has been circumstantial. For example, the Frome riots of May 1938 were spearheaded by workers who had migrated to the Tate and Lyle Frome sugar estates in response to advertisements placed by the company promising certain amenities to workers and their families. The labourers' protests were in large part due to the non-provision of the amenities upon their arrival. An article in the 26 March 1938 edition of the *Daily Gleaner* gives an idea of what migrant labourers were expecting: "Headline: Tate and Lyle Probably Spend 500,000 Pounds in Jamaica: Huge Development of Properties"; Subtitle: "Big Central Being set to grind these [canes?] now handled in small factories: Work for artisans . . . and labourers. Modern Cottages being erected for workers, with *school*, church and hospital; railway to link up estates" (emphasis added), *Daily Gleaner*, 26 March 1938; also see Hart (1989, 37).
25. The formation of trade unions in the island evolved from concerns of the lower middle classes. For example, the Jamaica Workers and Tradesmen Union was formed in 1936 by Allan George Coombs, a former police officer "of peasant stock" (Eaton 1975, 35).
26. Ken Post (1978, 206) argues that Garvey's advocacy of racial development through private enterprise resonated with small, usually black, business people of the island in the 1920s and 1930s.
27. This development was abetted by Garvey's departure from the island in 1935.
28. This was a Chinese lottery game; there was a pervasive xenophobic sentiment amongst the black petty bourgeoisie based on the perception that recent non-black immigrants, particularly Syrian and Chinese entrepreneurs, exploited the colonial economic structure to their own advantage.
29. This was Afro-syncretic revivalist religion which represented an "escape" from the oppression of the colonial establishment.
30. Rastafarianism is a millenarian doctrine which evolved during the 1930s whose anti-establishment message was instrumental in stirring grievances among certain elements of the lower class, particularly in the Kingston area (Gray 2004, 31).

31. To date, the author has found no evidence concerning the Rastafarian view of colonial education, but, in so far as the education system was seen as an institution of imperialism, the Rastafarians would have been against it. For discussion of the Rastafarians in colonial Jamaica, see Chevannes (1989) and Gray (2004, 31).
32. The 1943 census of Jamaica shows that non-blacks, specifically whites and, to a lesser extent, "coloureds", who engaged in agriculture were typically self-employed or employed in high-tiered positions.
33. During the 1930s, the ordinary male labourer in the British West Indies was remunerated at a maximum wage of 2s 6d (per day). See Orde-Browne (1939, 94–95). Anecdotal evidence suggests that wages paid to lower-end clerks were comparable to this.
34. In 1936, nearly 76 per cent of graduates of the Kingston Technical School, which offered significant clerical courses such as book-keeping and commerce, were listed in a government survey as "possibly not employed"; "Minutes of the Legislative Council of Jamaica for the year 1936", appendix 41, Report on unemployment, vol. 7 (1937), 5.
35. Member Canute Little of St Ann, who was most vocal on educational matters, believed that the elementary school syllabus, as it stood in 1938, would "direct the children aright" (*Hansard*, 18 May 1938, 327).

References

Besson, Jean. 1993. Reputation and respectability reconsidered: A new perspective on Afro-Caribbean peasant women. In *Women and change in the Caribbean: A Pan-Caribbean perspective*, ed. Janet Momsen, 15–37. Kingston: Ian Randle.
Bolland, O. Nigel. 1995. *On the march: Labour rebellions in the British Caribbean, 1934–39*. Kingston: Ian Randle.
———. 2001. *The politics of labour in the British Caribbean: The social origins of authoritarianism and democracy in the labour movement*. Oxford: James Currey.
Bryan, Patrick. 1991. *The Jamaican people, 1880–1902*. London: Macmillan.
Burton, Richard D.E. 1997. *Afro-Creole: Power, opposition and play in the Caribbean*. Ithaca: Cornell University Press.
Campbell, Carl. 1996. *The young colonials: A social history of education in Trinidad and Tobago, 1834–1939*. Kingston: The Press University of the West Indies.
Campbell, Chloe Deborah Margaret. 2001. Eugenics, race and empire: The Kenya casebook. PhD thesis, University of London–SOAS.

Carnegie, James. 1973. *Some aspects of Jamaica's politics, 1918–1938*. Kingston: Institute of Jamaica.

Chamberlain, Mary. 2004. *Narratives of exile and return*. New Brunswick, NJ: Transaction.

Chevannes, Barry. 1989. *The case of Jah versus middle-class society: Rastafari exorcism of the ideology of racism in Jamaica*. The Hague: Institute of Social Studies.

———. 1998. *Rastafari and other African-Caribbean world views*. New Jersey: Rutgers University Press.

Clarke, Colin. 1975. *Kingston, Jamaica: Urban development and social change, 1692–1962*. Berkeley and Los Angeles: University of California Press.

Cover, W.A. 1939. *The handbook of Jamaica for 1939*. Kingston: Government Printing Office.

Colonial Office. 1934. *Annual report on the social and economic progress of the people of Jamaica, 1934*. London: HMSO.

Cumper, George. 1956. Population movements in Jamaica, 1830–1950. *Social and Economic Studies* 5: 261–80.

Davis, J. Merle. 1942. *The church in the new Jamaica: A study of the economic and social basis of the evangelical church in Jamaica*. London: Department of Social and Economic Research and Counsel-International Missionary Council.

Eaton, George E. 1975. *Alexander Bustamante and modern Jamaica*. Kingston: Kingston Publishers.

Eisner, Gisela. 1961. *Jamaica, 1830–1930: A study in economic growth*. Manchester: Manchester University Press.

Freire, Paolo. 2003. *Pedagogy of the oppressed*. New York: Continuum.

French, Joan. 1988. Colonial policy towards women after the 1938 uprising: The case of Jamaica. *Caribbean Quarterly* 34, nos. 3 and 4 (September–December): 39–61.

Gordon, Shirley. 1963. *A century of West Indian education*. London: Longmans.

Goulbourne, Harry. 1988. *Teachers, education and politics in Jamaica, 1892–1972*. London: Macmillan.

Gray, Obika. 2004. *Demeaned but empowered: The social power of the urban poor in Jamaica*. Kingston: University of the West Indies Press.

Green, William A. 1986. The creolization of Caribbean history: The emancipation era and a critique of dialectical analysis. *Journal of Imperial and Commonwealth History* 14, no. 3: 149–69.

Hart, Richard. 1989. *Rise and organize: The birth of the workers and national movements in Jamaica (1936–1939)*. London: Karia Press.

———. 2001. *The life and resurrection of Marcus Garvey*. London: Karia Press.

———. 2002. *Labour rebellions of the 1930s in the British Caribbean region colonies*. Ceredigion: Caribbean Labour Solidarity and Socialist History Society.
Hill, Robert, ed. 1990. *The Marcus Garvey and Universal Negro Improvement Association papers*. Vol. 3. Berkeley and Los Angeles: University of California Press.
Holt, Thomas. 1992. *The problem of freedom: Race, labour and politics in Jamaica and Britain, 1832–1938*. Baltimore: Johns Hopkins University Press.
Howe, J.W., and B.H. Easter. 1934. *Some notes on vocational training as observed in the United States of America together with certain recommendations as to the development of the branch of education in Jamaica*. Kingston: Government Printing Office.
Isaacs, M.C.R. 1938. Our national crisis. *Cathoic Opinion*. August.
Jamaica. 1922. *Census of Jamaica and its dependencies taken on 25th April 1921*. Kingston: Government Printing Office.
Jamaica. Central Bureau of Statistics. 1945. *Eighth census of Jamaica and its dependencies 1943*. Kingston: Jamaica Central Bureau of Statistics.
Jamaica. Education Department. 1930. *Annual report by the director of education (S.A. Hammond) on the working of his department for the year 1929–1930*. Kingston: Jamaica Gazette.
———. 1939. *Annual report of the education department for the period 1st January 1938 to 31st March 1939*. Kingston: Jamaica Departmental Reports.
———. 1940. *Annual report of the education department for the period 1st April 1939 to 31st March 1940*. Kingston: Jamaica Departmental Reports.
Jamaica. *Hansard*. 1938. Proceedings of the Legislative Council of Jamaica, spring session, 8 March 1938–11 August 1938, vol. 2. Kingston: Gleaner Company.
———. 1940. Proceedings of the legislative council of Jamaica, spring session, 6 February–12 June 1940. Kingston: Gleaner Company.
Jamaica Union of Teachers (JUT). 1938a. *The Jamaica Union of Teachers memorandum of evidence to the West India Royal Commission*.
———. 1938b. *The Jamaica Union of Teachers' oral evidence to the West Indies Royal Commission*. CO 950/82.
James, C.L.R. 1963. *Beyond a boundary*. London: Hutchinson.
Johnson, Howard. 2002. Decolonizing the history curriculum in the anglophone Caribbean. *Journal of Imperial and Commonwealth Studies* 30, no. 1: 27–60.
Macmillan, W.M. 1936. *Warning from the West Indies*. London: Faber and Faber.
Mayhew, Arthur. 1938. *Education in the colonial empire*. London: Longmans, Green.
McKay, Claude. 1961. *Banana bottom*. New York: Harper and Row.
Miller, Errol. 1990. *Jamaican society and high schooling*. Kingston: Institute of Social and Economic Research.

Moore, Brian and Michelle Johnson. 2004. *Neither led nor driven: Contesting British cultural imperialism in Jamaica, 1865–1920*. Kingston: University of the West Indies Press.

Munroe, Trevor. 1974. The Bustamante letters 1935. *Jamaica Journal* 8, no. 1: 2–15.

Myrdal, Gunnar. 1944. *An American dilemma: The Negro problem and modern democracy*. Vols. 1 and 2. New York: Harper and Brothers.

Orde-Browne, Major G. St J. 1939. *Labour conditions in the West Indies*. London: HMSO.

Post, Ken. 1978. *Arise ye starvelings: The Jamaica labour rebellion of 1938 and its aftermath*. The Hague: Martinus Nijhoff.

Rampersad, Dave. 1979. Colonial economic development and social welfare: The case of the British West Indian colonies, 1929–1947. DPhil thesis, Oriel College-Oxford.

Reddock, Rhoda. 1989. Caribbean women and the struggle of the 1930s. *Caribbean Affairs* 1: 86–96.

Rury, John L. 1991. *Education and women's work: Female schooling and the division of labour in urban America, 1870–1930*. Albany: State University of New York Press.

Shepherd, Verene A. 1995. Gender, migration and settlement: The indentureship and post-indentureship experience of Indian females in Jamaica, 1845–1943. In *Engendering history: Caribbean women in historical perspective*, ed. Bridget Brereton, Barbara Bailey and Verene Shepherd, 233–57. Kingston: Ian Randle.

Sherlock, Philip and Hazel Bennett. 1998. *The story of the Jamaican people*. Kingston: Ian Randle.

Smith, M.G. 1958. *Politics and society in Jamaica*. N.p.

St Pierre, M. 1978. The 1938 Jamaica disturbances, A portrait of mass reaction against colonialism. *Social and Economic Studies* 27, no. 2: 171–96.

Sunshine, Catherine. 1985. *The Caribbean: Survival, struggle and sovereignty*. Washington, DC: EPICA Publication.

Thomas-Hope, Elizabeth. 2002. *Caribbean migration*. Kingston: University of West Indies Press.

Turner, Trevor. 1987. The socialization intent in colonial Jamaican education 1867–1911. In *Education in the Caribbean*, ed. Ruby King, 54–87. Kingston: Faculty of Education.

Watson, Keith. 1938. *Education in the third world*. London: Croom Helm.

West India Royal Commission (WIRC). 1945. *West India Royal Commission report presented by the secretary of state for the colonies to parliament by command of His Majesty*. London: HMSO.

Whitehead, Clive. 1988. British colonial education policy: A synonym for cultural imperialism. In *Benefits bestowed*, ed. J.A. Mangan, 211–30. Manchester: Manchester University Press.

———. 2003. *Colonial educators: The British Indian and Colonial Education Service 1858–1983*. London: I.B. Tauris.

Whitman, Charlie. 2002. *Bitter rehearsal: British and American planning for a post-war West Indies*. Westport, CT: Praeger.

Who's Who Jamaica. 1945. *Who's who Jamaica British West Indies, 1941–1946: An illustrated biographical record of outstanding Jamaicans and others connected with the island*. Kingston: Who's Who (Jamaica) Ltd.

Whyte, Millicent. 1977. *A short history of education in Jamaica*. London: Hodder and Stoughton.

Williams, E.S. Barrington. 1959. *Progress of a people*. Kingston: The author.

Wilson, Peter J. 1973. *Crab antics: The social anthropology of English-speaking Negro societies of the Caribbean*. New Haven: Yale University Press.

5

No Space for Race?
The Bleaching of the Nation in Postcolonial Jamaica

ANNIE PAUL

> It will be seen from what has been said that Jamaican society differs from other contemporary societies faced with colour problems chiefly in that the majority of the Jamaican population is black or coloured while the cultural background of these people is predominantly European . . .
>
> The public expression in newspapers and at meetings of views on colour prejudice is not as frequent as might be imagined from the evidence of strong colour feeling or consciousness. There is in existence a strong sense of constraint against speaking too openly about colour inside a group. Similarly individuals will not do so with members from another group. Thus a fair person would not discuss the position of the black people with a black individual. To discuss such matters in a newspaper or in a public meeting at which all colours may be represented is to offend the Jamaican sense of propriety.
>
> Editorial policy regarding such matters appears to be not to give undue prominence to "racial" items. On the other hand, the activities of "society" people occupy an extremely prominent position in the daily papers. This means that the activities of white and fair people are reported at great length in the papers the majority of whose readers are black. There seems to be no comment from any group on this anomaly.
>
> – Fernando Henriques, *Family and Colour in Jamaica*

If Selwyn Langley had been born in eighteenth or nineteenth century Britain and of upper-class parentage, he would have been called a black sheep. He would have been sent off to Jamaica and would have met Ella O'Grady and chosen her

from among his stock to be his housekeeper. He would have given her two children, made his fortune and returned to England as an ordinary sheep ready for his rightful place in the fold there and she would have been left with a small consideration, and her children, with what she could make of it, along with their very profitable skin colour.
– Erna Brodber, *Myal*

Jamaica's motto, "Out of Many, One People", suggests a multicultural, multiethnic society not unlike that of the United States or Brazil. It conveniently occludes the fact that "while nearly 80 percent of the population is unmistakably black some 95 percent of Jamaicans are people with some degree of African blood" (Nettleford 2003, 37). The "many" in the motto refers to what Rex Nettleford describes as "an intensely Eurocentric (predominantly white) upper class", one that, far from being homogeneous, incorporates "Sephardic Jews, Lebanese-Syrians, Whites of Anglo-Saxon or Nordic stock and some 'high-brown Jamaica (functional) whites' " whose entrenched common interests overcome their natural differences in relation to the rest of society. The "many" also includes the indentured labourers of Indian and Chinese descent who were brought to countries like Jamaica in the latter half of the nineteenth century after slavery was officially abolished. In the Jamaican context, however, unlike Trinidad or Guyana, the numbers of the indentured were minuscule compared to the overwhelming majority of African-descended people that constitutes the base of society.

It so transpired that the creolized culture that emerged from this population was overwhelmingly biased towards white or European culture "in terms of an abiding Eurocentrism which puts everything European in a place of eminence and things of indigenous (that is, native born and native bred) or African origin in a lesser place" (Nettleford 2003, 4). Writing in the early 1970s, Neville Dawes, one of the earliest black directors of that very colonial institution, the Institute of Jamaica, talked about two fallacies that operated in Jamaica. One was that "our culture is really European (which meant English or Anglo-Saxon) and that we must strive to make it more so" and the other was that "our culture is really African and we must strive to make it more so". A popular prejudice that "African" and "culture" were mutually exclusive categories was prevalent at the time, so that Dawes went on to talk about the widespread attitude of reverence for European culture:

[T]his total acceptance of the hegemony of "European" culture in Jamaica went much further and touched, in a curious way, our Chinese and our Indian cultural heritage. So that we had a situation of attitudes where the "cultured" person of Jamaican origin, black, white or mixed, if they thought of music considered that Chinese music sounded like cats fighting and that Indian music sounded like a dog howling in agony and that the music of the black majority of Jamaicans was like beasts fighting in a jungle but music was Bach, Mozart, Beethoven and Brahms. (Dawes 1975, 36)

The bleaching or whitening of official Jamaican culture away from its African origins persists today and manifests itself in all sorts of ways from actual skin bleaching to the seamless assimilation of colonial norms, values and practices on the part of the middle and upper classes. Nowhere is the persistence of these contradictions more visible than in the elite-controlled world of visual art in Jamaica, which recently threw up an exemplar in the form of the emancipation monument, *Redemption Song*, by Laura Facey-Cooper. Unveiled at Emancipation Park on 1 August 2003, the bronze monument depicts an eleven-foot-tall black male figure accompanied by a black female figure that is ten feet tall. Both are portrayed naked. The figures are thigh-deep in a pool of water, arms by their sides with faces uplifted to the sky. The base of the statue is inscribed with the words "None but ourselves can free our minds", a quote attributed to Bob Marley and Marcus Garvey.[1]

In keeping with the tradition of artist-produced public statuary in Jamaica, *Redemption Song* drew a wide array of negative responses ranging from protests about the graphic nudity of the naturalistically sculpted figures to concerns about how adequately the monument addressed the theme of emancipation from slavery. The emanating controversy, the passionate discussions in the public sphere for and against, the defence offered by the art establishment, the artist's explanations, the general reception of the artwork, in particular the response of journalists who mediated much of this debate, all provide valuable information on how Jamaican society functions and how issues of race and representation are mediated in the public sphere here.[2]

Interestingly, while issues of race and representation were clearly at the centre of the intense debate that took place in the Jamaican media around the emancipation monument, the nature of this public sphere precluded any straightforward discussion of the race factor. Thus the fact that the sculptor, Laura Facey-Cooper, was continuing the celebrated Jamaican tradition of white/light women sculpting black bodies or even the irony of a wealthy Jamaica white representing emancipation from slavery for an African-descended population in the twenty-first century was hardly discussed at all.[3] Instead, the discussion focused on the nudity of the bronze figures caught in a pose that seemed to bear little or no connection to the theme of emancipation; on its negation or disregard of prevailing local practices of clothing the body and ornamenting it into a stylish and stylized rejection of the strictures of the status quo; and on the numerous contradictions embodied by the two giant figures who, disregarding the sentiment inscribed on their base, looked heavenward for redemption.

The very title of the emancipation monument – *Redemption Song* – hints at the inherent problem of the work, for it betrays the reformist intent of the tradition Laura Facey-Cooper is honouring. This tradition or tendency, known informally as Drumblair,[4] "has depended upon the moral-political progressivism that inspired the nationalist-modern desire for a suitably reformed, disciplined and uplifted popular" (Scott 1999, 194). The spirit of Drumblair exemplified the middle-class Creole universalism assumed by the "Out of Many, One People" motto of the Jamaican state.

Writing in 1962 about "the political problems of welding a multi-cultural, multi-racial society into a homogeneous nation" (in the anglophone Caribbean), anthropologist Vera Rubin suggested three alternative tendencies such emergent postcolonial societies might adopt in response to the racist ideology that bolstered colonialism. The first option was open race conflict; the second, racism in reverse, as in the ideology of negritude; and third, the concept of non-racialism – "the denial of the existence of race in either a biological or a moral sense" (Rubin 1962, 434).

The Creole universalism of Drumblair was based on the third option, the denial or repression of race and a conscious policy of "non-racialism" which it was felt would promote cultural assimilation, this being the goal of Caribbean societies. The nationalism of Drumblair was a bourgeois one whose emphasis in producing suitable subjects for the new nation was on Jamaicanness, taken to be synonymous with non-racialism, denying the existence of discrimination based on race and claiming that, in countries such as Jamaica, all races exist in harmony. According to Deborah Thomas, "Creole multiracial nationalism was a narrower assertion of a specifically Jamaican identity more closely resembling classical European nationalism. That is, it was founded on a concept of common history and culture rather than race and, as in Europe, obscured the conflation of class with race" (Thomas 2004, 55).

In Trinidad, too, similar policies were adopted under the mantle of "cosmopolitanism" which was seen as being synonymous with cultural assimilation (Rubin 1962, 441). Nettleford, though clearly sceptical of claims about "multiracial" democracies brimming with racial harmony, quotes Norman Manley's explanation of Jamaica's unique position: "We are neither Africans though we are most of us black, nor are we Anglo-Saxon though some of us would have others to believe this. We are Jamaicans! And what does this mean? We are a mixture of races living in perfect harmony and as such provide a useful lesson to a world torn apart by race prejudice" (Nettleford 1998, 23).

In other words, Jamaica was imagined as a non-racial nation and non-racialism, besides being a distinctive feature, was described as an essential ingredient of Jamaican identity. According to Nettleford, by ignoring the reality on the ground, "Jamaican leaders make non-racialism into an important national symbol by declaring at home and abroad that 'nowhere in the world has more progress been made in developing a non-racial society in which also colour is not psychologically significant' " (Nettleford 1998, 23–24). Thus, "it is the Jamaicanness of the Jamaican that really matters rather than his being White (Euro), Black (Afro), Chinese or East Indian" (Nettleford 2003, 6).

Based on ideas of cosmopolitanism adopted as an antidote to the "presumed privilege" of the black majorities of postcolonial Caribbean society, it now becomes obvious how and why it is possible, indeed normal, in Jamaica for white artists to represent blackness and the histories thereof. Thus, when asked in an interview about the politics of white women representing black bodies, Facey-Cooper's response was:

> I am Jamaican – born, bred and schooled! Remember our motto – Out of Many One People – and I'm not as white as I may look. On my father's side, there is the English forebear, Sampson Facey born 275 years ago, who, in 1744 came to Jamaica at age 14 as an indentured person. With Phyllis Smith, a free Negro woman, he had seven children. From that time until my mother there has not been another Caucasian in the family. (Dacres 2004, 134)

Of particular interest here is the desire expressed for black identity, suggesting a need to pass as black in order to gain legitimacy as a white or light-skinned artist in a black society. What is curious is the claim, often proffered, that, despite their physical appearance, artists such as Edna Manley and Laura Facey-Cooper are actually black, because in both cases there was a foreparent – in Edna Manley's case, her mother – who, technically, had the requisite drop of black blood that would, in a country such as the United States, have justified their claim. In her 1992 book, anthropologist Lisa Douglass provided a wealth of information on white elites in Jamaica, making the distinction between white Jamaicans or local persons of European ancestry and Jamaica whites, "people of some African ancestry who appear white". Such persons, according to her, can decide to privilege their African ancestry, no matter how minimal, and claim blackness, an identity which they feel is more in line with Jamaican identity (Douglass 1992, 8).

The claim to having African ancestry, no matter how slight, suggests a belief that race is a biological category rather than a socially constructed one. Of course, the racial categories of "black" and "white" signify a variety of ways of belonging and being in the Caribbean that should not be taken as self-evident. Lisa Anderson-Levy rightly points out, for instance, that Caribbean whiteness implies an elasticity that may not be reflected in Euro-American notions of whiteness (Anderson-Levy 2005).

What is equally noteworthy in this respect is that it was just as common in countries like Jamaica for people of predominantly African ancestry to aspire to social "whiteness", though such claims were inevitably contained within certain limits. "Everywhere else," proclaimed Zora Neale Hurston, "a person is white or black by birth, but it is so arranged in Jamaica that a person may be black by birth and white by proclamation" (Hurston 1990, 7). There are numerous instances of such attempts on the part of black Jamaicans to become "census whites", some of them expressed in fiction and poetry. There is the hilarious poem by Louise Bennett in which Miss Jane's daughter writes proudly from "Merica" to say that, though she has failed her exams, "she passin dere fi white" (Bennett 1983, 101–2). An equally hilarious story is told by one of Edna Manley's grandchildren who described growing up completely confused because she was constantly confronted with the spectacle of her white grandmother claiming to be black while her brown/black grandparents resolutely maintained that they were white.[5]

Of course, in the rare instance when a black person is accorded white status it goes without saying that such a person has to display a mastery of white culture by the painstaking acquisition, by emulation, of European customs and culture and the discarding of Afro-Caribbean or black cultural traits. In general, blacks who aspired to social whiteness had to prove themselves worthy of it. As Neville Dawes observed, "black men who had 'achieved something' were always lunching at the Myrtle Bank but . . . the whites and very fairs who dined there had only achieved the colour of their skins" (Dawes 1960, 105). Sylvia Wynter refers to the incident where the comment of a young French boy, "Look a nigger!", brings home to Frantz Fanon his status as a "nigger". He had not realized this was his identity before, because his mother brought him up on the warning not to "be a nigger" since, as Wynter went on to point out, in the Caribbean, "you could *behave* in such a way as to prove you're *not* a nigger [Wynter's emphasis]" (Wynter 2000, 131). These are merely some of the asymmetries concealed behind the declaration and practice of non-racialism and cosmopolitanism in the Caribbean.

Anderson-Levy rightly emphasizes the importance of the processes through which whiteness is constructed and "the productive tension between non-whiteness and whiteness in varying historical or geographical locations". These categories, according to her, are "constructed by and through social relations of power, which change not only social (cultural) but also biological (natural) meanings mapped onto race. This broader conceptualization allows for the re-positioning of people formerly 'unqualified' for whiteness by virtue of their 'obvious' characteristics, fundamentally altering the category and hegemonic structures that depend on its existence" (Anderson-Levy 2005).

Thus, Marcus Garvey, that champion of black identity, observed that "Men and women as black as I, and even more so, had believed themselves white under the West Indian order of society" (Jones 1995, 6). This "West Indian order of society" was described by Elsa Goveia as being governed by "the belief that the blacker you are the more inferior you are and the whiter you are the more superior you are" (Goveia 1970, 10). According to her, this was the factor that continued to integrate West Indian societies, making the use of force unnecessary because "[t]he majority of the slaves on the whole tended to acquiesce in their condition as subordinates of the small minority of whites, and to help this acquiescence to become more internalized the whites insisted throughout the period of slavery on the inferiority of the Negro groups in the society, interpreting this inferiority once slavery had become well established as an inferiority of race not just of social position" (Goveia 1970).

There were numerous ways to produce and perpetuate inferiority. Erna Brodber, whose writings incisively and insightfully explore what she refers to as the "continent of black consciousness", touches on some of these:

> To make a human being into a slave, the enslaver has to reduce him, in Orlando Patterson's terminology, to "social death". This design involves: making him into an outsider in the society in which he lives; defining him as powerless within that social system; treating him as one without honour; presenting him within the society in terms of negative stereotypes; keeping him isolated from his kind by a partial integration into the master's group. (Brodber 2003, 24)

This self-regulating system was also recognized by Oliver Cox, who described the situation of modern slavery as requiring the definition of the enslaved as "irredeemably subsocial"; however, "the pith of this ideology is not so much that the coloured people are inferior as that they must remain inferior" (Cox 1970, 357). In return, members of the white ruling class are "envied, admired, and imitated religiously" by the remainder of the population which is portrayed as being obsessed with "achieving increments of whiteness" rather than challenging the status quo. Louis James describes how slaves, being deprived of their own culture, were continually fascinated and influenced by the ways of their masters. He quotes John Hearne as saying that "the white man and woman ate, conversed, dressed, fell sick, took their baths, quarrelled, courted, bore children and died before a large, interested audience . . . Familiarity with the European master's way of life did not breed contempt. Rather it bred respect and a desire to emulate it" (James 1968, 23).

Reading such behaviour as imitative and indicative of excessive respect for white customs and lifestyles may not grasp the complexity of the situation adequately. It is possible that, correctly gauging the high status accorded to whiteness, black slaves set out to acquire such status by emulating and acquiring white culture. Such an approach shows a sophisticated comprehension of the socially constructed nature of race and race position in society as opposed to the more simplistic one of biological determinism.

In H.G. de Lisser's novel *Psyche*, the protagonist, a newly arrived Mandingo slave girl who was a priestess of high status in her home territory is treated well by her master. Ignoring her slave status, he clothes her in dresses, stockings and shoes. Psyche assesses the lie of the land in her new country and calmly informs her master that she wants to be a white woman. He is amused by her presumption:

> "So you want to be white, is that it?" he asks.
> "No master for I can't be white in colour. But I want to be a white woman," Psyche answers.

Her master asks her to explain this enigmatic statement:

> "I mean," she said in a forthright fashion, "that I always want to dress like I am now and to wear shoes always, though they hurt. And I want to live in this house and look after you and it, and have slaves under me, like the wife of your headman . . . And then when we have children they too will be white, and they will grow up and be white." (De Lisser 1980, 28–29)

"All these frantic women of colour in quest of white men", as Fanon once remarked (1967, 49). But in stepping into white shoes, Psyche is forced to take off the anklets she arrived in from Africa, never putting them back on. It is clear that the reference here is to white as in status and not white as in colour, an ambiguous distinction Barry Chevannes draws attention to in his lecture "Ambiguity and the Search for Knowledge" (Chevannes 2001). What Psyche is demanding here are the privileges of whiteness, regardless of the fact that her skin is "quite black". Eventually, she receives all that she asks for, including a daughter by her master, Psyche Jr, who passes for white and grows up in England as an aristocrat. England is thus presented as a more enlightened society, calling for the emancipation of slaves, among other things, counterpoised against the hypocritical and corrupt plantation system that prevails on the island. This plantation society, ruled over by local whites, refuses to recognize Psyche's claims to whiteness or her superior status, recognized in England, accorded by her marriage to a European aristocrat.

Brodber, too, notes that concubinage with the master class delivered no change in status "vis-à-vis larger society", that is, plantation society, though it produced a perceptible boost in status for the slave concerned, within the ranks of the slaves (Brodber 2003, 23). How would such a society transform this iniquitous system of race relations into a viable and healthy polity in the twentieth century? That was the question facing the light-skinned ruling elites of this predominantly black country, echoing the question faced by their colonial predecessors: "How can we help these ex-slaves and their children develop their potential while seeing to it that they continue to serve us?" (ibid., 105–6). The solution was to erase race completely, to imagine Jamaica as a Creole nation, implying a supposedly neutral, colourless, raceless, secular space that, while claiming to erase all difference, actually privileged a Euro-American worldview. Officially referred to as non-racialism, this worldview insisted that, despite the racial background of the majority of Jamaicans, it would be most unnatural to talk of an African or black aesthetic and most natural to look to European and American heritage for fitting antecedents, resulting, as Nettleford put it, in the absurd situation where "a numerical majority is called upon to function as a cultural minority" (Nettleford 1998, xiv). Walter Rodney, the Black Power advocate, also remarked on this phenomenon, saying, "This is a black society where Africans preponderate. Apart from the mulatto mixture all other groups are numerically insignificant and yet the society seeks to give them equal weight and indeed more weight than the Africans" (Rodney 1990, 30).

This situation persists to this day. It was interesting that, in the whole debate surrounding the emancipation monument, the media was quicker to warn against the expropriation of the rights of those whose "melanin count may not reach, for the purposes of populist discourse, a critical threshold" ("Be careful of intellectual commissars", *Jamaica Observer*, 8 August 2003), that is, a high degree of solicitude for melanin-deficient minorities, while being downright hostile to expressions of African-Jamaican solidarity and difference.[6] Thus, in a bizarre inversion, the melanin-rich majority is treated as a minority, while society bends over backwards to accommodate elite minority groups whose wealth, power and prestige ensures their continued hegemony in the public sphere.

In fact, protests against Laura Facey-Cooper's depiction of emancipation were often trivialized in the media as racist objections to the fact of her whiteness. For, regardless of being able to claim a black ancestor in the distant past, the sculptress is undeniably a product of white Jamaica, a sociopolitico-cultural complex with a completely different relationship to slavery, emancipation, the teachings of Garvey or even to clothing than the majority of the people the monument is supposed to represent.[7] What, for instance, is the role of clothing in Jamaican society today?[8] Whereas for members of the elite, clothes may be nothing more than a practical encumbrance, the discarding of which represents a sort of freedom or emancipation, dress was used by ex-slaves to challenge the rigid social stratifications of post-emancipation Jamaica which still threatened to imprison and oppress them. For emancipated Jamaicans, clothing has been one of the "strategies of distinction" between their status as slaves and their newly bestowed status as freedmen.[9] With no other possessions to enable this distinction to be made, clothing, and a profusion of it, became and remains an active signifier of freedom and liberty, and an integral facet of black Jamaican identity. Clothing the body, lavishing time and attention on the immaculately manicured and encased physical self of the formerly enslaved, became a strategy in the practice of freedom. This can be seen historically in Garvey's adoption of resplendent military-like regalia for himself and his followers as well as in more contemporary rituals of dressing to be found in Jamaican workplaces, churches and the dancehall. David Scott also recognizes what he calls "the practice of *ruud bwai* self-fashioning" as an instance of what Foucault referred to as "an ethic of care for the self as a practice of freedom" (Scott 1999, 213).

An insufficient regard for the role of clothing in Jamaican society could also be the reason Edna Manley's 1965 portrayal of Paul Bogle, another historical monument, sparked such outrage in its day, for her sculpture showed Bogle shirtless, like a labourer, with a machete and very African features.[10] The only existing photograph of Bogle represents him, on the contrary, as a well-dressed, refined-looking individual.[11] In *Drumblair*, Rachel Manley recounts a conversation between her grandparents on the subject of the Bogle statue. Edna refers to Bogle as a "simple" man, comparing him to "the workers, the uneducated or the poor" struggling to find their voice; her husband Norman remonstrates with her, saying, "Deacons are not necessarily simple people" (Manley 1996).

According to Deborah Thomas, Bogle was "a black Baptist preacher and literate landowner with voting privileges" (2004, 32), but Edna, using the licence modern art allowed her, gave the people her vision of their hero, a hero stripped of the customary status markers and costume and endowed instead with a new set of signifiers – thick lips, broad nose, machete, muscular bare chest – considered suitable for a black hero. Although the public disapproval of the monument is often cited as an example of black self-hatred, it could just as well be interpreted as a protest against being represented in such stark, uninflected terms.[12] That the black underclass was not and continues not to be a homogeneous group is worth emphasizing. Brodber noted, for example, that Sam Sharpe and his 1831 rebellion represented "the upper reaches of the slave system, of people many of whom and certainly most of its leaders, had never had a lash on their back" (Brodber 2003, 49).

At a time when there were very few images of black people, Edna Manley considered it her mission to make "blackness" representable, as Krista Thompson outlines in her essay " 'Black Skin, Blue Eyes': Visualizing Blackness in Jamaican Art (1922–1944)". As Thompson goes on to say, "She and her contemporaries not only introduced black subject matter into art, but also had to encourage the local populations, particularly the island's black majority, to learn to see themselves as representable in the realm of art and as worthy of artistic representation" (2004, 3).

Ironically, Edna Manley, this generator of suitable black subjects and champion of self-government, was herself an incongruity according to her granddaughter Rachel who described the embarrassment she felt at her grandmother "standing there looking Caucasian, delivering her theatrics against British imperialism in her flawless English" (Manley 1996, 396). This was in the Black Power days of the late 1960s when a new radicalism was sweeping the Caribbean, putting race on the front burner and problematizing the policy of non-racialism that characterized the new ex-colonies and the elites such as the Manleys who ran them.

Vera Rubin noted that it was primarily in the British areas that the non-racial philosophy prevailed. According to her, "The concept of the non-racial society has flourished officially, has been written into political planks and proclaimed on public platforms . . . The concept of non-racialism is used primarily to denote race harmony and also to imply the lack of race discrimination and of racism and race conflict." Rubin then goes on to remark that "there are serious discrepancies between the real and the ideal of race relations in the West Indies is nevertheless revealed even by casual observation" (Rubin 1962, 437).

The role played by functional whites, such as Laura Facey-Cooper and Edna Manley, in the Jamaican art world *could* be seen as a triumph of the brave new social order the ruling elites had tried to usher in, one that purported to level the postcolonial playing field by eliminating racism and race discrimination. In actuality, however, the social framework strategically constructed and painstakingly maintained through colonial times into postcoloniality ensured "the subsumption of the race question under the national question" (Puri 2004, 54).[13]

Thus, the very natural race consciousness of a black population was systematically overwritten in the formatting, as it were, of the new Jamaican subject. Writing almost forty years after Fernando Henriques (see epigraph), Lisa Douglass also noted that colour is practically a taboo subject among Jamaicans who prefer to believe that inequalities in status are the result of class hierarchy rather than colour hierarchy.

> They want to believe it seems, that people earn their social position through class mobility rather than inherit it through the meanings attributed to colour and gender. Thus, they say social power and prestige differences are a result of education or proper socialization rather than consequences of colour or status at birth . . . By focusing on class as an achieved quality unaffected by colour or gender, Jamaicans promote their belief in a meritocracy and in egalitarianism. In this way, responsibility for a person's situation, or for its transformation, lies in the effort, striving and disciplined behaviour of the free individual, not in the power relations of the social order at large. (Douglass 1992, 9–10)

So-called non-racialism also occluded the variance in "cultural ideas and social institutions" between the different groups making up Jamaican society. M.G. Smith noted, for instance, that at the very apex of Jamaican society stood "a tight handful of expatriate and Creole whites who, by virtue of their economic assets and contacts, are largely able to dictate economic conditions to the people and government . . . This white section, despite its divergent economic and other interests, also shares a very distinct complex of values, ideas, interests and understandings which, together with equally distinct patterns of social relations and interaction, constitute and perpetuate their de facto corporate core, in contraposition to those of the black/Indian populations and the coloured Creole section of this society" (Smith 1990, 34–35).

Widening the parameters of racial definition to include individuals such as Manley and Facey-Cooper, functional whites, as "black" requires that the category of blackness undergo a kind of cultural bleaching, as it were.[14] Since such a "universalistic incorporation" demands a steadfast denial of the importance of race and ethnicity, sociocultural nuances such as local attitudes to clothing and nudity were systematically ignored and sidelined in the emancipation monument debate. This repression of race and ethnic difference can also result in a sinister silencing of uncomfortable/inconvenient cultural histories. Thus, as one letter writer on the subject of the emancipation monument pointed out, "[n]owhere in Emancipation Park [the location of the monument] do we see a display of the history of plantation slavery, the liberation struggle that was energized when the evangelical missionaries began preaching to the slaves in the late eighteenth century, or of how it culminated in Emancipation and the enduring challenge to live in a free and well-ordered community" (Mullings 2003, n.p.).

Nor, he goes on to say, are any of the nation's symbols represented in the park. "Given the resonance of emancipation in our as yet unhealed history, such a cluster of omissions is utterly astonishing . . . it is then no surprise to see the emerging consensus that the commissioned statues are irrelevant and offensive to *a broad but often derided, censored and ignored cross-section of the community*" (ibid.; emphasis mine).

The erasure of race and the history of slavery from the discourse of nationhood and national belonging requires that traumatic subjects such as emancipation be rendered palatable by de-emphasizing and neutering crucial aspects of it. Thus, as Narda Graham observed after noting Laura Facey-Cooper's deliberate decision to anchor the monument to a narrative of personal liberation and healing:

> What is highly interesting is that in this description, the sculptor, a Jamaican of predominantly European ancestry, claims a stake in Emancipation in two ways: First and more simply, she reveals that, despite her physical appearance, one of her ancestors was in fact African and a slave. Secondly, and more significantly, she converts Emancipation to a theme that is individual and, paradoxically, therefore universal (that is, that which can be experienced by individuals of all types, everywhere). In doing so, she removes the specificity of Emancipation from its context as the end of a painful, specific period in history, as experienced by a specific group of African peoples. She has also removed the collectiveness of the Jamaican Emancipation experience, replacing it with a personal inner journey to freedom, which she has experienced and hopes others will duplicate for themselves. However, a monument is nothing if it is not a community experience. (Graham 2004, 176)

It is the elision of such community experiences in the official sphere of Jamaica that is the problem. In addition, the ability of those already in positions of privilege to extend this privilege by "claiming an identity we thought they despised" is troubling.[15] David Scott cautions against the

> now tediously familiar postmodern (and liberal) view according to which the unencumbered self can step back from the identifications that have, so to speak, imprinted upon it the form in which it finds itself at any conjuncture and choose from among the elastic range of available options . . . We do not simply choose our selves. One is not black simply by choice; one's identity is always in part constituted – sometimes against one's own will – within a structure of recognition, identification and subjectification. (Scott 1999, 125)

Unlike the literary field, the field of visual art in Jamaica is still very much shaped by the reformist vision of Drumblair, one that strives for "a Creole cohesion" at the expense of marginalizing the majority identity. As Scott points out:

> the project of this middle-class nationalist-modern was to integrate progressively the social and cultural formations that composed the plurality of Jamaica around a single conception of the national good and a single portrait of the national citizen-subject. So that by Independence in August 1962 the new nation could congratulate itself on its achievement of a seemingly viable pluralist consensus (that is, the "Out of Many, One People", proclaimed by the national motto). (ibid., 191)

As Wynter has noted, this ideal of Creole nationalism envisioned democracy *not* as a social system incorporating human beings at large but as one that represented only "those categories of people who attain to our present middle-class or bourgeois conception of being human" (Wynter 2000, 157). The problem with this was that "you cannot have a middle class as the norm of being human without the degradation of what is not the middle class, which is the working class and the jobless" (ibid., 136). Scott observes that the dissonant voices of the popular modern, as represented by singers such as Bob Marley, Anthony B and other dancehall DJs, reflect a popular desire "to resist precisely this integration into the available forms of middle-class identification offered by the postcolonial state". Increasingly such voices are refusing to be "made over into a liberal citizen-subject who knows to leave his disreputable, unrepresentable difference behind when he enters the public realm" (Scott 1999, 216).

What is needed, it seems to me, is a genuine pluralization of the nation-space, one that enables the different communities that make up the Jamaican nation to coexist on a basis of equality and mutual respect. Instead of problematizing and trying to erase difference, this nation-space should enable identity transactions to take place without demanding the erasure or bleaching out of particular social and cultural identities that may be viewed as threatening or inconvenient to powerful minorities. Such a nation should produce a public sphere where no axis of difference, whether race, class or gender, is considered taboo or proscribed from public debate and contestation.

In the absence of such a pluralized polity the outcome is predictable. Deborah Thomas discusses the ascendance of what she calls "modern blackness" – "a bracketed blackness that continually deconstructs the creole nationalist motto by calling attention to the relations of power that are often erased within the creole formulation" (Thomas 2004, 12–13). This "unapologetically presentist and decidedly mobile" blackness is a rejection of Drumblair's "utopianist vision of what blackness could do, could be, if it were to get with the creole program, a vision of a 'tamed' blackness that mirrored the values that have come to be associated with the creole professional middle classes" (Thomas 2004, 13).

A good example of one such eventuality has occurred in the discourse of visual art in Jamaica which rests on the fault lines of an unreflexive middle-class Creole universalism. Thus, it is not surprising that an institution such as the National Gallery has largely run aground today, floundering in its own irrelevance to a large and vibrant body politic vigorously representing itself in music, dance and video both locally and internationally. The question is no longer the early-twentieth-century one of "making blackness representable"; the popular classes have arrogated that right to themselves for some time now. That it is time to officially start privileging Jamaica's African heritage is something the state has begun to concede. As Deborah Thomas points out in relation to the country's new cultural policy titled "Jamaica: Towards a Cultural Superstate", "A delicate balance is being performed here, a two-step that seeks to privilege the histories, cultural practices, and experiences of black Jamaicans without undoing the Creole model of national cultural identity" (Thomas 2005, 112). Whether this balance will be achieved in the future remains to be seen; the case of Jamaica's 2003 emancipation monument made it clear that the Creole vision of Jamaicanness still prevails, in the field of artistic representation, at any rate.

Notes

1. In the wake of the furor caused by Facey's sculpture, the Bob Marley Foundation's proprietary claim on the line quoted on the monument's base "None but ourselves can free our minds" has proved punitive enough to convince the sculptor to efface the words in question completely. The Marley line was itself a quote from Marcus Garvey, though one word made all the difference. The Garvey original exhorts the freeing of "the mind" while Bob sang of "our minds". This solitary collective noun allowed the Marley Foundation to demand JA$300,000 for the use of the quote. The sculptor having declined to pay the fee, the words were accordingly removed from the base of the monument.
2. For a discussion of some of these, see Annie Paul (2004).
3. The tradition started with British-born Edna Manley who is described as the "mother" of Jamaican art. Manley's 1936 sculpture *Negro Aroused* virtually enjoys sacred status as a nationalist icon. Her cousin and husband Norman Manley was Jamaica's first premier and is known as the father of the nation. According to Sylvia Wynter, the Manleys represented in Jamaica what the White Anglo-Saxon Protestants (WASPs) represented in the United States. "We tend to forget that in an ex-British colony like Jamaica, hegemony was not merely defined by the colour white but rather by the entire WASP/English complex. Only *its* style of life, *its* mode of being, was truly normative" (Wynter 2000, 171; emphasis in the original).
4. Drumblair was an influential cultural/political movement associated with the Manleys whose house, the locus for their meetings, it was named after (Manley 1996; Buddan 1997).
5. This story was recounted to me by a friend who heard it first hand from the Manley grandchild. For reasons of privacy, I do not wish to disclose the name of either individual.
6. Professor Carolyn Cooper, a vocal critic of the monument, was dismissed as an "intellectual commissar", curtailing the freedom of artists to express themselves.

7. Nettleford refers, for example, to "functional whites" and "the cultural commitments such persons betray". According to him, the term "Jamaica White" covers "those with the tarbrush (however minuscule), to the 'genuine articles' as well as persons of Jewish and Lebanese extract and some of the in-between mixtures that have graded skin tones" (Nettleford 1998, xxxiv).
8. For an entire thesis on the subject see Buckridge (2004).
9. Tarlo quotes Pierre Bourdieu's concept of Distinction, and the strategies thereof, in relation to Indian sartorial practices. The concept is equally applicable in the Jamaican context (Tarlo 1996, 318–19).
10. Paul Bogle, national hero, is celebrated for having led a landmark insurrection against the colonial authorities in Morant Bay in 1865.
11. I am indebted to Faith Smith for this insight into Bogle's social status as represented in the photograph in question.
12. Similarly with the Christopher Gonzalez's statue of Bob Marley, which also portrayed Marley in uncompromisingly black terms, the protest was characterized as another example of black self-hatred rather than a desire for visual veracity.
13. Puri (2004, 54), citing Vera Kutzinski, discusses the claims of racial transcendence in Cuban nationalist discourse in which "the idea of cultural synthesis encodes a strategic avoidance of race".
14. At a forum titled "Edna Manley Today" held at the Edna Manley School of Art on March 6, 2006, David Boxer protested a panelist's reference to Manley as a white Jamaican, claiming that Edna would have been horrified, as she never thought of herself as white; she was a coloured hybrid.
15. In this essay, Kim Robinson makes a case for the legitimacy of white West Indian writers such as Winkler, Michelle Cliff, Robert Antoni and others on the basis of their identification with and sympathy for the black population as indicated by their assumption of black identity. Robinson claims that "the manipulation of one's identity may be, and most often is, an external imposition, but to some extent it is an internal manipulation, a matter of personal choice" (Robinson 2003, 96).

References

Anderson-Levy, Lisa M. 2005. Place-(ing) race, race-(ing) place: The role of citizenship in the (re)production of whiteness in Jamaica. Paper presented at the Caribbean Studies Association conference, Santo Domingo.

Bennett, Louise. 1983. Pass fi white. In *Selected poems: Louise Bennett*, ed. Mervyn Morris, 101–2. Kingston: Sangster's Book Stores.

Brodber, Erna. 2003. *The continent of black consciousness: On the history of the African diaspora from slavery to the present day*. London: New Beacon Books.

Buckridge, Steve. 2004. *The language of dress: Resistance and accommodation in Jamaica, 1760–1890*. Kingston: University of the West Indies Press.

Buddan, Robert. 1997. Locating Drumblair in Jamaica's social history. *Small Axe* 2 (September).

Chevannes, Barry. 2001. Inaugural lecture as professor of social anthropology. University of the West Indies, Kingston, Jamaica.

Cox, Oliver. 1970. *Caste, class and race: A study in social dynamics*. New York: Monthly Review Press.

Dacres, Petrina. 2004. An interview with Laura Facey Cooper. *Small Axe* 16 (September): 125–36.

Dawes, Neville. 1960. *The last enchantment*. London: Macgibbon and Kee.

———. 1975. The Jamaican cultural identity. *Jamaica Journal* 9, no. 1: 34–37.

De Lisser, H.G. 1980. *Psyche*. London: Macmillan Caribbean and Kingston: Novelty Trading Company.

Douglass, Lisa. 1992. *The power of sentiment: Love, hierarchy and the Jamaican family elite*. Boulder: Westview Press.

Fanon, Frantz. 1967. *Black skin, white masks*. New York: Grove Press.

Goveia, Elsa. 1970. The social framework. *Savacou* 2 (September): 7–15.

Graham, Narda. 2004. Whose monument? The battle to define, interpret and claim emancipation. *Small Axe* 16 (September): 170–78.

Hurston, Zora Neale. 1990. *Tell my horse: Voodoo and life in Haiti and Jamaica*. Perennial Library Edition. New York: Harper and Row. (Orig. pub. 1938.)

James, Louis. 1968. Introduction. *The islands in between: Essays on West Indian literature*, ed. Louis James. London: Oxford University Press.

Jones, Ken, ed. 1995. *I, Marcus Garvey*. Kingston: The author.

Manley, Rachel. 1996. *Drumblair: Memoir of a Jamaican childhood*. Kingston: Ian Randle.

Mullings, Gordon. 2003. Looking for emancipation in the park. *Daily Gleaner*. 16 August.

Nettleford, Rex. 1998. *Mirror mirror revisited: Identity, race and protest in Jamaica*. Kingston: Kingston Publishers.

———. 2003. *Caribbean cultural identity: The case of Jamaica. An essay in cultural dynamics*. 2nd edition. Kingston: Ian Randle.

Paul, Annie. 2004. Emancipating ourselves . . . in post-slave societies of the New World. *Axis: Journal of the School of Caribbean Architecture* 7 (June): 122–35.

Puri, Shalini. 2004. *The Caribbean postcolonial: Social equality, post-nationalism and cultural hybridity*. New York: Palgrave-Macmillan.
Robinson-Walcott, Kim. 2003. Claiming an identity we thought they despised. *Small Axe* 14 (September): 93–110.
Rodney, Walter. 1990. *The groundings with my brother*. London: Bogle L'Ouverture Publications.
Rubin, Vera. 1962. Culture, politics and race relations. *Social and Economic Studies* 11, no. 4 (December): 433–55.
Scott, David. 1999. *Refashioning futures: Criticism after postcoloniality*. Princeton: Princeton University Press.
Smith, M.G. 1990. *Culture, race and class in the Commonwealth Caribbean*. Kingston: School of Continuing Studies, University of the West Indies.
Tarlo, Emma. 1996. *Clothing matters: Dress and identity in India*. London: Hurst.
Thomas, Deborah. 2004. *Modern blackness*. Durham, NC: Duke University Press.
———. 2005. Development, "culture", and the promise of modern progress. *Social and Economic Studies* 54, no. 3 (September): 97–125.
Thompson, Krista. 2004. "Black skin, blue eyes": Visualizing blackness in Jamaican art (1922–1944). *Small Axe* 16 (September): 1–31.
Wynter, Sylvia. 2000. The re-enchantment of humanism. Interview with David Scott. *Small Axe* 8 (September): 119–207.

6

Museography and Places of Remembrance of Slavery in Martinique, or the Gaps in a Memory Difficult to Express

CHRISTINE CHIVALLON

Since the 1990s, Martinique, the overseas French *département* in the Americas and on the "extreme periphery" of Europe, has undoubtedly entered into the era of patrimonialization.[1] This phenomenon is hardly original considering that, as J.F. Bayart puts it, our age is marked by the "generalization of mnemonic experience" (2004, 84). Contemporary societies, having lost the serene confidence in a future of progress, relentlessly museumify their past, showing in the context of globalization the reassuring landmarks of deeply rooted localism. Martinique is no exception to this trend.

The patrimonialization phenomenon in Martinique could become as generalized as the infamous "cultural consequences of globalization" (Appadurai 2001) if it did not also have to rip away from a completely different process: one of having not been able to constitute with any certainty what could be considered today as heritage.

Martinique's collective past and history are made of buried memories, diffused and diluted by the dominant colonial discourse that has been better able to impose its official chronology.

Patrimony, constructed as a way "to recognize, to defend, and to make fruitful one or more common heritages" (Le Goff 1998, 9), cannot be conceived as a tool endowed with the possibility to attain, as if by magic, transparency and the truth of the past. Through patrimonial action, with museographical language as one of the major components, "the past is what the present needs to legitimize, standardize and create itself" (Preziosi 2004, 76). This museal self-examination stems from rupture. It intervenes at the moment when the collective needs to locate, name, collect and categorize everything that is supposed to have come from the past, as if memory was no longer able to circulate on the habitual paths of intergenerational transmission (Halbwachs 1997).

These remarks, within the context of Martinique, indicate how complex the problem of heritage is in societies where memories were maltreated, crushed by colonial powers and produced in the violent conditions of slavery, which can be called a "social death" (Patterson 1982, 38). Societies that display a full mastery of their collective path – the French nation, for example – resort to patrimonial language to create an illusion of identity and use it as a "reservoir to feed historical fictions constructed about the past" (Guillaume 1990, 18). What does this mean for societies that use the same procedures based on a past buried, dominated and trapped by the authority of the colonial system? Does one create a double illusion, one of a reinvented past based on a past that has never been? Or rather, is one right to wait for patrimonial action to participate in the emancipation of memory and its extirpation from the places where it was reduced to silence?

What does today's patrimonialization bring to the outing of Martinique's slave past and its consequences on social formation? Our study was conducted in 2002 in Martinique, involving patrimonial establishments, including genuine museums and old plantations that had added to or substituted their agricultural activities with a focus on museum activities.

Rooting up a buried heritage?

Official Oblivion and Buried Memories

To talk about heritage in Martinique is to unavoidably bring up the question of collective memory. Rather than enter into the terms of a debate that has widely occupied the social sciences, we will simply recall, especially for non-specialist readers, that this memory is considered to have been so maltreated, crushed by the yoke of slavery and colonialism, that it led to no form of community cohesion.[2] The approach of Édouard Glissant (1981, 130–31), with his still famous expressions such as the "deletion of collective memory", "non-history" and "obscured history", is well known. His approach leads one to believe that no "sedimentation" was possible, and thus the collective becomes simultaneously scattered, "compartmentalized", and lost by the "practices of separation and dispersion" (p. 68).

Collective memory goes so far as to be perceived as "an emptiness" in the endeavour that aims to denounce the errors of the slave system. This perception is as easy to develop as the official discourse, endowed with a formidable efficiency, that extols the fusion of Martinique's destiny with that of the French Republic. At the heart of the powerful process of assimilation – transmitted through different government apparatuses (the educational system, but also the church and the moral values of French culture) – one finds the extremely official version of history that attempts to weaken the impact of slavery's heritage and turn it into fiction.

One can thus understand that memories directly formed from within the slave system are buried by the diffusion of the official narrative framework massively occupying Martinique's public space. For this reason, most analyses converge today to interpret the relationship with the heritage of slavery in terms of "oblivion" or "silence" (Chivallon 2005a; Cottias 1997; Price 2001; Schmidt 1999).

Though we can characterize official memory policy and reduce it to a strategy of systematic undervaluing of folk cultural practices, we still know very little about collective memories built within or against the establishment. Research in progress (Chivallon 2002, 2004a, 2005b), or prior research (Chivallon 1998), tends to show the existence of solidly resistant cores formed beyond the policy of oblivion. Further exploration, however, is required in this field to know the terms of the memorial project carried out by the descendants of slaves. Was the intense patrimonialization deployed over the last few years a way to "discover" these buried memories as well as the way they lived, transmitted and expressed the reality of the history of slavery?

ENTERING THE ERA OF PATRIMONIALIZATION

To measure the scope of this new era, it would not be superfluous to consult the *Guides bleus* series of tourist guidebooks first published in 1986. In this edition, there are six museums listed in Martinique, none of which is consecrated even partially to the history of slavery. None of these heritage sites are meant to highlight the physical traces of lifestyles structured by the slave economy. We had not yet come to the turning point marked by the symbolic decapitation of the statute of Joséphine in 1991 at the Savan Square in the heart of Fort-de-France. At that point the bust of Napoléon Bonaparte's wife became headless and its body smeared with blood-red paint – the people knowing that, in 1802, the emperor reinstituted slavery (which had been abolished under the Convention[3]) and maintained it in the colonies through the Treaty of Amiens.[4] Its explanatory plaque was crossed out with the terse comment: "Esklavaj Krim Kont limanité."[5]

This type of action constitutes the radical side of the appearance of another memorial discourse in Martinique's public sphere. This new phase was accompanied by many institutionalized and standardized initiatives that mark the transition to a new "regime of historicity" (Hartog 2003) known as "the museum perspective" (p. 201) and, for about fifteen years, has included the slave period. In 2001, there were forty-two museums, seven times more than in 1986 (ARDTM 2001), of which five dealt explicitly with the history of slavery. By adding other memorial markers – such as the building of monuments (like the "Memorial to Brotherhood" [Le Mémorial de la fraternité] at the Diamant, created in 1998 to honour the memory of enslaved Africans); the naming of streets (like in Rivière-Pilote, where all the streets of the town were renamed according to the history of the local colonized populations); the days of commemoration (like 22 May, celebrating abolition won in 1848 by slave revolts); associated activities (like those of the House of Bélé [La Maison du Bélé] in Sainte-Marie, where "masters" of this traditional dance, passed on from the world of African slaves, initiate those who have forgotten its rhythms and gestures) – it is not a stretch to speak of an unprecedented frenzy of heritage projects.[6]

Current heritage policies have also become an affirmation of an identity under the constant threat of prolonged colonialism and heightened dependence on the context in continental France. During his speech at the permanent inauguration of the Regional Museum of History and Ethnography (Le Musée Régional d'Histoire et d'Ethnographie) of Fort-de-France in 1999, the president of the Regional Council (Conseil régional), Alfred Marie-Jeanne, an emblematic figure of the independence movement, insisted that the heritage project must be "a solemn service, for the people, giving them back a part of themselves through works of the past" (Museum of History and Ethnography brochure, 1999). What has become of this restitution, of this opening up of memory? Do the classic tools of patrimonialization reach the desired goal of "making woman/man historically or culturally conscious and reconciled with herself/himself" (ibid.)?

Patrimonialization in Action: A Past That Remains Submissive to the Language Expressed by the Other

The question of "making historically conscious" overlooks the uncovering of a past that has been hidden by official memory policy. This effort must inevitably reference the institutions of slavery that remain the primary matrix of Martinique's social formation. The following analysis is restricted exclusively to establishments that affirm or maintain, even in what goes unsaid, an explicit relationship with slavery. Establishments include either newly founded museums that are often created on historical sites to reconstruct the history of the slave era, or sites where the slave experience actually happened, primarily in *habitations*,[7] and that could be converted into "places of remembrance" through the patrimonial activity.

Saying Slavery? Recent Museographical Language

Out of forty-two museum establishments, twenty-four should explicitly take into account the experience of slavery, considering the theme they examine or the location that they represent. It is possible to distinguish two broad categories: museums that make slavery visible and those that make it invisible. Only five museums are included in the first category. In the second are the nineteen others, including almost the entirety of all the *habitations*. In other words, out of all of the recently surveyed museum establishments in

Martinique, and despite the frenzy of heritage projects, only a feeble proportion of them – 11 per cent – deal with slavery.

At this stage in our progression, we must turn to the extremely relevant typology elaborated by J.L. Eichstedt and S. Small (2002) in their study of museums created on former slave plantations in the southern United States. Created to interpret what the authors call "white-centric representational strategies", their typology distinguishes five categories: (1) one involving the erasure of slavery and the valuing of plantocracy; (2) one that makes slavery trivial and distorts its meaning; (3) one that uses a "segregated" mode, juxtaposing emphasis on the white world against information about the world of slaves; (4) one, qualified as "relative incorporation", that resolutely incorporates slavery into its narrative framework, thus destabilizing the glorification of the white world while sometimes, forgetting this incorporation, moves into previous discursive forms; and (5) one known as "in-between" where the strategy of looking beyond the wondrous descriptions of the plantation's golden age is not yet fully reached, thus excluding it from the previous fourth category (pp. 10–11). The authors were only able to evaluate the majority of the museum sites from the first two categories. Only 3 per cent of the "plantation museums" in the southern United States qualify for the fourth category: the one that takes the legacy of slavery into account (p. 65). This approach, focused on "white" plantations, was complemented by a study of twenty additional sites that the authors qualify as being "black-centric" (p. 40). These sites develop "counter-narratives" that "contest the dominant narrative and are organized around a different set of valorizations – of struggle and resistance against brutality, of resilience in the face of injustice and of dignity in the face of inhumanity" (p. 233).

Can such a typology be transposed to Martinique, whose history ends up melting into the destiny of the Republic that maintains the vision of a social world where the category of race is held as being absent? Do the differences between the United States and the French Antilles – on one hand, a clear racial bipolarity and on the other, the principle of equal integration "without distinction of origin, race, or religion" according to the French Constitution – show how "the heritage industry" in the southern United States creates a "racialized regime of representation" (Eichstedt and Small 2002, 6, 9)? Though one cannot ignore the fundamental differences in question (Chivallon 2004b, 71, 75, 130–31), it is also not possible to ignore the large contradiction that crosses Martinique's society: the republican system fixed onto a social situation whose structure creates a strong, permanent legacy tainted by racial division. The presence of the *béké* group, who are direct descendants of the masters and colonists in Martinique, is a reminder of racial hierarchy. This group, that continues to base its strategies of social reproduction on the strict observance of conserving racial status, still maintains a place among the dominant elite at the head of Martinique's primary economic engines and thus confirms the surprising longevity of its survival (Chivallon 2004a; Pivois 2000).

This legacy, because it is continually updated, allows the typology elaborated in the context of the United States, though quite different, to be transposed at least partially to Martinique. As we will see, it allows one to recognize unambiguously the first rhetorical strategy – the one of effacement – as it was used within the *habitations* that were themselves owned by the *béké*.

For the five museums that were identified as visibly displaying slavery's past, one would logically expect that they would create an equivalent to the African-American "counter-narration" and create opposition to the colonial pole. Nothing could be less certain, however, because the message produced is embedded in the texture of classic museographical language, thus creating an obstacle to an approach more faithful to the sensitive realities of slavery. Adding to this characteristic are what could be called "lapses": involuntary gaps in language or even "missed acts" that make attaining the goal of expression impossible. These five museums were created by the following four public establishments: the Sugar Cane Museum (La Maison de la Canne), the Fonds-Saint-Jacques, the Eco-museum of Martinique (L'Écomusée de Martinique), the Regional Museum of History and Ethnography. The Museum of Folk Art and Tradition (Musée des Arts et Traditions Populaires) in the town of Saint-Esprit, a small association-run museum that is small scale compared to the other four, also seems to belong in this category.

The Sugar Cane Museum is without contest the museum most oriented to the restitution of the slave experience. Installed in the restored buildings of an old distillery, it is the result of work done by an association of history and geography teachers from the prestigious *Lycée Schœlcher* that began their work in 1981. The museum opened its doors in 1987. This project, whose primary vocation was pedagogical, was hailed as a success when the Regional Council officially acquired it in 1992. The presentation of the museum's materials, articulated through the trilogy "One Land, One Plant, One People", is organized on a classic chronological axis that goes from the discovery of the island to the end of the reign of centralized factories and also on a thematic axis comprising the two main products resulting from the transformation of sugar cane: sugar and rum. The story of slavery, because it is intrinsically linked with the culture of sugar cane in the New World, cannot be left out of an exhibit meant to recount the agricultural and industrial heritage that created it. For this reason, slavery naturally figures in its own chronology beginning in the middle of the seventeenth century and ending with abolition in 1848. Almost nothing is omitted from the exposition itself nor from the documents made available by the museum, including the treatment, sale, price and marking of slaves, the Code Noir,[8] the freeing of slaves, marronage, the hierarchy of slaves on plantations, attributing names, and so on.

The exhibit is accurate, precise, well researched, and includes high quality objects and texts. Though slavery is unambiguously present, it is not, however, central or presented as the substructure of the societies presented. Slavery is associated instead with a category of history – a period – and has the same status as the era that precedes it ("the period of centralized factories"). None of this allows the spectator to grasp the phenomenal dimension of the experience of dehumanization.

The Sugar Cane Museum, like the other four museums, operates by immersion in "something else", in this case technical heritage, which ends up supplanting the message about the institution of slavery. This immersion reveals an identical shift toward a domain other than the foundational domain of the slave system. Both the Eco-Museum in Rivière-Pilote and the Museum of History and Ethnography of Fort-de-France take the same care to express slavery with much historical accuracy, especially with the exposition catalogues and the signs that explain the course of the exposition.[9] The Museum of Ethnography regularly organizes expositions on the theme of slavery. They correspond perfectly with the desire to expose the historical reality of slavery by compiling archives and establishing collections. From this point of view, the "scientific" goal is reached, but what about the understanding of human lives and the depth of the experience of beings confronted with imprisonment in slavery? Emotion is permanently left out of the framework, inspired by strict adherence to chronological archives.

It is not for lack of will that the goal of exposure is not reached. Nevertheless, permanent museum exhibits only exacerbate the absence of the lives of slaves and their descendants. This is how the shift works. In Rivière-Pilote, the slavery display of the Eco-Museum, which was opened in 1993 and installed in an old distillery, whose restoration was accompanied by the renovation of an Amerindian archaeological site, has become swallowed up by the pre-Columbian period. Only one display in the exhibit is dedicated to slavery and the slave trade by a symbolic presentation of shackles. At the Museum of Ethnography in Fort-de-France, which is inside a Second Empire[10] colonial house, the subject is avoided by focusing on the lifestyle of the mulatto bourgeoisie.

The modest Museum of Popular Art and Tradition in the town of Saint-Esprit is quite different. Compared to the other museums of this category, its means are very modest and popular but successful enough to emphasize folk lifestyles. Consequently, this place has a rather believable ambiance that displays objects whose logic breaks with that of the strict organization of the other museums. Though a shift also takes place at this museum – by focusing on the post-abolitionist period – it creates, nonetheless, the disorganized poetry of the peasant countryside of Martinique: the world of liberated slaves and their descendants par excellence.

Le Fonds-Saint-Jacques stands alone. More of a monument than a museum, it is the architectural Mecca of ancient *surcrôtes*,[11] the first units in the production of sugar that are associated with the Reverend Father Labat, a historical figure who resided in Martinique from 1694 to 1705. The site's existence goes back to the origins of colonization. The *département* has owned it since 1948. Since 1987, a Cultural Centre, whose vocation is the "management, animation and promotion of the historical domain", has been created. At le Fonds-Saint-Jacques, it is the quasi-cult, dedicated to Father Labat, that blocks the message. This priest, who was responsible for a *habitation* that possessed 389 slaves at his departure (Queinnec 1999, 26) – and not "90 workers" as the site's official brochures claim[12] – is the author of a famous travel account (Labat 1993) whose "descriptions provoked the indignation of Europe" (Queinnec 1999, 26).

As it is, a new genre of discourse in Martinique, constructed over the last fifteen years, resembles the category "of relative incorporation of slavery" and even more often the "in-between" category described by Eichstdet and Small (2002) and explained above. Given the decision makers who undertake these museum projects, it is not the idea of breaking with the golden age of plantations that is difficult to accept (although the "Labat cult" could hint at this) but rather it is the projection into the world of the "pre" or of the "outside" slavery: the pre-Columbian age, industrial technology, the "free people of colour" (*libres de couleur*) the post-abolitionist period. One wonders, however, if museographical language itself, by inevitably inferring the aforementioned diversions, creates the major handicap to dealing with slavery. Paula Findlen (2004, 28 and 33–36) shows clearly how museums rely on "encyclopedic strategies". The museum, as Donald Preziosi (2004, 71) reaffirms, "is one of the most central and indispensable framing institutions of our modernity". It is a place of spatial-temporal classification and ordering. It is a powerful instrument of visualization that renders tangible, through material signposts, the categories of vision and division of the modern world, "of societies, ethnicities, races, classes, genders, individuals, of history, progress, moralities; of nature itself" (p. 80). As "an encyclopedic theater of memory", the museum is "the veritable house of opticality, of vision, and consequently a place for blindness and masquerade, where what is visible is also invisible" (pp. 76 and 80).

What Martinique's museum makes invisible is precisely a culture that cannot be translated by a language so indebted to the rhetoric of modernity. Does Paul Gilroy (1993, 37, 38 and 221) not speak of a black cultural ensemble of the New World as a "counterculture to modernity"? For him, it is not about suggesting an anti-modernist discourse but rather a culture that is able to defy the illusory divisions of modernity. Slavery – by placing horror and terror at the heart of the ideology of progress – predisposed the men and women that endured it to hold "the capacity to explode the pretensions of the 'Modern' ".[13] This explosion is translated as the emerging of a "polyphonic" culture that cannot be trapped into the ethnic, political and territorial categories of modernity (Gilroy 1993, 19 and 28). This situation permits one to describe the difficult encounter between museums and the collective memory of slavery in Martinique in terms of a hiatus.

Erasing Slavery? Places of Colonial Memory

Two public establishments enter into the category of "erasing slavery": the Museum of the Pagerie (Musée de la Pagerie) and the Château Dubuc site. The first is installed in the birthplace of Empress Joséphine, an old sugar plantation owned by the Tascher de la Pagerie family. In 1944, the veterinarian Rose-Rosette, a local history enthusiast, acquired the estate that had belonged to the *békés*. This amateur museologist, presented as a "descendant of slaves" (*France-Antilles*, 1 January 1999)[14] and at the same time admitting to an "adoration of the '*belle créole*' " (Madras 1996, 62), was able to create, as early as 1954, one of the oldest museums in Martinique. It was, until recently, the most visited museum, but its attendance has been steadily declining. Intended to present the two sides of the site's history, the world of slaves and the world of masters, according to its founder's testimony (*France-Antilles*, 1 January 1999), the museum, belonging to the General Council (Conseil Général)[15] since 1985, is still under the stranglehold of the emphasis on Joséphine's personal trajectory. Several paintings in the entryway depicting cruelty towards slaves and the shackles on display in the single room dominated by Joséphine's personal effects are not enough to make up for the overall tone of the exhibition, because we are on the very premises where the decisions regarding the destiny of slaves were taken. Nothing is used to clearly interpret Joséphine's husband's decision to reinstitute slavery. The contradictory information about Bonaparte, too complex to cover in detail here, tends even to exonerate him.

The Château Dubuc is an even more painful example of the expression of what goes unsaid. This location is cut off from the others and ends up creating a symbiosis with its surrounding natural environment. It is the only site to bear witness to an old past come back to the present through traces and ruins barely maintained and is the only site where the slaves' confinement cells are still visible. The Château Dubuc could have had the chance to be unencumbered with so-called gestures of heritage had an exhibit not distorted the way one sees it. "Exposition" is much too big a word to describe what is little more than three informational signs – "Morals and Customs of the eighteenth century"; "The Dubuc *Habitation*"; and "Sugar Production Methods" – several engravings about the flora and fauna and three small displays filled with untagged objects: fragments of pipes, rusted tools, pieces of dishes or chipped pottery. Everything becomes clear about what goes unsaid when one notices the absence of the word "slave" from the text about the "Morals and Customs of the eighteenth century".

The other seventeen establishments that are also in the category of "erasure" all consist of private *habitations*, the domain above all of the *béké* group and more rarely of the bourgeoisie of colour. The majority of them (twelve in total) are distilleries that have opened their doors to guided tours followed by tastings in a clear commercial attempt to attract a tourist clientele. From these sites – la Mauny, Trois-Rivières, Depaz, Dillon and so on – there is nothing to expect in the way of efforts made to unveil anything other than the method for producing rum except for the sometimes more elaborate staging of exhibits that take into account the spatial structure of the *habitation*. This staging, like at the Depaz plantation at the base of the Pelée Mountain, can hint at the characteristic layout of these old properties where the splendour of the master's house incarnates creole elegance.

Two distilleries stand apart from the others due to the scope of their heritage project. The Saint-James and Sainte-Marie Plantations have a distillery that is endowed with a museum that welcomes the largest number of visitors out of all of the other museum sites put together, with ninety thousand per year, compared to thirty-five thousand at the Sugar Cane Museum (*France-Antilles*, 21–22 August 1999 and 28–29 August 1999). It must, however, be pointed out that the rum tasting is free. The museum is installed in the old master's house as well as in the distillery belonging to the Cointreau Group. The commercio-heritage strategy guided by folklorization will become more intense with the announced, but still unfinished, project of creating a "veritable traditional village of artisans" that will belong to a "zone dedicated to the culture and tradition of rum" (ibid.). In this case, the erasure comes from both the exclusive focus on the *béké* perspective and from the charming and exotic vision, deplored by Myriam Cottias (1993, 265), that creole ethnography borrows from patrimonial action.

Adding less to this quasi-popular folklore, the Habitation Clément, at François, displays much more ostentatiously "its" historical truth that caters to the tourist industry. This distillery-*habitation*, belonging to the most powerful *békés* in Martinique, the Hayot Group, whose rum is now produced on a neighbouring site, is on the inventory of classified monuments and historical sites (like most of the museums examined here: Château Dubuc, la

Pagerie, Fonds-Saint-Jacques, and so on). This case gets at the heart of the rhetoric, so well described by Eichstedt and Small (2002, 107), of the symbolic annihilation of slavery by focusing exclusively on the materials that deal with plantation lifestyle but omitting any relative mention of slaves. The Habitation Clément – despite the fact that it takes its name from a mulatto who headed it at the beginning of the twentieth century – is a reminder of the "white gold" period, the centuries of the "grand era of economic growth" and the illustrious proprietors, all *béké*, who have succeeded one another at the head of the estate.

This second museum group, which does such a good job of erasing the reality of slavery, makes us confront the patrimonial strategy that brings us back to the idea of the quest for identity, as some authors would describe it. This kind of museum hides fractures and reposes in the warm idea of continuities. It "comes to be an instrument of that [bourgeois] self-fashioning in the sense that artworks, museological objects of desire are constructed as objects whose style or grace is worthy of emulation, whose spirit and vivacity one might admire, whose uniqueness is worthy of remembering" (Preziosi 2004, 79). Here, the logic of producing identity in the making of heritage is used to the extreme. In the privacy of the island, where blacks and *békés* still confront each other, this logic allows the symbolism of hierarchal values linked to socioracial groups to endure by almost completely denying the deep rooting of slavery. The gap created by such a use of the heritage-making machine is that this identity strategy makes museums reinforce the social order rather than educate. Paradoxically, it could be said that they do create "places of memory" according to Pierre Nora's definition (1984, xx–xxii). The historian believed, in fact, that there were two phases in the making of these places: a first phase attributed to a living collective memory, and the second phase where memory is supplanted by the staging of history. In Martinique, this double "reign" over "places of memory", that makes them both "natural" and "artificial", is only found on the *béké* plantations. This situation comes about because the collective memory of the slave descendants never had the chance to make visible those places that would allow it to circulate. Such places do not run the risk of being (re)fabricated and shown as "places of memory" since, even today, we hardly know where they are to be found. This situation is the most likely explanation for "new" elements – frescos, statues, monuments and newly renamed streets – that quite often have the role of taking into account the memory of slavery. When it comes to the plantations, they maintain complete sovereignty as the places where the particular culture of emphasizing racial domination has been handed down. Today, the patrimonial rehabilitation of these plantations bears the mark of the double reign over places of remembrance: they are the repetition of colonial memory that continues to affirm its white supremacy in the museographical context.

PATRIMONIALIZATION IN MARTINIQUE: AN UNCONSUMMATED DIVIDE?

The inability of patrimonial language to allow expression of the living memory of slavery in Martinique must be addressed as we reach the end of our exploration. The characteristics of patrimonial gestures – the fact that these gestures always stem from a strategic appropriation of the past to be used by the present – are not what are being questioned. Rather, it is the language itself, its mechanics and conventions, that makes the job of rehabilitating the history of slavery almost useless. On one hand, this language confines discourse to a framework that is not adapted to the teeming cultural worlds that it undertakes to lay down. These worlds end up shying away from the *chronophage* logic that is enamoured with the categorizing order of the history-writing process. On the other hand, the strategic potential of this language allows for the manipulation of identity articulated on the binary separation of "shown-hidden". The rhetoric of places of colonial memory, developed in the world of plantations-as-museums, does nothing more than express the presence of creole whiteness by erasing the existence of black worlds, whether of slaves or even of "workers".

As far as the statistics on attendance at these sites are concerned, it can be concluded that few people living in Martinique are actually concerned by these heritage projects. In fact, 87 per cent of visitors to these museums are tourists.[16] Knowing that only 15 per cent are natives of Martinique visiting the country,[17] one can no longer doubt that museums, and other establishments acting as such, address themselves to a foreign audience, thus practically making the island's population a distant spectator to these actions. The reach of this patrimonial projection, however, undoubtedly has other resonances caused simply by its presence alone without Martiniquans needing to go and visit the museums themselves. Indeed, in Martinique, everyone knows who does what and what belongs to whom. The structure of the patrimonial field says more than the message emitted by the museum system. The division between project makers, specifically their membership in clearly typified groups – the *békés*, the bourgeoisie and the black political class, and associative leaders from modest communities – reproduces an order that the republican model's veneer has difficulty wiping out. Here, at the beginning of the twenty-first century, the words of Roland Suvelor (one of Martinique's most influential intellectuals) which were reproduced in the newspaper *Libération* (Pivois 2000), reiterate an old statement that is still made relevant, even in the ultra-modern heart of the island: "We are living in a country where the notion of race plays an essential role, permeates our daily lives and influences almost every one of our gestures." If the patrimonial message creates a rupture in the way that it takes possession of the past – with the museal perspective that seeks out archives rather than intergenerational transmission – those who create it are placed in the continuity of the social arena where patrimonial competence is distributed. Museographical creations, therefore, arise more from the reproduction of social race relations than from a divergence from the remembered history. Through these creations, a new but efficient way of leading back to and maintaining old and archaic social positions is passed on. This unconsummated patrimonial divide thus makes it possible to use Eichstedt and Small's (2002, 9) analysis, despite all expectations, to see in Martinique, as in the United States, that a "regime of racialized representations" enters the museum framework.

Acknowledgements

All citations of this text have been translated from the French. This text is a short and different version of a more developed study published in French, "Rendre visible l'esclavage. Muséographie et hiatus de la mémoire aux Antilles françaises", *L'homme* 180: 7–42.

I would like to extend a warm thanks to my colleague Stephen Small at the University of California at Berkeley, who shared his research with me during his two year stay in Bordeaux as the director of the Centre d'études californiennes. He allowed this work, carried out in Martinique, to have an interpretive and methodological dimension, and for that I owe him.

Notes

1. The term "patrimonialization" in this case, and throughout the text, means the creation or development of cultural and historical heritage.
2. For a more in-depth examination of the question of collective memory as it relates to slavery's past, see Chivallon 2002, 2004a, 2004b, 2005a and 2005b.
3. Slavery had been abolished for the first time in 1794 under the "Convention", the period where the French revolutionary assembly governed.
4. Regarding this issue, consult the article by Champion (1995).
5. Translated, this means "slavery: crime against humanity".
6. For an example of the objects, sites and events that are now considered to be patrimonial, consult Martinique's official tourist website (http://martinique-tourism.com). Regarding the heritage of the bélé dance, see the online interview with the choreographer Sonia Marc at http://afrik.com.
7. Term used to describe plantations in the French Antilles.
8. *Le Code Noir* ("The Black Code") was a French decree initiated by Colbert and promulgated in 1685 just after Colbert's death. Colbert was Secretary of State of the Navy and Minister of commerce under Louis XIV. The Code Noir was one of the most sophisticated laws addressing the status of the slaves, defining their conditions as "movables" (*biens meubles*) having virtually no rights.
9. See in particular the catalogue "Ecomusée de la Martinique: Histoire vivante d'une culture et d'une communauté".
10. The "Second Empire" under Napoléon III covers the period from 1852 to 1870.
11. A type of sugar mill.
12. Note the euphemism "workers" to replace "slaves" used in the site's official brochure ("Fonds-Saint-Jacques: Archéologie et histoire sur les traces du Père Labat", 4).
13. Expression taken from Lazarus (1995, 331) in his commentary on Paul Gilroy's work.
14. *France-Antilles* is the local newspaper of Martinique.
15. Conseil Général: the institution corresponding to the management of the Département of Martinique. The Conseil Régional is its counterpart for the

Région of Martinique. Since the Région Martinique has only one *department*, the expression Région mono-départementale is used.

16. According to the 2001 survey conducted by l'Agence Régionale de Développement Touristique de la Martinique on museum attendance.
17. Statistics from 2003 provided by the statistical service at l'Agence Régionale de Développement Touristique de la Martinique. Regards to Bruno Marques for having sent them.

References

L'Agence Régionale de Développement Touristique de la Martinique (ARDTM). 2001. Anse Gouraud-Schoelcher. ARDTM.
Appadurai, Arjun. 2001. *Après le colonialisme: Les conséquences culturelles de la globalization*. Paris: Payot.
Bayart, J.F. 2004. *Le gouvernement du monde*. Paris: Fayard.
Champion, J-M. 1995. 30 floréal An X: Le rétablissement de l'esclavage par Bonaparte. In *Les abolitions de l'esclavage*, ed. M. Dorigny, 265–71. Paris: UNESCO et Presses Universitaires de Vincennes.
Chivallon, Christine. 1998. *Espace et identité à la Martinique: Paysannerie des mornes et reconquête collective (1840–1960)*. Paris: CNRS Éditions.
———. 2002. Mémoires antillaises de l'esclavage. *Ethnologie Française* 32, no. 4: 601–12.
———. 2004a. Espace, mémoire et identité à la Martinique: La belle histoire de "Providence". *Annales de Géographie* 113, no. 638–39: 400–423.
———. 2004b. *La diaspora noire des Amériques: Expériences et théories à partir de la Caraïbe*. Paris: CNRS-Éditions.
———. 2005a. L'usage politique de la mémoire de l'esclavage dans les anciens ports négriers de Bordeaux et Bristol. In *L'esclavage, la colonisation et après . . .*, by S. Dufoix and P. Weil, 533–58. Paris: PUF.
———. 2005b. Résurgence des mémoires de l'esclavage: Entre accélération généralisée et historicités singulières. *Diasporas. Histoire et sociétés* 6: 144–55.
Cottias, Myriam. 1993. Société sans mémoire, société sans histoire: Le patrimoine désincarné. *Encyclopédie Universalis*. 263–65.
———. 1997. L'oubli du passé contre la citoyenneté: Troc et ressentiment à la Martinique (1848–1946). In *1946–1996: Cinquante ans de départementalisation outre-mer*, ed. F. Constant and J. Daniel, 293–313. Paris: L'Harmattan.

Eichstedt, J., Small, S. 2002. *Representations of slavery: Race and ideology in southern plantation museums.* Washington, DC: Smithsonian Institution Press.

Findlen, Paula. 2004. The museum: Its classical ethymology and renaissance genealogy. In *Museum studies: An anthology of contexts*, ed. B.M Carbonell, 23–50. Oxford: Blackwell Publishing. (Orig. pub. 1989.)

Gilroy, Paul. 1993. *The black Atlantic: Modernity and double consciousness.* London: Verso.

Glissant, Edouard. 1981. *Le discours Antillais.* Paris: Seuil.

Guides Bleus. 1986. *Antilles française, Guyane, Haïti: Croisières aux Caraïbes* . Paris: Hachette.

Guillaume, M. 1990. Invention et stratégies du patrimoine. In *Patrimoines en folie*, ed. H.P. Jeudy, 13–20. Paris: Mission du Patrimoine ethnologique, Cahier 5, Éditions de la Maison des Sciences de l'Homme de Paris.

Halbwachs, Maurice. 1997. *La mémoire collective.* Paris: Albin Michel. (Orig. pub. 1950.)

Hartog, François. 2003. *Régimes d'historicité.* Paris: Seuil.

Labat, J.B. 1993. *Voyages aux isles: Chronique aventureuse des Caraïbes, 1693–1705.* Paris: Phébus. (Orig. pub. 1722.)

Lazarus, Neil. 1995. Is a counterculture of modernity a theory of modernity? *Diaspora* 4, no. 3: 323–40.

Le Goff, J., ed. 1998. *Patrimoine et passions identitaires.* Paris: Fayard.

Madras. 1996. *Dictionnaire encyclopedique et pratique de la Martinique.* Éditions Exbrayat: Fort-de-France.

Nora, Pierre. 1984. *Les lieux de mémoire*, tome 1, *La République.* Paris: Gallimard.

Patterson, Orlando. 1982. *Slavery and social death: A comparative study.* Cambridge: Harvard University Press.

Pivois, M. 2000. Couleur békés. *Journal Libération.*

Preziosi, Donald. 2004. Brain of the earth's body: Museums and the framing of modernity. In *Museum studies: An anthology of contexts*, ed. B.M Carbonell, 71–84. Oxford: Blackwell Publishing. (Orig. pub. 1996.)

Price, R. 2001. Monuments and silent screamings: A view from Martinique. In *Facing up to the past: Perspectives on the commemoration of slavery from Africa, the Americas and Europe*, ed. G. Oostindie, 58–62. Kingston: Ian Randle.

Queinnec, M-L. 1999. Le notariat des îles et l'esclavage. In *Esclavage, résistances et abolitions*, ed. M. Dorigny. Paris: CTHS.

Schmidt, N. 1999. Commémoration, histoire et historiographie: A propos du 150e anniversaire de l'abolition de l'esclavage dans les colonies françaises. *Ethnologie française* 29, no. 3: 453–60.

7

"Reflection" from the Margin
Jah Cure and Rastafari Celebrity in Contemporary Jamaica

JAHLANI NIAAH and SONJAH STANLEY NIAAH

WHO IS THE STAR OR CELEBRITY?

There is increased focus on celebrity culture in books, films, conferences, and sociological, cultural and media studies. There is significant interest in the role played by the celebrity and stardom in contemporary societies, including, but not limited to, questions about the changing history and role of the celebrity or star in the twenty-first century, the role of the media in the commercial and symbolic significance of celebrities, and the connection between audiences and celebrities. Key questions include: How do we analyse the performances of celebrities? How do they articulate constructions of national, gender, age, class and sexual identities? How do celebrities function as brands? How important are celebrities to a sense of national or cultural identity? Are there alternative forms of celebrity, and is celebrity constructed in the same way everywhere? Are celebrities credible as leaders and role models for the wider society?

Following the early works by Daniel Boorstin (1971); Richard Dyer (1979, 1986) whose focus was on the film star as a semiotic system, including Marilyn Monroe; and Joshua Gamson (1994) whose focus was on the industries that manufacture the celebrity product, recent attempts to define celebrity have come from Rojek (2001), Marshall (1997), and Turner,

Bonner and Marshall (2000). These new definitions of celebrity will be examined further.

In *Understanding Celebrity,* Turner notes that there is concern on the part of "columnists and other public intellectuals" who estimate the contemporary celebrity syndrome as a "symptom of a worrying cultural shift: towards a culture that privileges the momentary, the visual and the sensational over the enduring, the written, and the rational". Conversely, there are those who see celebrities as extraordinary people exposed by industry officials. He also notes that the "defining qualities of the celebrity are both natural and magical" (Turner 2004, 4). According to Turner, "The contemporary celebrity will usually have emerged from the sports or entertainment industries; they will be highly visible through the media; and their private lives will attract greater public interest than their professional lives. Indeed the modern celebrity may claim no special achievements other than the attraction of public attention" (2004, 3).

In an age characterized by the loss of community at several levels, scholars have posited that the attention paid to the celebrity and the increase in the "investment in our relation with specific versions of this figure" can be attributed to the compensations we make for the loss of community. Chris Rojek (2001) and John Frow (1998) (whose works are discussed by Turner) believe that "the cultural function of the celebrity today contains significant parallels with the functions normally ascribed to religion" (Turner 2004, 6). Various figures, and the effects of these figures on their audiences, have been ascribed godlike qualities or fame (see also Chevannes 1999b). Even as these views are held, others critique the celebrity for their fickle nature, faddishness and "constructedness".

It is important to note the media's role in the production of celebrity. For example, the manufacture, trade and marketing of celebrity is the result of strategic commercial plans. Andrew Wernick (1991) defines a star as "anyone whose name and fame has been built up to the point where reference to them, via mention, mediatized representation or live appearance, can serve as a promotional booster in itself" (quoted in Turner 2004, 9).

Taken in its most general sense, the terms star and celebrity are used synonymously by those who ascribe greatest importance to celebrity as a mechanism which functions within the ambit of the mass media. The terms star and celebrity will be used interchangeably throughout this chapter.

Defining Jamaican Stardom

As we move to map the untold stories of how celebrity is constructed outside of Britain and the United States, we focus on various genres of fame, modes of production and the role of the celebrity in Jamaican culture. Arguably, Jamaican culture is replete with examples of how ordinary people create and maintain the status of hero, star and actor and produce and consume celebrities, in such areas as film, sports, music, rebellion, and community activism or leadership. Visual representations of Jamaicans in the twenty-first century have not come from Hollywood, Broadway, or the French Riviera, even though they might have been influenced by these spaces. Rather, they are more localized, fashioned by the people for the people. Perhaps one of the most profound statements about celebrity in Jamaica comes from the lyrics "I'm broad, I'm broad, I'm broader than Broadway", by Barrington Levy. The simultaneous use, rejection and gigantic leap beyond Broadway in the lines is corroborated in Jamaicanisms such as "wi likkle but wi tallawah", larger than life when necessary, powered on the engine of ancestral struggle and memory.

Jah Cure's case may be used to make statements about or distinguish different modes of celebrity production and celebrities' relationship to audience or fans, promotion, as well as their role in the media, the economy and the wider society. Mapping the incorporation and differential use of technology (especially the camera) is also necessary.

Jah Cure as Star?

Jamaican born Jah Cure, Siccaturie Alcock at birth, was convicted and sentenced to thirteen years in prison for abducting, robbing and raping a female and her aunt somewhere in St James. He has so far served seven years in one of Jamaica's maximum security prisons, and his earliest possible release date was 28 July 2007. There are different opinions surrounding Jah Cure's innocence or guilt, whether he was a "real gun-toting badman" from Flankers, in the parish of St James, or an innocent man dealt a raw deal in the representation he got from lawyers. Some wonder whether the alleged victims' links to a powerful "money man" influenced the strength of justice brought to bear on Jah Cure. By his moniker, Jah Cure self-identifies as Rastafari, and there are questions about whether a "real Rastafari" would commit such a crime. The intention is not to dwell on the legal case surrounding Jah Cure, however. Instead, we will focus on how Jah Cure has come to the attention of Jamaicans and fans around the world.

When the song "True Reflection (Prison Walls)" hit the radio waves in Jamaica there was agitation underway for freeing Jah Cure, but the song made it to every sound system, radio and television station and sidewalk cassette-man, thereby sending the singer into the realm of fame. Almost everyone heard and loved the song and wanted to hear it over and over again. Jah Cure, who has his own music company – I Cure Music Company – is said to be worth over J$1 billion. Cure admits that his fans have a central place in what keeps him going in prison, though access and communication with his fans is significantly different from the traditional celebrity: "hearing the fans singing my music, and knowing that there is someone out there who hears me, loves me [is important]" (Jah Cure 2005).

In society the prisoner is often voiceless, but not Jah Cure. He is talking to the world from prison where no one else is. Whereas Bob Marley, Garnet Silk, Buju Banton, Sizzla and Capleton, Rastafari icons at the turn of the millennium, have operated within life and in some cases death, with voices in Rastafari's proverbial "Babylon",[1] Jah Cure has been the caged bird, caged in Babylon, the Rastafari bird that must sing to rehabilitate himself through prison sentence. The sentence is about reformation through reflection; reflection behind prison walls – real walls within "Babylon". The margin of prison is a space of containment, isolation within isolation as part of the experience of being an African imprisoned in the West. The songs recorded by Jah Cure from prison and released to the world constitute a return of voice to the voiceless. Jah Cure can escape from the cage to the world through song. Rastas have always understood this, because song has been a primary route through which the culture and ideology of the movement have been disseminated. There has been a history of music and song making since the convergence of Rastas such as Mortimo Planno in Trench Town and Count Ossie in East Kingston. These musical camps were virtually ideological schools churning out reggae music and musicians that were trafficked to the world.

Rastafari Leadership and Stardom

Anyone can be a star in Jamaica, but it is the musicians who are at the centre of that definition. The leadership they provide through lyrics, ideology, lifestyle and inspiration far outweighs the role of key institutions of socialization, such as the school, church and family, for many disenfranchised youth. Chevannes (1999b) highlights this new dimension of leadership through *popular* heroism and how it became manifest in the need for funeral rites, particularly since superstar status at this point requires "[an] instrument for negotiating the passage of heroic Rastafari from the land of the living through to the land of the dead" (p. 337). Rastafari icons, such as the Honourable Robert Nesta Marley, as well as Peter Tosh, Garnet Silk and Dennis Brown, are no longer seen as "socially dysfunctional" and undesirable, as they were at the dawn of independence in 1962. Indeed, at the funeral of Garnet Silk, the celebrant from the Ethiopian Orthodox Church described the Rastafari artist Marley as "fulfil[ing] the prophecy as the Psalmist put it: The Lord gave the word: Great was the Company of those that published it. We give thanks to God for the works of Bob Marley, because he was able to bring a consciousness of God to the people. Thus we say he was like a prophet unto us" (ibid.).

In referring to Marley, Silk, Tosh and even Brown in this way, Chevannes posits the Rastafari (musical) leadership as being of a particular category among great people. He describes the Rastafari hero as having attained an apotheosis or deification, where the dead hero becomes the object of popular veneration (Chevannes 1999b, 352).

The Rastafari movement presents a rare opportunity to study the construction and development of popular leadership and stardom through its practice in Jamaican society. Marley's case is iconic but not unique, as he represents a range of scholarship and discourses that not only predate the turn of the twentieth century, but also constitute a system of thought and articulation that is continually evolving and fine-tuning itself to match the prevailing conditions, locally and internationally. At the same time, Marley brought to the fore a new brand of thinking and articulation that assaulted the conservative traditional system of governance. Marley and the Rastafari, in general, represent a critical point of social engagement in the business of leadership. We argue that the African-Jamaican situation is largely that of a margin-driven Gnosticism[2] from which has emerged a vision of alternative African being, and ultimately an alternative leadership.

This alternative leadership is explored by Chevannes (1981), who identifies the Rastafari as having provided the dominant ideological force among the urban poor. According to Chevannes, the movement inhabited the spaces where "town and country met by the great markets, where the railway station was located . . . close by the waterfront" (p. 392). This, despite the fact that the movement is acknowledged as being acephalous, firmly rejecting the idea of centralized administration and leadership, while still proselytizing and popularizing the claims of the movement. Importantly, Chevannes (1981) attempts to apply grounded research to an appreciation of the impact of the Rastafari movement on the urban youth population. He does this by analysing the alternative leadership, especially that produced in the West Kingston area by the "leading Rastas". This is similar to the approach taken by Owens (1976) in the late 1960s.

Chevannes (1981) describes the early character of the inner-city youth: their ideas, organizational logic and idiosyncrasies. He also gives an account of the politicization of the youth throughout the 1960s and how it is that increased criminal behaviour becomes the norm. Using Chevannes's framework, we can engage the logic of the Rastafari experience in the construction of alternative solutions for the youth and understand how these solutions resolve themselves in an increasingly politically charged environment, including spaces such as the prison. Although his work is not explicitly a study of leadership, Chevannes concludes that the contribution of the Rastafari movement in the poor communities of West Kingston created sympathy for them among community youth. The period of Chevannes's analysis – the 1960s and 1970s – is the time of greatest activism in that area by key Rasta leaders, particularly Prince Emmanuel Charles Edwards, Mortimo Planno, Sam Brown, Bongo Watto and Prophet Gad. Chevannes identifies their influence as a natural part of growing up in the inner-city lanes, helping to develop a routinized sense of Rastafarianism as part of the total articulation, part of a whole experience of the community. This presence of the Rastafari teacher–leader allowed for the discourses they promoted to become a part of the discussion and interpretation of other things including politics, hunger and unemployment during these two decades. Within the Rastafari worldview exists a developed system and practice capable of training and engendering folk/alternative leadership which has spread all over the world.

Buju Banton, Rastafari singer/songwriter, contemporary reggae artist and leading Rasta youth leader, demonstrates the discourse extant among the people and aids us in trying to picture and understand the spirit of the social dialogue as the voice of the people in his song "Untold Stories":

> While I'm living
> Thanks I'll be giving
> To the most high
> I am living while I'm living to the father I will pray
> Only him know how we get through every day
> With all the hike in the price
> Arm and leg we have to pay
> While our leaders play
>
> . . . .
> No love for the people who suffer real bad
> Another toll to the poll may god help wi [our] soul
> What is to stop the youths from get out of control
> Filled up of education yet don't own a payroll
> The clothes on my back have countless eye holes
> I could go on and on the full has never been told
> I say who can afford to run will run
> But what about those who can't . . . they will have to stay
>
> . . . .
> It's a competitive world for low budget people
> Spending a dime while earning a nickel
> With no regard for who this may tickle
> My cup is full to the brim
> I could go on and on the full has never been told

Rastafari artistes such as Buju Banton, Sizzla, Capleton, Anthony B and Jah Cure are, by acclaim, among the leading Rastafari youth leaders today, with influence and adherents not only in Jamaica but also across the African diaspora and the world over. They constitute a representation discourse related to identity and self-expression. The project of representation of African discourse, what Erna Brodber (1996) identifies as "Re-engineering Black Space", allows the majority black population to begin to construct and negotiate a space that had not previously existed, and which, in fact, had been violently denied. The articulation of the Rastafari people, therefore, takes place from a different perspective: the focus on their systems of teaching and knowing, their loci, perspectives and interpretations are brought to light from the point of view of the oppressed and marginal.

African diasporan folk spirituality generally tells a story of a benevolent, all-powerful father creator in whom complete faith must be placed. It is to this, "the most high", "the Father", that Rastafari musician Buju Banton turns his and our attention, and his song therefore reads more like a prayer of faith. His "untold stories" choose familiar points of reference as they lament the plight of the people through familiar idioms, such as those of the Bible. Many of the popular masses today would identify politicians as those who lead them, while at the same time – like Buju – admitting that they have been ineffective as leaders because they bring "no love for the people who are suffering" ("Untold Stories"). This absence of "love" for the people speaks to the insignificance of the people to the leaders and the lack of commitment to improving conditions for the oppressed. The traditional leaders of Jamaica are increasingly being called villains: musicians call them "vampires", "the beast", "the wicked", "Babylon", "downpressors" and various other permutations of evil to represent how people feel under their leadership. The leaders are seen to be acting unjustly, presenting the oppressed with a reality that is unchanged or worsening. Folk discourses pick up on this "seeming rat race" by thinking critically about this condition. The solution to the "corruption" of power and leadership is founded in the "Father" in Zion, from which/whom solutions will flow. Who is this eternal Father conceived to be? This is where the Rastafarian contribution has been especially poignant in reconstructing the father image.

There are clear connections with the Christian monotheistic imagination within the Rastafarian worldview, taken from the standpoint of the leadership emanating from the All Mighty Father God (Niaah 2005a). The original and "brazen" contribution here is what Nettleford recognizes as a quantum leap forward in the black liberation discourse, brought not only in the interpretation of God but in the discernment of his presence. To this extent, some have had the privilege to behold the face of God, to eat with him and to talk with him in the flesh. Noteworthy are the three Rastafari brethren, Mortimo Planno, Douglas Mack and Philmore Alvaranga, who went to Ethiopia on the first official mission to Africa in 1961 (Planno 1996; Mack 1999). Such individuals are perceived to have received a lifelong blessing to have been in the company of the king, Emperor Haile Sellassie. According to Planno, "I consider [him] my God." Individuals such as Planno would be clear agents or servants of the living God within the interpretation of many in the movement including Marley, Tosh and Jah Cure. These opinions about servants of God and the character of their work may or may not be endorsed by the other Rastafari brethren, as this is a part of the dialogical character of the movement, much of which is often rife with contestation. Cleavages can occur around individuals with intellectual and material resources, leading to the emergence of camps where such individuals are domiciled or meet on a day to day basis (Yawney 1980). In this regard, Planno became one of the earliest such figures to emerge, coming to national attention through his leadership in West Kingston's Rastafari communities and especially after his participation in the 1961 Mission to Africa. The Rastafari celebrity therefore becomes potentially a new paradigm – based on the schooling the movement's ontology affords, and through its activism and conscientization, celebrated icons have a unique character as leaders in some of the most crucial sectors of contemporary Jamaica.

RASTAFARI LEADING REFORMATORY PRAXIS

Chevannes identifies a type of lower class, margin driven leadership prototype that has been emerging since the eighteenth century and which has steadily consolidated and matured throughout the twentieth century. He describes this leadership as being charismatic, deriving from inborn ability versus one that is constructed. Chevannes's (1971)[3] work is useful in connecting the folk ideas concerning "leadership", and he provides an elaborate engagement of the phenomenon of leadership, the Africanization of religion, and, by extension, its leadership pattern and aesthetic. He cites Revivalism and Rastafarianism as two forms of lower-class Jamaican religions which have partially or entirely rejected white European culture and political power as well as the entire philosophical system of governance. Chevannes looks at a possible explanation for the newly emerging character of leadership and postulates a location in the notion of "charisma", as debated in sociology. He highlights shepherding and the ingredients for its success. He mentions (1) a mission identified, (2) a message, (3) notion of a gift, (4) recognizable authority, and (5) receiving a gift. Further, he notes that if greater importance is attached to the message than the person of the prophet, the "movement" could see its leadership dispersing.

Rastafari, in its connection to earlier folk religious forms, has systematically constructed a new paradigm. The more common feature around which leadership is constructed relates to that of leading Rastas who are responsible for what would amount to small cell groups. This is seen as early as G.E. Simpson's (1956, 1962) observation of about twelve such groups existing in and around the West Kingston environs. Later, in the late 1960s, Joseph Owens (1976) demonstrated that there were approximately sixty such cell groups spread across the Kingston Metropolitan Area. After the decade of the 1960s, leading Rastas increasingly became consolidated into what emerged as mansions or tribes. To this extent, Prince Emmanuel became known in connection with his affiliate organization in the Ethiopia Africa Black International Congress; the Rastafari Movement Association associated with individuals such as Planno and Sam Brown; Prophet Gad became known through Twelve Tribes; Abuna Blackheart through the Judah Coptic House; and Claudius Henry through the Ethiopian International Peace Association Foundation. In the literature, this tendency is reflected through research looking at specific organizational groups, for example Yawney (1980), Homiak (1985), Pulis (1990) and Chevannes (1994).

By the end of the 1950s, a tradition of songs started to emerge (Reckord 1982). This became refined in the 1960s after technological advancements propelled a new shape of musical production, and a strategic use of what is a multimedia mode of production and transmission. Specific oratorical capacity and a voice that commands attention are significant and considered, in the modern context, as a gift. In the early days, the oratorical capacity was confined to the ethos of preaching (street preachers) as the significant feature of the movement – following on from the Revivalist tradition of engaging the crowds where they were gathered in public to bring messages. Music became the charisma, eventually, and the ability to bring together song writing genius plus vocal ability were key features of the success and impact of the new leadership.

Generally, the idea of lower-class leadership is viewed as a type of margin, operating outside of the mainstream. Whereas leadership is central to most lower-class or working-class religions, the experts agree that, where the Rastafari is concerned, there is a deconstruction of leadership as we generally recognize it, the movement having acephalous tendencies generally unlike that of Revivalism and Pentecostalism in particular.[4] Chevannes (2002) confirms Rastafari as a genuine folk religion due to this acephalous character. Indeed, this is considered the movement's strength, its autogenesis for awakening the framework of Rasta consciousness. The gift, unlike other accounts from Revivalism or Kumina, requires little trance-inducing experience, but more is dependent on maturation and livity. This is often preceded by the use of marijuana or ganja which is often ascribed as being the source for creating this consciousness. Chevannes (2001) speaks of the Rastafari movement as the gateway between an unschooled and a schooled tradition in critical imagination, thus placing Rastafari as the threshold of knowledge production for New World re-imagination. This he updates in the chapter entitled "Paradox of Disorder" (Chevannes 2006), as he seeks to locate the movement's operationalization of fundamental critique within Jamaican/Babylonian space rife with disorder, chaos and corruption on which the popular culture feeds.

However, Chevannes (1999b) registered perhaps the most specific update on Rastafari leadership within the society when he addressed the Rastafari movement at a crossroads between the living and the dead. We return to the account of Garnet Silk to highlight the insights about commemorative funeral rites among Rastafari. Chevannes himself returned to the field to survey the dead hero of the movement. He encountered a movement at a crossroads between confronting death and the reality of the society's acclaim for a passing icon, a Rastafari leader worthy of celebration. The high acclaim for a son claimed by the nation resulted in the imposition of a final rite on a movement reputed to reject death.

> Left to very orthodox Rastafari teachings alone, there would have been no rite of final passage for any of these superstars. However, through the ethical content of their music and their identification with Africa, Ethiopia and nationalist defence of black people, they earned a local reputation as prophets. Silk was being hailed as the next Marley, following the decade-long dominance of dance-hall music in Jamaica, which had turned from the conscious lyrics of Marley to the bawdy trend begun by Yellow Man. That they should be accorded a fitting rite of passage was a cultural imperative of the Jamaican people, who having idolized them

in life as prophets, must now enshrine them in death as ancestors. (Chevannes 1999b, 337)

Chevannes concludes that Rastafari had become the apotheosis of hero, and he embarked on a view of Marley and Garnet Silk to prove this point. The hero Rastafari had become was, however, that of an irony, especially given the fact that the movement originated from the margin and, to a great extent, remains there with respect to the official society. Bob Marley, King of Reggae, Order of Merit, the Legend, Tuff Gong had indeed demonstrated his visionary pedigree: the society had been forced to celebrate him, indeed, the society was bombarded by his face. Marley had not only become the iconic image of Jamaica, but he had become the voice of the millennium. New liturgies, new iconographies, new ambassadors, new cultural meanings, new economic foundations, ultimately a new decolonizing liberation theology, a leadership from the margin among the lower classes had emerged.

Where Does Jah Cure, or Siccaturie Alcock, Factor in This?

Jah Cure has become one of the most popular voices of the time. He moved from the margin of the society's attention with his chart-topping release of "Love Is" (see below) and, later, "True Reflections".

> Love is much more to life than just words . . .
> Love is call on me brother
> Love is call on me sister
> When you love someone love from the heart . . .
> Love is the answer for every question
> Just ask yourself why, why, why
> Love is the key to open the door
> When they are closed in your face
> Love shows you the way
> When you are lost, lost, and can't find your way
> ("Love Is")

Jah Cure presents some old but new concerns about the margin. It is from the margin of his prison cell that he has made his mark. This prison margin is the most accessible black male space available.

Behind these prison walls
Doing my paces, doing my time
I'm spending my restless nights
Visioning faces, all day I cry, cry
Prison a no bed a roses
Di livity it makes me bawl
I wish that Jah could come and take us
Back in time
Cause I swear, I can be a better man
Yes I swear, if only you could understand
The faith in me shall set me free, reflection (2x)

Behind these metal bars
To jah jah I'm chanting
Pray for your love divine
I'm oh so sorry a man
Deeply I'm hurting
The price ordained to be mine
Impossible to see the changes
That I made in my life
All they see is just a boy they left behind
But I swear, I can be a better man
Yes I swear, if only they could understand
The faith in me shall set me free, reflection (2x)
("True Reflections")

What surfaced as a frequently posed question in developing this chapter was "whether Jah Cure was Rasta or Rascal". This is not only a question asked of Jah Cure, but a common point of scrutiny or engagement from the rest of the society about the Rastafari who is constantly being measured up from the wider society against a mandate or expectation which the society believes the movement should abide by. Wittingly or unwittingly, such scrutiny recognizes that there is a quality or an undeniable "inner landscape" that the movement is assessed to have, and thus its membership, if not called up by its affiliate organizations, is required by the wider society to uphold a higher level. Within the society, the movement has seemingly attained a social high water mark for upliftment, and this is imposed on all the movement's members. Being acephalous, this begs of all of its members the ingrained ability for leadership of self.

LEADING BY ACCLAIM: "PEOPLE BECOME ATTRACTED TO OUR FASCINATION"

Jah Cure is the bearded man, the Brother Man[5] of the times past, an outcast of the society but also an exemplar of positive change and advocate of love. This raises two important issues: the idea of the man versus the message as an issue which has been steadily debated with regard to Marley and what some may consider his promiscuous lifestyle. Perhaps even more importantly, it brings into focus the routinization of Rasta worldview and contribution when one examines the popularity of Jah Cure and the performance of his songs in popular competitions such as the recent Digicel-sponsored Rising Stars competition. Christopher Martin, Digicel's Rising Star 2005, by opting to do cover versions of "True Reflections", gave face to Jah Cure's sounds.[6] Martin, an innocent "Christian youth", was now being asked to transfer the sentiment of the time not only from the point of view of Jah Cure but also that of the system of Babylon's prison in which the composition "True Reflections" was authored. Jah Cure is now the shining example of the Babylonian functional "reform programme". But this is not so unusual, because Rastafari music and its artists have moved from that station of being unfit for airplay to that of being primary mediums of hope for the society. One example is the way in which Sizzla's tribute to mothers, "Thank You Mama", became one of the most requested songs in that particular year for Mothers' Day.

All of this is important because the Rastafari movement's exponents are not usually theorized within the understanding of leadership (or stardom), but this is at the heart of the movement's inscribed history and self-designation. In the same way that the society is eager to provide that measure to identify Rastafari as a potential guardian of the society's righteousness, it is perhaps also too eager to condemn the Rastafari, hence condemnation surfaces if there is the slightest doubt regarding the integrity of the Rastafarian. In the case of Jah Cure, and Marley before him, image and potential are affected by a charge of rape (posthumously alleged in the case of Marley). Or if not condemning the Rastafari, the society is happy to place the movement in that category of "cultural workers" with peculiarities who can only but assist and surface in the rendering of cultural productions (for example, drumming and singing).

Jah Cure has become a cultural item in prison. A modest pre-jail career has mutated into a major career with his incarceration. The oft-invoked slogan attached to his name – "the world awaits the release of the Cure" – has potential millenarian resonance. There are a number of contemporary Rastafari artists who vie for leadership spotlights based on their musical contributions. This includes a spectrum of artists from Beenie Man or Ras Moses to Sizzla, Capleton, Anthony B and Turbulence, to mention a few. We wish to posit that the Rastafari connection and the cosmological resource it has marshalled have given the movement primacy as a serious voice of youth leadership. This validates Chevannes's (1981) earlier observation about the reformative influence the Bobo Shanti provided in West Kingston during his fieldwork there. This position, however, takes that argument further by identifying the movement as a key, dynamic and accessible resource for relevant leadership praxis or a livity. Turbulence, one of the artists mentioned previously, provides this testimony in the lyrics to "Notorious":

> I could have been one of the most notorious
> I got saved by the king and his grace is so glorious
> I could have been one of the most devastating
> I got saved
> By the king and his love is everlasting
>
> Burn away the wicked lifestyle and the wicked image
> And the wicked man dem profile
> I'm so happy to be Rastafari child
> And me ova come the wicked with just a smile
> Den me start to live and do things worthwhile
> In a love an' harmony I try to be vital
> nah bow to wealth
> Selassie will provide

Given the public debate surrounding the national honour that Bob Marley should receive (that is, whether he should be conferred with the status of national hero), and the association of Rastafari with traditions of dreadlocks, ganja smoking and outspoken anti-systemic critique, there is seemingly something of a general reluctance to accept or recognize the Rastafari within the overarching official leadership space of the society. To some extent, the Rastafari engenders a position that transcends the mundane, suggesting an "in earth but not of the earth" mentality as far as the usual channels of governance are concerned. Therefore, though central to the demise of the Babylonian system and critical of its order, some would say Rastafari does not seek to step up to the table and offer its personhood as an alternative, but this is increasingly being challenged.

Political road bands, football matches, community events and gatherings in general cannot appropriately develop if there is no staple of Rastafari artists to ensure that the appropriate rites, word-sound and aesthetics of a new black selfhood are presented. Indeed, if it were not for the cultural leadership that the Rastafari provided through the playing of instruments and singing, many a function would be a non-start. This was perhaps understood quite early (1969–72) by the organizers of the political road bands: had there been no hope of breaking the political monotone through cultural items, many meetings would otherwise not have succeeded by way of numbers.

The image of Bob Marley uniting the political leadership of the Jamaican population in the 1970s has been immortalized in various forms (television, books, newspapers and documentaries). The perpetuation and transformation of the leadership is apparent with the Rastafarian teacher–leaders seemingly holding greater influence in the society. The prison space indicates that the social space from which the cadre of African diasporan males operate has been under siege. The prison space has become the latest point of pressure to thwart the emerging leadership from the margin. Chevannes is correct, Rastafari will emerge and prosper any time and anywhere, even without the physical presence of its exponents, because the movement has become a part of who we are. Perhaps as a result of this, as well as other influences, broader issues now face the movement's leaders and these indicate a deepening of the issues that confront the development struggle of religio-political movements. The identity, character and practice of the affiliate bodies become of concern, especially in this instance, in determining who is the Rastafari voice of the people in this time.

Notes

1. "Babylon", here, is Rasta-speak referring to the Western system of hegemony, that imprisoning nature of societies through man-made laws reinforced by governments, the traditional church and apparatuses of the state that oppress the disenfranchised. There are historical connotations linked to hegemonic forces from the time of the Biblical Babylon.
2. This new research about God, according to Planno, has come from the sidewalk intellectuals.
3. Other works by Chevannes (1976, 1981, 1999a) are also important in understanding the nature of Rastafari leadership. In his 1981 article, Chevannes makes the case for the movement in Kingston as being the chief means of reforming the youth who had gone astray in crime and violence.
4. Hierarchy is, to some extent, different and, largely, not explicitly encouraged, as Rastafari journeying through its dialogical approach provides a levelling playing field for individuals. Eldership or elders/leaders are being redefined. Planno, for example, introduces the notion of "young elder" to explain the ability to organize and lead a flock of students. With this understanding comes a localization of power not requiring any overarching genuflection. Reasonings are a levelling ground and bring, potentially, all age groups of the movement into communing with each other. The Bobo Shanti are somewhat more explicitly rigid as far as leadership is concerned and perhaps hold a more identifiable system of trained leadership and hierarchy recognized through the prophet, priest, king system. See Chevannes (1994) and Newland (1994) for ethnographic fieldwork on the Bobo Shanti.
5. See Niaah (2005b) who argues that the character Brother Man is an early presentation of the leadership mode of the Rastafari.
6. Dania Deacon, one of the runners-up in the same competition, used the music of another young Rastafari singer/composer, Gyptian, to secure her place as one of the top performers.

References

Boorstin, Daniel. 1971. *The image: A guide to pseudo-events in America*. New York: Athenium.

Brodber, Erna. 1996. Re-engineering black space. Plenary presentation at the Conference on Caribbean Culture, University of the West Indies, Mona. March.

Chevannes, Barry. 1971. Jamaican lower class religion: Struggle against oppression. MSc thesis, Sociology Department, University of the West Indies.

———. 1976. The repairer of the breach: Reverend Claudius Henry and Jamaican society. In *Ethnicity in the Americas*, ed. F. Henry, 263–98. The Hague: Mouton.

———. 1981. The Rastafari and the urban youth. *Perspectives on Jamaica in the seventies*, ed. Carl Stone and Aggrey Brown, 392–422. Kingston: Jamaica Publishing House.

———. 1994. *Rastafari: Roots and ideology*. Syracuse: Syracuse University Press.

———. 1999a. *What we sow is what we reap: Problems in the cultivation of male identity in Jamaica*. Grace, Kennedy Foundation Lecture Series. Kingston: Grace, Kennedy Foundation.

———. 1999b. Between the living and the dead: The apotheosis of Rastafari hero. In *Religion, diaspora, and cultural identity*, ed. J. Pulis, 337–56. Amsterdam: Gordon and Breach.

———. 2001. Rastafari and the critical tradition. Paper presented at the Society for Caribbean Research Seventh Interdisciplinary Congress. University of Vienna, Italy.

———. 2002. Roaring lion: The rise of Rastafari. Unpublished interview transcripts. Frontline production.

———. 2006. *Betwixt and between: Explorations in an African-Caribbean mindscape*. Kingston: Ian Randle.

Dyer, Richard. 1979. *Stars*. Rev. ed. London: BFI.

———. 1986. *Heavenly bodies: Film stars and society*. London: BFI Macmillan.

Frow, John 1998. Is Elvis a God? Cult, culture, questions of method. *International Journal of Cultural Studies* 1, no. 2: 197–210.

Gamson, Joshua. 1994. *Claims to fame: Celebrity in contemporary America*. Berkeley and Los Angeles: University of California Press.

Jah Cure. 2005. Jah Cure speaks from prison. Interview by Josef Bogdanovish. 13 August. http://www.yardflex.com

Homiak, John. 1985. "The Ancients of days" seated black: Eldership, oral tradition and ritual in Rastafari culture. PhD diss., Brandeis University (microform).

Mack, Douglas. 1999. *From Babylon to Rastafari: Origins and history of the Rastafari movement*. Chicago: Research Associate School Times Publishing.

Marshall, P.D. 1997. *Celebrity and power: Fame in contemporary culture*. Minneapolis: University of Minnesota Press.

Newland, A. 1994. The life and work of King Emanuel Charles Edwards. Typescript, author's personal collection.

Niaah, Jahlani. 2005a. Absent father, Garvey's children and the back to Africa movement. In *Negotiating modernity: Africa's ambivalent experience*, ed. E.S. Macamo, 19–43. London and New York: CODESRIA Books/Zed.

———. 2005b. Sensitive scholarship: A review of Rastafari literature(s). *Caribbean Quarterly* 51, nos. 3 and 4: 11–34.

Owens, Joseph. 1976. *Dread: The Rastafarians of Jamaica*. Kingston: Sangster's Book Stores.

Planno, Mortimo. 1996. *Earth most strangest man: The Rastafarian*. New York: Institute for the Study of Man.

Pulis, John. 1990. Gates to Zion: Historical vision and community in rural Jamaica. PhD diss., University New School, New York.

Reckord, Verena. 1982. Reggae, Rastafarianism and cultural identity. *Jamaica Journal*, no. 46: 3–13.

Rojek, Chris. 2001. *Celebrity*. London: Reaktion.

Simpson, G.E. 1956. Jamaican Revivalist cults. *Social and Economic Studies*, 5, no. 4: 321–440.

———. 1962. The Ras Tafari movement in Jamaica in its millennial aspect. In *Millennial dreams in action: Essays in comparative study*, ed. S. Thrupp, 160–65. The Hague: Mouton.

Turner, G. 2004. *Understanding celebrity*. London: Sage.

Turner, G., F. Bonner and P.D. Marshall. 2000. *Fame games: The production of celebrity in Australia*. Melbourne: Cambridge University Press.

Wernick, Andrew. 1991. *Promotional culture: Advertising, ideology and symbolic expression*. London: Sage.

Yawney, C. 1980. Lions in Babylon: The Rastafari movement of Jamaica. PhD diss., McGill University. Microfiche. University of the West Indies.

8

If Yuh Iron Good You Is King
Pan in 3-D

KIM JOHNSON

The steelband I shall speak about is something which only exists in one country: Trinidad and Tobago. There are steelbands all over the world today, and some are quite good, especially those in New York and London, and many are affiliated to steelbands in Trinidad, and there are virtuosos who play jazz, such as Othello Mollineux and Rudi Smith. But the beating heart of the steelband movement can only be found in Trinidad and Tobago, where there are miraculous organizations which are known as "conventional steelbands" and are as different from other steelbands as their majestic symphonies are different from the elevator muzak performed for tourists by most small pan ensembles. This is how the instrument was invented to be played.

In Trinidad, the word "pan" is used to refer to three different aspects of the steelband music, and, in deference to the wisdom of my people, I shall present my overview along the lines of those three categories. They are, first, *pan* as the overall steelband movement, which includes everything and everybody to do with steelbands; second, *pan* as the instrument itself, a tenor pan, a bass pan, and so on; and third, *pan* as the music produced by the conventional steelbands I mentioned above.

Good. Now, let us begin.

Inclusion: The Band

"It brings people together, both playing and listening, in a way no other kind of music seems to," said Lady Berkley, wife of the twentieth Baron Berkley and member of the London Melodians, in the *Times* of 7 December 1994.

Lady Berkley, an Englishwoman and, at the time, a recent enthusiast of pan, was a novice. She knew nothing about pan in its Trinidad and Tobago context, its history or contemporary significance. Her statement in the *Times* was, therefore, to Caribbean people, exaggerated, trite and obvious. For that reason, it is the most fruitful place to start a chapter addressed to a readership that includes those who are undoubtedly more familiar with pan: because, usually, the fish do not see the water.

The first thing to note is that the steelband that Lady Berkley was enthusing over was the London Melodians. That is a branch of a band I knew well, the Melodians. It is a small steelband based in Arima. You do not have a New York branch of the Rolling Stones or a London U2 or a Trinidad branch of the Wailers (although there were at one time a few Jamaican Lord Kitcheners).

This transnational spread of the not-particularly-good Arima band is far from unique. There are New York branches of Desperadoes, All Stars, Phase II Pan Groove, Invaders and other Trinidad steelbands. In Japan, I think, there is a branch of Renegades.

Those are real branches of the main tree. At carnival, their members come to Trinidad. Sometimes a few players may perform in the mother band. Often, they assist in fund raising. Reciprocally, the arrangers for the main bands visit New York or wherever to assist satellites in their music. Renegades had one member who lived for months every year in Japan. So we can make our first obvious point: a steelband is more than a musical ensemble. It is a community.

Think of a steelband as a series of concentric circles. If the outermost circle is the overseas members or supporters, the innermost circle comprises the core players. I say core, because the number of players in a steelband waxes and wanes. At Panorama, if we take one of the large bands, there would be up to 120 players on stage. These players might change for the three rounds of the competition. So, if we include reserves, there might be 140 players in the carnival season. But in the rest of the year, the figure is much smaller. Usually it shrinks to around twenty or thirty members of the "stage side". These are the players who play at gigs outside of the carnival season and who usually tour with the band. They usually include the leaders of the big band's various sections.

I located the players at the innermost circle because, ultimately, a steelband produces music. Music is the glue that holds the band together: music brought these groups into existence, and the production of music is their *raison d'être*. But I could have put at the centre another group who are often not musicians. What to call them? The die-hards, the hard-core members? Usually they are older – because music making is a time-consuming young-people's business that detracts from more domestic obligations. Yet these hard-core members are, in another sense, the continuity of the band. Most were, at one time, players. Now, they comprise what might be considered the executive and stakeholders of the band.

If you use the analogy of a limited liability company, the players are the workers who produce the goods the company sells. The other core groups are the executive and the shareholders who own the company. It is not a one-on-one analogy, because in this band company the directors were all once workers, and many workers will in time become directors, and all are shareholders.

An analogy can help us to see, both in the likeness it brings to light but also in the dissimilarity. For instance, the "shareholders" in this company, those closest to the inner circles, also have functions to perform. There are clear-cut functions: public relations, fund raising, building racks, painting, designing costumes or T-shirts. There are also amorphous, ad hoc and unspecialized functions, such as cleaning up before a function, loading the racks on trucks, preparing food for the band, and so on.

The wider circles comprise supporters, who range from the fanatic to the fair-weather fan. My cousin Wayne, known to the Renegades inner circle as John Wayne, was a player thirty years ago, and is now a fanatic supporter. He listens only to Renegades. Every year before Panorama he goes to church – he is a devout Catholic – and lights a candle for Renegades. At the competition, after Renegades plays, he leaves, whether they appeared first on the list and early in the evening or last in the wee hours.

The importance of such support cannot be underestimated. I have likened it to love, because of its non-rational, distorted perspective. My band is my band, whether they are first or last, good or bad, large or small. It is akin to a mother's unreasoning love for her child, because in both cases it is based on giving and self-sacrifice, which is necessary for the helpless infant to grow. In the case of a steelband, this dependency is not an initial phase but a continuous need. The continued existence of every steelband is permanently contingent on this support. Every steelband exists on the brink of collapse. Since the birth of the steelband movement in the early 1940s, countless steelbands have come into existence, grown, matured, wilted and suddenly died. Many were small (I will not say insignificant, because they were significant to their members), but others wilted and died after blossoming with tremendous panache and beauty. Indeed, if I were to list the top ten greatest bands ever, I would include Sun Valley, Tripoli, Casablanca and North Stars, yet none of these exists today. I can still recall the deep sadness I felt one year in the 1970s when I visited Casablanca's panyard before Panorama and found it silent.

The miracle, then, is that the movement endures, that bands continue to endure; indeed, some have done so since the birth of the movement. All Stars, Invaders and Desperadoes were formed (under different names) as early as 1941. It would be a remarkable thing to meet a person who is strong and healthy and 140 years old, but it is even more remarkable to see how the species has evolved and thrived. Similarly, the continued existence of the steelband movement is more remarkable than the longevity of individual bands. Let me give some facts which might illustrate how remarkable is this steelband movement:

- Trinidad and Tobago has a population of 1.5 million people, nineteen large steelbands which can each field 95 to 120 players (fourteen of these have the full 120) for Panorama. Then there are twenty-one medium bands of 60 to 90 players (thirteen of which have 90) and twenty-nine small bands of 35 to 55 players. That does not include the school bands.
- London has 10 million residents, five symphony orchestras and a dozen chamber ensembles.
- No symphony orchestra in London is larger than a medium-sized steelband. A small steelband is at least three times the size of a chamber ensemble.
- The Panorama finals has an audience of around ten thousand in the North Stand and eight thousand in the Grand Stand, in addition to at

least as many who prefer to hear the bands on the track. There are thousands of players, tens of thousands of patrons – no other art form in Trinidad and Tobago involves as many people.

This is remarkable because, although they have survived for a long time, as I said, every steelband is permanently poised on dissolution. Steelbands are large and expensive to maintain. Expensive in terms of hard cash and expensive in terms of sweat. Many people must give long hours of labour, and many others must give many dollars to keep a single band alive. Yet they earn not a fraction of their keep. They are voluntary, non-profit, high-maintenance organizations (and hence different from companies). Their continued existence is fed by the only force which is greater than commerce and which I have mentioned before: love.

As opposed to *eros*, this is not the romantic love a man may have for a woman (and vice versa), such as the poets and pop singers rhapsodize about, but something equally profound and seemingly more long-lasting. The Greeks called it *storge*, the love of siblings or comrades-in-arms who have together endured much. It is this love which made the steelbands such fearsome organizations in the 1950s and 1960s. Now it fuels the intense rivalry of the Panorama competition.

What is the attraction that draws Trinidadians into steelbands? What is the source of pan love? When we discover that, we discover what animates a band; that is, what sustains its life and promotes growth. Here let me quote one of the most evocative and incisive answers to that question, given by the mighty poet David Rudder:

> Hear the tenors rolling
> People on the floor
> The guitar pans grumble
> The crowd in an uproar
> All of a sudden everything just up and chill
> Everything just gone to a standstill
> The crowd start to cuss
> They say: "Whe wrong with the band?"
> It was the rack with the iron gone and fall
> The vibration bus' way the welding
> When the iron fall it humble the pan

> And everything start to crawl
> Everything start to fall
> And the truth was plain to see
>
> The Engine Room
> Is down there whey does cause the bacchanal
> Pan is the body but rhythm is heart of the thing
> The Engine Room is the soul of Carnival
> Korey did damn well say if yuh iron good you is king.
> ("Engine Room")

I could discuss that calypso at length and not exhaust the richness of its insight, here I shall focus on Rudder's central point, the truth he makes so plain to see (and hear), and make it our second obvious point: pan is the body but rhythm is heart of the thing.

The pans in a steelband are all melodic instruments – they play the range of tones which constitute the melodies of songs – whereas the iron, formerly the brake hub of a car, is purely a producer of rhythm. It is also the loudest instrument in the band. As such, it controls the entire band. Many of the great steelband captains, such as Ellie Mannette from Invaders and Bobby Mohammed from Cavaliers, even when they were gifted on other instruments, played the iron. When yuh iron good you is king.

In Cuban music, the same central role is performed by the man knocking together two pieces of wood, which are significantly called "claves": keys. (In Trinidad they are called the "toc-toc".) The claves lock the music together by providing the central timing, which is vital because there are many different rhythms going on at the same time.

Rhythm brings us together. As individuals it brings our bodies together, coordinates our muscles, our legs, arms, heads, hearts. We dance because we walk. As a collectivity it brings us together and coordinates our collective movement. We dance or, to a more mechanical, unsyncopated rhythm, we march. Rhythm moves us, both emotionally and physically. In Trinidad, this was quite literal: steelbands used to be a means of transportation on carnival day. People far away from home waited until a band was going in their direction to take them home. Many people have told me "I was waiting for a band to take me home", as if they were referring to a taxi or a bus.

As its volume increases, so too our minds are taken over by our bodies' urge to move, and more and more people are drawn in. Much West African traditional drumming is intended to draw a wider audience through an overpowering volume and rhythm. If a village is conducting some ritual, everyone – man, woman and child – is expected to join. Abstention is meant to be impossible.

To counteract the centrifugal force of Trinidadians' natural anarchism, the gravitational force of a steelband's rhythm has to be all the stronger. In the early days, when two steelbands met, each tried to drown out the other, disorient the other's players and take away the other's revellers. This often caused bands to clash violently. (When that happened, the mark of courage, almost never attained, was for the band to continue playing throughout the melee.)

The power of a steelband's music is manifest in its tendency to expand. The earliest bands had around fifteen players. They grew larger and larger until they embraced communities and, finally, collectively, they included the entire nation. This process has taken place over and over in different countries. For instance, in the early 1960s there was a small garden party organized by a woman of Polish Jewish background for underprivileged children in London. Until, one year, she invited a small three- or four-member steelband to play for the party. As the band played on the road leading to the party, more and more West Indians joined in. Some thought it was a demonstration. A moving crowd congealed around the tiny band and tramped along to the party. Thus was born the street parade that is now the single largest street festival in Europe: the Notting Hill Carnival.

Such a strong gravity does not discriminate. This is found in all black music of the Americas, which was able to break down the apartheid in countries such as the United States. In the steelband movement, this inclusiveness is especially apparent, because people from all spheres are not only drawn to the music but are also drawn into the music making itself.

It is not uncommon to see in a band pre-pubescent children, octogenarian men and young men of African, Indian, Chinese, Syrian, European stock. There are upper-, middle- and lower-class members. There are members from the United States and from England, from Japan and from Holland. Phase II has around five or six Japanese members. One black girl from New York is around twelve years old. One white boy in Renegades, the first year I saw him playing, had to stand on a box because he was too small to reach the tenor. A Belgian woman who teaches music in Amsterdam used to play for Phase II, but now she has moved to Desperadoes. And so on. These players can be seen on the finals night of Panorama, which means they are there for one reason only: they are the cream of the crop.

No other institution I can think of anywhere else in the world has so thoroughly broken down every major social barrier: sex, age, class, race and nationality. It is a perfect meritocracy. As Lady Berkley puts it: "It brings people together, both playing and listening, in a way no other kind of music seems to." She, too, apparently, discovered that "when yuh iron good you is king".

Improvisation: The Instruments

The African-derived music of the Americas is improvised. That much is well known, and it does not apply only to jazz. There are the other obvious examples: the lyrical extemporization of calypso and the non-lyrical vocals of scat. But the improvisation runs deeper. For instance, at a famous concert in Berlin, Ella Fitzgerald forgot the lyrics to "Mack the Knife", so she extemporized and made a hit. That would be considered an abject failure within a European aesthetic. But the African aesthetic emphasizes that every song should be different every time it is performed, even by the same performers. Every musician is expected to bring their own interpretation of a song, and that should change (within limits) every time it is performed. (That is the ideal, of course, which is compromised by nightly repetition and by recording.)

Such improvisation is not restricted to melodies and lyrics, however, but characterizes the African approach to every aspect of music making. Instruments, for instance, are used in different ways. James Brown turned the whole band as a rhythmic instrument to back up his screams and screeches. On his first great hit, "Please, Please, Please", he pushed to the forefront the rhythmic backup lines from the standard "Baby, Please Don't Go" and relegated its melody into the chorus. Dancehall performers have turned even the voice into a percussive instrument.

Pan music is not improvised. But it is not a great leap from using an instrument differently from how it was intended to be used, such as beating on the side of a drum (or the box of a guitar), to making an instrument out of an object not intended to be one, such as the brake hub of a car, a schoolboy's desk, a gin bottle, a dustbin or an oil drum. When the teenaged James Brown was in reform school, he formed a gospel group with a paper-and-comb harmonica, a drum kit of old tins, and a broom and washtub bass. With this approach, the squeak of a hand sliding along guitar strings can become part of the music, like the intake of a Baptist singer's breath, or her moans and groans, like Brown's keening wail or the foot-shuffling of an audience.

Now, get one thing clear. Such instrumental improvisation is not based on an idea that any sound from anything will do. Rather, it is a functional aesthetic which accepts that the *right* sound can come from anything. That is an important distinction, because an imagined "right sound", insofar as it exists platonically in the musician's mind, guides his search for the object that would produce it.

Because it was formed in the crucible of plantation slavery, people conceptualize Afro-American music as a *syncretism*, a sort of alloy created by European hegemony over Africans and resulting in a bit of this and a bit of that all mixed up. That idea rests on a vision of slaves being compelled to learn European instruments and music, perhaps to play for European masters.

I differ, based on my research into the evolution of creole music in Trinidad and other parts of the New World. You can make someone learn an unfamiliar music, but you cannot make black people adopt a music they do not like; their musical aesthetic is too deeply rooted for that. More likely, as history shows, they will take what they find useful and can fit into their aesthetic, but reject the rest and turn around to make you adopt their aesthetic. If Africans heard European sounds and instruments which fit into the evolving vision of music they sought to produce, they stole them. Stole in the way that a good artist steals (whereas a bad artist borrows), according to T.S. Eliot.

In other words, an important aspect of the African musical tradition involves using whatever is considered useful. So if an African composer steals a few bars from Beethoven's Fifth Symphony, it does not make the composition less African because those bars are spliced into an African framework by African means.

Take, for example, Anthony Williams, the greatest all-round panman in terms of developing the instrument, arranging the music and leading a band. Very early in his career, Williams decided that he needed to know more about music, how it worked, the relationships between notes and the theory behind it. So he signed up for voice classes. He did not want to waste time learning the fingering necessary for an instrument. Williams also studied European art music. Not because white people claimed that was the highest point of musical evolution (as they still do), but because European art music has wonderful things to teach us that cannot be learned from simple three-minute folk songs and popular music. There's no compromise with cultural oppression and no serendipity involved: just a rational quest for artistic transcendence inspired by a vision of genius.

Interestingly, one of Williams's brilliant innovations was his placement of notes on the pan, which he named the *spiderweb*. He took the twelve outer and inner rings of notes and placed them in the following order, starting at the bottom (counter-clockwise):

C G D A E B F# C# G# D# Bb F

Without knowing it, he had arranged the notes of the tenor pan (which is actually soprano in range) in a circle of fifths, with each note being five tones away from the next (moving counter-clockwise), which represents the basic principle of Western harmony. Comparative musicologist Eugene Novotney, for instance, told me years ago:

> It is no new idea, this circle of fifths. It is the way music theory has been taught for generations now. I do not know one culture that studies harmony that does not present the circle of fifths as the model. When we had our first conversation, the thing that fascinated me: when I walk up to a tenor pan and see that as an object, rather than just a theory in my head, I fell in love with it. I fell absolutely in love with it. My God, this is an idea that I thought only existed in somebody's head and I'm playing it. My God, I'm playing it. I feel like I had a natural affinity to the tenor pan ... When I first saw a tenor pan, I absolutely saw the tenor pan as my friend. Oh yeah. Because the model of that pan, the fourths and fifths, the circle of fifths, it had been in my head since probably I was seven or eight years old and the means of, the practicality of, the circle of fifths the way it's taught in Western music theory, is it's a tool. It's a philosophical tool to help students remember how to form scales.

So we can make another obvious point: Afro-American music making is a rational improvisation towards an aesthetic goal. Again, let me quote David Rudder:

> After yesterday's rejection
> On towards a new perfection
> From a hunger came a feel
> From the feel we shaped the steel
> ("Dedication")

What was this hunger? How did they shape the steel? The hunger of the early panmen was to create a music that could represent and respond to the world in which they lived. That is the ideal of African music, at least what was left of it that came to the New World: to absorb and turn into art the environment in which it finds itself. This is no art that floats above the lives of people. The sheer persistence of that aesthetic is what makes its fruit differ in different places. It is a seed whose tree produces fruit that varies with the soil in which it is planted. If Africans lived on Mars, their music would be like nothing on earth, because it would be shaped by and for life on Mars; yet it would only be so because of the aesthetic brought from Africa. It changes because it remains the same. Syncretism is no part of the equation.

Before 1940, when young men suddenly become obsessed with metal percussion, Trinidadians drummed as we do today. Schoolboys drum. Excursionists drum. Orisha devotees drum. At carnival, they pounded bamboo stalks on the ground or knocked them together. Percussion was pervasive. But it was not enough, not for the young generation, the first to be cut off from the French patois of their parents, and they hungered for something more or something different. Why? Because their world was different from that of their elders. The old structures of colonial domination had been shaken. The Second World War had begun. Even before the servicemen arrived, American docksite workers were flooding the island and introducing their brash, loud culture. People were moving, families resettling in new neighbourhoods. Organized labour was flexing its muscles. Avant-garde artists were challenging the stasis of middle-class culture. Even the physical environment was changing; it was becoming littered with metal debris. The pace of life and communications was faster. Dance music, influenced by swing, was different, louder, more complex and totally modern.

The adoption of metal percussion was instantaneous, love at first sight. In 1939 the all-metal band that inspired the others first appeared, and by 1940 all-metal percussion could be described as "the real native music that is so characteristic of the Trinidad Carnival" (*Port of Spain Gazette*, 15 February 1940).

Those percussionists drummed bits of metal: dustbins and a wide range of other metal containers and parts of derelict automobiles. Their rhythms were louder, sharper ones which contained tonal variations, but otherwise the bands were beating rhythms much like their predecessors did. It was not different enough, though, they hungered for more.

Today, a steelband comprises several different pans (in addition to the Engine Room of percussion). Its main pans are as follows:

Lead Section: tenors, double tenors, second pans, double seconds
Mid-Range: guitar pans, and so on
Bass: Cello pans, bass pans

I say main because there are slight variations between bands, with some having certain pans, mainly in the mid-range – say, triple cellos – which other bands may not. All are made ("tuned" is the word used) the same way, although some tuners specialize in making only certain pans.

The process of tuning a pan involves choosing the drum, sinking it, marking the notes, backing and grooving them, levelling the drum, cutting the skirt, tempering it in fire, tuning it, boring holes for hanging it, fine tuning, finishing, blending and making sticks. Every stage of this is a highly skilled craft whose mysteries I can only hint at, but maybe a hint is enough to excite your wonder and curiosity at what two heroic generations of Trinidadian tuners have wrought by inventing and developing the instrument, expanding its range, clarifying its sound, changing its timbre, making it easier to tune, and making it more durable and louder.

Sinking the face of the drum with a hammer or a shot put, *marking* and pounding up sections to form convex bulges (*backing*) are technical jobs that stretch and change the molecular structure of the steel. This is why different drums with different kinds of steel require different treatment. Pans with higher notes require deeper sinking than those with lower notes: a modern tenor goes nine inches down, whereas a bass no more than five inches. The notes vary in size: the higher the tone the smaller the note. And none of this admits precise measurement. Pounding the notes up into soft bulges creates tensions within the steel and enables it to vibrate. Then outlining the notes with a groove of softened metal (*grooving*) allows the vibrations of one note to be separated as much as possible from another.

After this tempering comes the task easiest to describe and most difficult to do: actual *tuning* – *coarse tuning* to soften the metal until it vibrates at the right pitch; *fine tuning* to adjust its pitch and timbre; and *blending* to ensure the pans are tuned and blended with the other instruments of the band, after having been chromed.

Every note you hear on an instrument, say a guitar, is composed of the fundamental note along with several other different overtones known as *partials*. The partials are what allow us to identify the particular timbre of the note – that is, what kind of instrument is playing the note – and its brightness. The importance of partial overtones is indicated by the fact that small speakers, such as those in telephones and portable transistor radios, cannot produce low fundamental notes, but because they do produce the appropriate overtones, you "hear" the correct sound – even though its main part does not exist. The fundamental is the outline, the partials the chiaroscuro. Without overtones, you get the horrible, tinny sound of a cellphone melody. With inaccurate partials, you get the hazy sound of pre-1950 pans.

Now, to tune a guitar you tighten or slacken the string and, in so doing, you adjust its tone. All the rest, the partial overtones, comes automatically and indeed can be explained by a simple mathematical formula. But the fundamental note on a pan and its partials must be tuned separately from one another.

The discovery that this could be done, and its necessity, was the accomplishment of two men – Tony Williams and Bertie Marshall. Yet, how it is actually done today has to be rediscovered anew by every tuner on every note of every pan. The tuner taps this part of the note, taps that part, trying to get a particular sound, moving the fundamental, shifting first the octave partial (that is the same note only higher, the way a man and a woman could sing the same note but an octave apart), then the various overtones, moving one up, pulling another down, until they "marry" at the right spot. "That's why every note on every pan is an experiment," says Gerard Clark, Starlift's tuner. It is also why the world of tuners is full of anecdotes of how difficult notes were tuned in the zaniest ways, stories like the one, for instance, of the tuner who lost his temper after days of failure with a note and flung his hammer at the pan only for it to hit the note and knock it right in tune.

Nowadays, this is done with electronic strobes which allow notes to be tuned to precise concert pitch: middle C is 220 Hertz. But it still requires a sharpness of ear which takes up to a decade to learn. How can I demonstrate the mystery of this achievement? A conductor can listen to an orchestra and distinguish if a single string on a violin is out of tune; so too a tuner can hear a pan and tell if the partial of a single note is off. It is the aural equivalent of how a painter can look at a pigment and see the colours which were blended to produce it.

Previously, notes were placed in arbitrary order. Very early, tuners had discovered that notes could not be tuned in consecutive order: each one put its neighbour out of tune. So a tuner would put a note wherever he or she could get it to sound okay. An early primer on pan making, written by Hilanders founder Kim Loy Wong, recommended that the tuner "trade the note's place with another . . . if for example you cannot get middle C on the Ping Pong to go below D, then let it stay D and see if you can get D two sections to the right of it" (Seeger 1964, 23).

The genius of Tony Williams was, first, to discover the partial octave in the note, and then to design the spiderweb pan, which has become more or less the "Fourths and Fifths" tenor pan design (modified by Lincoln Noel) used by all tuners today. This cycle-of-fifths arrangement of notes places adjacent notes either an octave or a fifth apart, so that their partials support one another in harmony. That king of the iron brought his notes together in placing and tuning them in a way no other tuner did.

IMMEDIACY: THE MUSIC

The hunger in those youths drove them to shape the steel into a new instrument, a melodic one, so that from banging noisy rhythms on old dustbins, they moved within ten years to, for instance, Chopin's *Nocturne*, which Casablanca essayed in a 1950 recital with a pianist and lyric tenor.

This Casablanca example raises again the issue of white hegemony. When it comes to pan, many writers have considered Afro-Trini's liking for European art music to indicate some sort of subservient betrayal of black culture or mark of European cultural dominance. (Would the same be said about the great jazz tenor saxophone virtuoso and innovator Coleman Hawkins, whose hero was Pablo Cassals, and whose record collection consisted entirely of classical music?) The truth is, if you asked the panmen, as I have, you would discover that they liked a wide range of musical styles, because it was part of their environment, which was in some ways more varied in the 1950s than it is today. In other words, before African music is nationalistic, hegemonic, even before it is functional, it must work as an art. This art really knows no boundaries; the artist steals whatever he comes across and thinks might be of use, and this is especially true of African musicians, who respect no boundaries other than aesthetic ones, which is why the music cannot be itself bounded. (I say this in the light of modern Trinidadian music, soca, which is often incapable of working in aesthetic terms and, instead, is determined by its function to induce collective frenzy, largely through a simple pounding beat and aerobics instructions. Such music, I would argue, is a betrayal of African principles of music making.)

The hegemony paradigm has a mirror image, which is equally misled. If Afro-American music is not the product of white hegemony, neither is it the result of black (or creole) "resistance". True, it grows and is shaped by its environment, including the psychic environment of oppression, which it is both limited by and transcends. The stoic austerity of the blues and the revolutionary message of reggae are both influenced by and a transcendence of the oppression of black people in the southern United States and Jamaica respectively. They were also a product of other traditions such as the spiritual traditions in gospel music and Rastafarian drumming. Music created in an environment of black resistance will reflect the politics of the community. But the reason that music can reach anyone, anywhere is because of its integrity and beauty as a work of art.

"Resistance" is reactive, a response to something; the elaboration of an art form can never be resistance alone, unless by that you mean a resistance to the human condition of mortality and absurdity. It may be influenced or limited by circumstances, but ultimately it is a positive striving to absorb and reshape everything in the environment, including the beliefs of the musician.

In the case of pan, it was the product of the African aesthetic as nourished by the cultural ambience of Trinidad in the 1940s and onwards. Instead of reacting to their highly circumscribed lives, the young inventors of pan, who boldly went where no man had gone before, were driven by their need to improvise an instrument, an ensemble and a music that related to their thoroughly modern lives. They did not just want a louder, more resilient drum to back up their singing, they wanted one to encompass the full range of their musical environment; they wanted an instrument that could play melodies as well as rhythms. Let me state this fact baldly and then move on: African instrumental improvisation has generally transformed melodic instruments into rhythmic ones; pan, however, moved in the opposite direction. But the impulse was the same; that is, to produce a music that reflects the environment.

What is this environment? Some of its components I have mentioned: the other kinds of music that is heard; the social, economic, cultural and political conditions faced by the musicians; and the musical traditions they have inherited. But ultimately the environment which creates and is created by African-derived music is the most immediate: the community where it is being heard at any moment in time. It could be at a funeral, at a party, at a football match, on the streets during carnival or on the corner. That is the environment where it will succeed or fail; that is the acid test.

African-derived music creates communities. Every youth movement since the Second World War has gelled around some type of popular African-derived music. Early December 2006, for instance, two hundred politicians petitioned to Prime Minister Dominique de Villepin to take legal action against several French hip-hop musicians whose music had inspired the exploited migrants to riot all across France.

Steelbands came to represent neighbourhoods and, eventually, the entire nation. Recall Lady Berkley: "It brings people together." But the real community which the music creates is the ephemeral community of people within earshot, those swept along by its rhythms, the mobile and transient community of now.

That community is generated by the music: the party, the concert and, in the case of pan in the early days, the carnival band on the road, and now the audience at Panorama. This community is not just people within earshot but people who have been transformed from being individuals into a group of people moved by the music being performed at that moment. They have been moved, both literally and figuratively.

This is achieved through two main modalities. The first is the various forms of musical improvisation in which the musicians shape the music to suit the audience and the other performers. This is a two-way relationship, and the better both parties are at it, the tighter the relationship. This relationship is between the musicians and the audience, but also within the audience itself. We are all here grooving collectively to the beautiful sounds being produced specifically to evoke and touch the mood we are in at this moment in time.

This includes more than the melodic improvisation of jazz and most African-American music in performance, where every performer is expected to give his particular interpretation of a song; it is also the lyrical improvisation of extempo and the non-lyrical vocal improvisation of scat. Jamaicans inject this immediacy into recorded music through the improvised chat of deejays, who have themselves become the artists and created their own art form.

The second is the visceral compulsion of rhythm and volume. (Lesser artists such as disco musicians of the 1980s and soca musicians of the present rely on a simple pounding beat; additionally, soca musicians use aerobics instructions – wave something, move to the left or wherever – and deafening amplification to achieve the community they are unable to generate through their art.)

Whatever the method, the intent is the same: to match the music and the mood of the moment so performers and audience fuse into a single community. Steelbands on the road used some improvisation (Cobo Jack made Invaders famous for that) on the road in the late 1950s, but mainly it was the rhythm and the slow foot-scraping chip of the followers which fused the crowd and the band. Now that bands are no longer on the road and their music is often too complex and too orchestrated for improvisation, the togetherness and unity is generated through competition, which, today, means Panorama.

Even that has changed. Steelbands no longer flood the roads of Port of Spain with rivers of music: all their eddies and rapids, sluggish shallows and dramatic cascades. That swirling, rolling sound suited a time when the huge, awkward bands were themselves mobile and trundled along the streets, powered by the pan-pushers, who were in turn powered by the music which also whisked the vast crowds like they were no more than the leaves in a flood. Indeed, when Panorama first started in 1963, the steelbands performed on the move. But them days done. Steelbands now remain firmly anchored on the Panorama stage, shaking furiously until each one's ten minutes have expired.

Instead of pouring torrents on to the streets, steelbands now erect baroque cathedrals, each vibrating stone individually carved and embellished. It is an elaborate, ornate style, intricate motifs within intricate motifs, a music which, in the 1990s, suited Jit Samaroo's genius and Renegades's more than anyone else's, until that gave way to the slower, rougher power of Clive Bradley and Desperadoes, and the stylish elegance of Boogsie Sharpe and Phase II Pan Groove.

This competition is a sublimation of the older warfare and street clashes, which were in turn an outcome of informal street competitions. How does this generate the immediacy of improvisation?

Great music is the creation of surprising inevitability. Where will the piece go next? And when we hear, we are surprised at first because we did not foresee that. But immediately, or even simultaneously, the surprise is resolved by the correctness of what follows. Ah yes, we feel, it had to be that.

Today, steelband music cannot surprise you through improvisation, so it has turned itself into something akin to a sport, with its supporters and exciting finals. They say football is the greatest sport because it offers the most scope for surprise, for the underdog to win. Most sports began as war games, and so too Panorama is a battle; only, here, the armies are musical ensembles, their generals the arrangers and their weapons are music.

Let me conclude with David Rudder's commemoration of Exodus Steel Orchestra's victory in the 1992 Panorama, "Dus' in Deh Face":

> Big fete, like the whole of the East gone mad
> People – the traffic police had it hard
> Prancing, some man get on like leggo beast
> Boasting, how proud they is to come from the East
> They say tell Port of Spain we coming again, that was a warm up
> And then they went down to Point, mash up the joint, the lick-up was non-stop
> Respect now is what we want, they cyan take we light again
> We eh taking no prisoners, so sorry, we soakin we belt in cut-tail pee
> So when we reach it go be: Whap! Whap! Whap! Whap!

When you see we come down
Tell them war declare in town
Dus in they face
Guns will be blasting for sure in this musical war
Dus in they face
We looking for fight it's trouble tonight
We feeling all right
It's a panman war
We come out for war to settle the score
The tenors sawed off
And it's doy doy doy doy doy doy

All Stars, Desperadoes and Renegades
Quiet, but they sharpening their musical blades
Fonclaire, the Phase and the Humming Bird,
Waiting for the judges to give the word.
And Lincoln and Bertie and Birdie and company
They love the bacchanal
Them who tune the pans
Now they watching the jam
In this pannist Carnival
Now it come to this after two months of labour
Living on nuts and corn from dusk till dawn
We must refuse to think bout lose
Nobody could beat we, I tell you: na na na na na.

References

Seeger, Pete. 1964. *The Steel Drums of Kim Loy Wong: An Instruction Manual to Accompany the Folkways Records FI-8367 and FS-3834 and the Movie* Music from Oil Drums. New York: Oak Publications.

9

Don Drummond
Just How Good Was He?

HERBIE MILLER

Concurrent with the 2000 musical symposium held at the University of the West Indies Mona, "Don Drummond Musical Genius", the *Jamaica Observer* published two articles which were critical of the ska trombonist and composer. In them, two prominent Jamaican musicians, Sonny Bradshaw and Headley Jones, challenged the merits of Drummond's musical abilities, calling into question the overwhelmingly positive light in which the symposium had placed the popular musician. But what is ability? By what standards do these critics pass judgement? The fact that two of Drummond's contemporaries could advance such serious criticism solicits my response, using the question posed by one of the articles, "Just How Good Was He?"

My response addresses the dismissive claims and the accolades placed on Drummond by both his adversaries and supporters, and engages in a critical reappraisal of his music in the context of time and place. I posit that Drummond's genius, like that of his predecessor Count Ossie and his successor Bob Marley, was not only musically innovative but conveyed sociocultural enlightenment as well. Using a value system that opposes Jones's, I make an assessment of Drummond's work by looking beyond the values associated with the rigid harmonic structures and methods that govern the Eurocentric musical analysis favoured by Jones.[1] I locate Drummond in the more fluid complex of African diasporic musical trends. His musical contribution and cultural significance are evaluated through those lenses, thus establishing him and his music's role in that context.

Jones raised the first critical question about Drummond in the article "Another Side of the Coin" (*Daily Observer*, 29 March 2000, 13) when he justifiably asked: Where is the Drummond genius? He then proceeded to answer his question by discrediting Drummond's musical ability. Jones stated that he "regarded Drummond as possessing a poor musical harmony concept", a fault he reasoned "that all the researchers possible at whatever level will find it impossible to correct". What Jones did not recognize was the desire by many jazz musicians in the late 1950s and 1960s[2] to simplify or completely discard the standard harmonic element that helped shape their music. To understand the relationship between musicians of that period and harmonic ideas, an investigation of the modern jazz scene of that moment is helpful.

This is necessary since Drummond, like the jazz musicians of that era, organized in relation to the fervour of the time – a belief by blacks in America that, by mobilizing around the civil rights movement, racial equality could be a reality. Likewise, Drummond reflected a communal desire and expression for political and social equality, as well as the recognition of Afro-Jamaican aesthetics, historical memory and traditional values. These were basic principles of the Rastafarian community, the communal circle of Don Drummond. These jazz musicians felt it was essential to bring back a primal expression to the music, and to achieve that goal it was necessary to de-emphasize harmony as the primary building block in black musical expression.

"The idea of selected notes sounding together to form chords is the great European additive to Afro-American music" (Carr, Fairweather and Priestley 1988, 216). This was the opening sentence of Brian Priestley, the British jazz musician and writer, when describing harmony. Priestley's statement, like those of so many jazz historians, suggests that the African element – their preference for melody and rhythm – lacked harmonic ingredient. Various stringed instruments including the banjo – indigenous to Africa – capably functioned as a harmonic guide in music ensembles. The kalimba, or thumb piano, and the marimba, which Dennis deCarli, the seventeenth-century European observer to west and central Africa, thought "resembles the sound of an organ, and makes a pretty agreeable harmony" (Rath 1993, 719), are indications that African music – though not stressing its value – did include harmony. Jazz has always ambivalently utilized harmony since its beginnings.

However, as it developed, greater emphasis was placed on harmonic sophistication among American jazz musicians during the bebop (1943–48) and so-called third stream (1948–50s) movements. At that point, "[m]uch of modern jazz, for instance, starting with [Duke] Ellington and moving through [Charlie] Mingus, [Archie] Shepp, Albert Ayler and groups like the Pharaohs of Chicago and the Mystic Revelation of Rastafari in Kingston . . . returned to the essence and origins of black music in the community sounds of church, gospel, work-songs . . . [and] blues" (Brathwaite 1994, 186).

This response was an indication that there had developed a widening distance between the black community and jazz. Jazz had ceased being a music for social dance as well as a way of listening that involved the emotions associated with, at once, the relentless joy, swing and release related to the blues. What jazz had become, or was in fear of becoming, was an intellectual, musical aesthetic that involved a cerebral relationship, akin to the attitudes of patrons of European concert music and devoid of the pure emotion that was emblematic of its identity. Within its musical precision, jazz's most basic element was the blues. It was the raw passion of a people; its syncopation, improvisation and relentless swing gave it its identity.

Toward the end of the harmonically challenging bebop era, between 1943 and 1949, instigated by Thelonious Monk, Charlie Christian, Kenny Clark, Dizzy Gillespie and Charlie Parker, the established paradigm of the period emphasized harmony as the direction for modern jazz. This was followed by a period when the pianist Lennie Tristano pursued an "intense examination of jazz's current state, and introduced the scalar and harmonic approach he developed. It was a harmonic language that adapted the practices of contemporary classical music, polytonal effects, suggested Stravinsky, and like mid-century art music, exhibited an extensive use of counterpoint" (Kelsey 2005). Tristano was accompanied by a handful of disciples along this path.

This period was also encouraging to other jazz artists. Mostly classically trained and experienced, some drew from European musical influences that challenged harmonic conceptions. To those such as John Lewis, the leader of the Modern Jazz Quartet; pianist Dave Brubeck; and musicologist and music organizer Gunther Schuller, the harmonically layered European avant-garde was appealing. This group of jazz musicians based their system of advancement on harmonic textures that elevated jazz to newer heights that were more demanding. Lewis's "Orchestra USA" was a showcase for his forays into the "introverted, complex and structured" compositions that were his specialty. (Fraim 1996, 58). And, "influenced by European composers such as Darius Milhaud", with whom he studied, Brubeck "imported many classical devices into jazz" (ibid.). Gunther Schuller arranged recording sessions and live performances that challenged the idea that jazz was not concert music and therefore not high art. By infusing complex European harmonic structures and employing skilled musicians with the most developed conservatory competence, Schuller introduced the "third stream" movement. He also enlisted the most accomplished and technically equipped jazz musicians as participants. Though intricate and challenging, this music nonetheless lacked the harmonic freedom that essentially allows jazz its expressive qualities. In the hands of these musicians, modern jazz was locked in an elaborate cerebral space, arranged with dense textures, unusual time signatures, difficult chords and harmonies and little space for spontaneous improvisation. It was caught up "in a type of dilemma, a musical straight jacket, [the idiom was] stuck in the intricate, intellectual textures of complex chords and harmonies" (ibid.).

To rescue jazz from this musical predicament, its most rooted musicians were already questioning the necessity of harmony. "Harmony lost its primacy as the key to the evolution of jazz," states Peter Townsend in his essay "Musical Style and Liberationist Ethic, 1956–1965". "What to do about harmony became one of the central issues for musical practice and theory during the stage of radical innovation of the early 1960s," he states. Ornette Coleman, for instance, "distinguishes harmony (which he refers to as 'background') from the music, and urges his musicians to play the music not the background" (Townsend 2001, 150). It was a time for "cutting back, opening up and airing out the density of modern jazz", argues critic Martin Williams. It was also a time, which "involved less emphasis on complex harmonic background and a greater emphasis on melody" (Fraim 1996, 67). Writer Amiri Baraka supported the discarding of harmony, considering it "European, western and an obstacle to the rediscovery of African musical values" (Townsend 2001, 151). Saxophonist Archie Shepp makes the point that while African music does have harmony, its emphasis was "a western musical phenomenon", since for Africans the highlight was their "tremendous melody and rhythm" (ibid.).

To address the emphasis on harmony, two alternative schools of thought became the vogue. One set of jazz musicians, notably, the Adderley brothers (Nat and Julian "Cannonball"), Bobby Timmons, Art Blakey, Lee Morgan and Oliver Nelson, were of the belief that to escape the quagmire, jazz's progress must be linked to more accessible forms of African American music. As a result of their ideas, the gospel flavoured, blues spiced, hard bop style – sometimes called soul jazz – that they developed became popular. Its popularity was primarily because it was a style of music that had a raw, natural soul to it, a feel closer to the blues and the spirituals that appealed to the African American emotional sensibility. Harmony, Priestley stated, "may have been less than totally essential to blues although, by the time they were first recorded, a succession of accompanying chords was fairly standard" (Carr, Fairweather and Priestley 1988, 216). George Russell, who by 1953 had developed his *Lydian Chromatic Concept of Tonal Organization*, had influenced another alternative. His lydian concept is credited with opening the way into modal music for jazz musicians, and provided Miles Davis and John Coltrane, on the album *Kind of Blue*, with a new approach to jazz improvisation. While modal music was nothing new,[3] it was now being put to new use. *Kind of Blue* "contains modal pieces with harmonic challenges cut to a minimum. This allow[ed] the soloist to invent on a single chord or scale for sixteen measures or as long as [they] wished" (Fraim 1996, 63).[4]

Like these artists, Don Drummond's knowledge of harmony was indeed quite solid. For evidence, one only has to listen to tunes like the romantically warm "Green Eyes", taken over a Latin rhythm, or "What Is This Thing Called Love", "Sometimes I'm Happy" and Horace Silver's "Bernie's Tune". All these songs are based on standard harmonic progressions. One should also be mindful that during this period (1962), Drummond was among the vanguard of those musicians performing jazz on the local Jamaican scene and, simultaneously, creating ska. It is all but certain he would have been aware of the different directions jazz was taking and the advancements of its current musical thinkers. Musically, Drummond was rooted in melodies, rhythmic elasticity and the importance of the music's African derivation. In that regard, he immersed himself in the Nyabinghi rhythms of Count Ossie, effortlessly floating melodies over ringing Rasta drums (for example, "Smiling", "Duck Soup" and "Mad, Mad World").

Like the American hard boppers, soul jazz and modal school of musicians, Drummond must have come to the belief that by deconstructing the harmonically sophisticated approach of the beboppers, the modernists and the third stream schools, he could better emphasize a sensibility based on the rhythmically rich but harmonically uncomplicated ska figures. This would have been so whenever he performed with Count Ossie and his drummers, since there was usually no chord instrument – piano or guitar – to suggest harmonic directions. Without instrumentation that directs chord movement, Drummond was able to investigate fresh paths that would lead to ska. Rico Rodriquez, who partnered Drummond on some of these excursions, explains: "When you play music with Ossie you kinda *create* music more . . . You see, when you don't hear no chords is like you 'ave a wider scope fe development" (Hebidge 1994, 59). However, it is to particular songs in Drummond's repertoire that we must turn in order to reveal the proof.

"Mesopotamia", "Down Beat Burial" and "Addis Ababa" are compositions by Drummond that demonstrate this point. However, discussing Drummond's harmonic intelligence, Gordon Rohlehr established that harmonic sophistication did not necessarily have to be dense and complex. Using a number of recorded sources, Rohlehr illustrated some of Drummond's musical ideas. He recognized that to express emotion, musicians sometimes were required to possess fuller community awareness rather than overt conservatory training. Drummond's interpretation of the atmosphere that was part of Kingston's communal energy, and how capturing that feeling – through music – related to harmony and emotion, was pointed out by Rohlehr in the song "Man in the Street":

> I hear all kinds of things here. I hear the noises of the streets. I hear the country buses – kinda rounding the corner and you hear those horns blasting. In other words, he is fusing music out of the sounds, out of what he is hearing around him . . . Drummond is transmuting those sounds around him. And the assertiveness to it – the assertiveness of the life force, the energy that is so typical of Jamaica. It's one of the greatest qualities of Jamaica, that powerful, affirmative sense of life. And that's what he's capturing in the music. It's not a question of . . . whether he had subtle harmony or unsubtle harmony. He's dealing with the raw experience of people and he's transmuting that into sound. That is what he is doing. (Rohlehr 2000)

"This validates what Drummond was doing and sets him even into European context," remarks musicologist Marjorie Whylie (personal correspondence, 25 November 2005). "What he was doing is no less potent than the creative offerings of composers of musique concrète, creators who were using environmental sounds and early synthesizers to do exactly what Drummond was achieving with conventional instruments."

Drummond's musical thoughts are evident on other recorded sources as well and are similar to what others were dealing with in the jazz world. On his compositions "Green Island", "Reburial", "Down Beat Burial", "Mad, Mad World" and "Confucius", Drummond had the bassist employ a pedal point throughout, adding to the hypnotic effect of these tunes and structuring them within the open-ended modal format similar to what Miles Davis did with "All Blues" (1958) or John Coltrane with "My Favorite Things" (1961). These approaches to composition and performance linked Drummond to the then radical movement toward modality and a sense of freedom from strict harmonic structures by stripping songs to minimal chord progression. "Perhaps the truth is", according to Brian Priestley, "that the use of harmony in jazz is less a guiding light than in most European music and more a matter of texture" (Carr, Fairweather and Priestley 1988, 17, 216). However, the ability to make such musical modifications required, first and foremost, a thorough grounding in harmonic knowledge.

In his critique, Headley Jones stated that Drummond's best solo work was "based on the simple root subdominant-dominant chord pattern (which is) quite elementary", and asked, "Where's the genius in that?" Cuban (Montuno) and Haitian music; and, again, modal jazz like Miles Davis's "So What"; and definitely the jump blues popular in Jamaica in the early 1950s were often based on the I–IV–V tonic, the "subdominant-dominant harmony chord patterns". Also, I–IV–V harmonies have been a fundamental aspect of music making for centuries; this progression has been the output (standard) in the Western canon for musicians from Bach to James Brown. Why then is it important that Drummond be held to standards of harmonic practices beyond others regarded as geniuses? Without further elaboration, I suggest that Drummond was incorporating all these elements into fulfilling his vision of creating a sound that would become essentially Jamaican. That is also one of his outstanding contributions to the island's popular music.

Jones then argued that "the best of [The] Skatalite[s'] recordings were limited to a 1–6–2–5 pattern with fading endings", while suggesting that that formula was simplistic. All musicians, in all genres of music, at times fade endings. But more importantly, Jones, who places much emphasis on harmony, should know that the simplistic I–VI–II–V is the *most* common chord progression used in jazz, particularly among beboppers. Called "rhythm changes" after the George Gershwin song "I've Got Rhythm", the harmonic progression is one of a handful that jazz musicians of almost generation have turned to first as the basis for melodic invention. Furthermore, it should be pointed out that the renewed "simplicity" that musicians as respected as Art Blakey, Oliver Nelson, Horace Silver, Julian "Cannonball" Adderley, his brother Nat, Lee Morgan and Bobby Timmons, among others, played did not result from an inability to perform more complex pieces. Rather, it came from a desire to reassert jazz's place as North America's equivalent to the European classical tradition:[5] originality, American identity, rhythmic elasticity and propulsion, also called syncopation – which is what we call swing, that magical feel that elicits the head nodding, finger snapping and foot tapping reaction in which one is engulfed before one is aware. Note also the term used by musicians to describe this idea was "freedom", a word that, by the 1960s, signified the emotions of a politically charged "Third World" movement and African American communities across the United States of America in their call for social change. Charles Mingus, among jazz's most complex and prodigious composers, was not against using simplistic formulas. His 1960 recording of the tune "Folk Forms", explains Brian Priestley, "is a simple blues in the key of F, spontaneously organized around a couple of simple rhythmic figures" (Townsend 2001, 148).

In the article "Just How Good Was He?" (*Jamaica Observer*, 12 May 2000) the influential veteran musician, bandleader and observer of musical trends, Sonny Bradshaw, took to task the merits of Don Drummond. Published anonymously, but written by Basil Walters, the article described Bradshaw as "one of those who believes Drummond has been romanticized". The article later quoted Bradshaw: Drummond "was a good musician but he has become a folk hero because of his location". Bradshaw's statement implied that because of Drummond's less than privileged socialization, his mental illness and the tragedy that ended his career,[6] the trombonist was accorded favoured ranking. In the same article, Bradshaw further stated that Drummond "was a budding composer but never attained his potential as an outstanding musician internationally like his contemporaries Joe Harriott and Wilton 'Bra' Gaynair".

When I discussed these opinions with him, Bradshaw said: "Jamaicans always had a soft spot and love affair with the underdog" (personal communication, spring 2004). I found Bradshaw's statement provocative and somewhat contradictory. In an earlier opinion, he wrote that, following the migration of the island's best jazz musicians, among the "new crop [it was] . . . fabulous Don Drummond who in spite of continued ill health manages to produce the most satisfying performances on trombone in the West Indies" (liner notes, *Jazz Jamaica from the Workshop*, 1962). Bradshaw also told me in an earlier discussion (April 1998) that Drummond was such an outstanding musician that he, Bradshaw, pursued the trombonist for inclusion in the 1956 edition of the Jamaica all-star big band. Bradshaw's disappointment in Drummond therefore implies that the trombonist's popularity is "romanticized" and thus unwarranted, since he did not fulfil his promise. His reaction seems to rest on the idea that, to fulfil that potential, Drummond would have had to pursue a career in European music or that he should have migrated, like Harriott and Gaynair, with the intention of becoming a bona fide jazz musician. Drummond might not have achieved the promise envisioned for him by Bradshaw and, indeed, the Jamaican social elite, but he certainly achieved the status worthy of the discussions in which Bradshaw and the participants at the University of the West Indies conference engaged.

Drummond's only confirmed trip outside Jamaica was in 1951, when he spent about a year with Eric Dean's Orchestra performing in Haiti, though he may have been a member of that band when it spent six months there on a previous engagement during 1949 (*Daily Gleaner*, 23 February 1951). It was while performing with Dean's and other jazz type groups around that time that Drummond was first noticed. He increasingly gained critical attention and wider popularity as word about his musicianship started to spread. He also established an early reputation as a talented composer, a gift at which he became quite prolific as his career developed. It was also a craft for which he would later gain popular and critical recognition. Again, Rico provides insight: "He was such an advanced musician that after he played with Eric Deans and touring Cuba and Haiti and all those places, . . . he learn[ed] a lot of the melodies, so he could write whatever he need[ed] to write, so him write a lot of things for himself, [rather] than play people's tune, but he knew all the standards" (telephone interview, 2005).

On 15 April 1955, "With the Stars" by Bat Man, a column in the *Star* newspaper which covered the entertainment scene, enthusiastically reported: "Bournemouth Club has got a band which is the creamiest thing this night spot has seen since the halycen [sic] days of Roy Coburn's Blu-Flames. Don Drummond leads this real gone group, and the cats are purring with noisy joy" (p. 7).

However, like Jones and Bradshaw, there were those critics in the 1950s that found it necessary to review Drummond without the appreciation for modern expressions, individual interpretations and compositional originality. They expected Drummond to conform and cater to the demands of those whom entertainment writer Spence McLure described as "the upper crust of society who were waltzing in the spacious ballroom", at clubs like Bournemouth (*Music Sheet*, 6 May 1955, 3). The *Music Sheet*, a popular entertainment paper during the 1950s, for which Bradshaw did most of the writing, was at the same time somewhat indifferent and encouraging in its review of Drummond's new band:

> In our band box this week is the Don Drummond All-Stars . . . This group is specifically a jazz group and is not an ideal dance band but boasts a wealth of talent in their line up which includes Cluet Johnson bass; Papa Son drums; Janet Enright guitar; Jack Jones alto sax; Foggy Mullings piano; Jerome Walters vocals and leader Don Drummond trombone.
>
> Main fault with this group is that their tunes are too long as each soloist plays at least two choruses much to the embarrassment of [those] who are in [the] majority to [the] genuine jazz fans in Jamaican dance halls.
>
> The music of this group is different as they do not bury themselves in worthless stock arrangements but work out exciting riffs on the spot. With some neat arrangements coupled with the necessary rehearsals this group would be a tonic to the music business.
>
> Again, the deportment of this little band is poor. There is no uniformity in their dress and their stand behaviour is strange, but we look forward to rapid improvement in this department of Jamaican music.
>
> Donald Drummond is the greatest trombone potential the island has discovered since the memorable days of Peter Baker, but he should set the proper example for his musicians to follow, if he is to achieve the success he so much deserves. (6 May 1955, 2, 3)

It was with an eye on the creative and aesthetic control of the artist, and the concern for the comfort of those fans more interested in dancing and less attuned to spontaneity, that the writer critiqued Drummond. They were an audience who, obviously, were more disposed to the music of dance or swing bands, with their neat arrangements and mannered, uniformly rehearsed presentations. The writer found Drummond's tunes "too long", too "spontaneous" and "different", since they did not use the stock arrangements the audience was accustomed to hearing. Because they were "specifically a jazz group", the members of Drummond's aggregation "work[ed] out exciting riffs on the spot". Composing on the spot, or head arrangements, and the individual's solo remain two of the main elements that distinguish the jazz musician. These are prized skills in the jazz musician's arsenal, and they were tools mastered by the best Jamaican instrumentalists, including Gaynair, Harriott, Harold "Little G" McNair, Dizzy Reece and Don Drummond. As well, the writer complains about band deportment and "strange behaviour". Since the actions of the musicians were not described as bad behaviour, and that strange implies weird or eccentric, this calls into mind the peculiar manners of Parker, Gillespie and Monk. I am not suggesting Drummond and his band were in any way mimicking the idiosyncrasies of the beboppers, but I am mindful that Drummond would be certified mentally incapacitated in time to come. However, it was clear the reviewer recognized the talent in Drummond and his group and, instead of gratuitous dismissal, offered encouraging wishes that they would conform to the examples that guarantee success, the recognition of Don Drummond's preeminence among his peers notwithstanding.

Throughout his career, Drummond recorded extensively, making, by some estimates, over five hundred studio recordings; of these, approximately a third were his own compositions. Students and fans of ska are aware of numerous classics composed by Drummond: "Addis Ababa", "Confucius", "Far East" and "Eastern Standard Time" are a few. Less known are "Mr Wonderful", "A Sound Is Born" and "Gipsy Song", a composition based on Scheherazade. However, I will focus on one Drummond composition, "The Message", a jazz number he never recorded, but which is talked about whenever old timers reminisce about the trombonist's early years. Almost fifty years after, and with a sense of delight, Rico remembers "The Message" as a showstopper at the Carib Theatre when Drummond performed it with the all-star big band led by Bradshaw. "The crowd really went wild with that one," said Rico with a chuckle in his voice. Neville "Brammy" Bramwell was a regular on the jazz scene in the 1950s as well, and he witnessed Drummond's performance at that event. He described the occasion thus: " 'The Message' was played at the 1956 Carib concert which was a near riot as the massive crowd outside exceeded the capacity and the iron grilles on the outside were bent by the throng . . . Don started playing . . . from the balcony . . . and then gradually made his way to the stage" (e-mail, 5 August 2005). Bassist Lloyd Mason was then an aspiring musician who followed Wilton Gaynair and other jazz musicians around in the early 1950s. He later recorded on some early ska tunes with Drummond and played bass on the two jazz albums on which the trombonist appeared. In an interview in 2005, Mason recalled: "At Bournemouth, 'The Message' was always requested and Drummond's band had to play it over and over until one night the management banned them from playing it since people just got caught up in listening instead of dancing when it was played." The *Star*'s entertainment reporter wrote a similar story in his column (7 March 1958, 7):

> [Don D] excited the Carib crowd with his original composition "The Message". Since then, the arrangement has gone the rounds of musicians and at every dance date it is a must. At one nightspot, however, a jazz fan requested the item from the Orchestra and it was played much to his joy. A couple of nights later he returned and requested an encore, only to be told that the management had banned it. Reason? Too fast for comfortable dancing.

Performances that encouraged comfortable dancing were the "tonic to the music business" that Drummond's jazz group did not provide. It was not considered "good time" or entertainment music, developed to sell drinks and background music for dancing, or music reduced to little or no artistic merit. But these were precisely among the reasons Parker, Gillespie and Monk devised the fast improvisational and fluid style called bebop. It was their way of performing jazz that would project mastery of group cohesion, showcase individual virtuosity and be recognized as art. They were rebelling against the commercial style of music played by dance bands like Glen Miller, Artie Shaw, Benny Goodman and others, the kind of music that was copied by their Jamaican admirers. Local bands, such as Roy Coburn, Eric Deans, Milton McPherson and Sonny Bradshaw, styled themselves after these American orchestras. It was those bands that the Jamaican elites wanted musicians like Don Drummond to continue imitating. Obviously, artistic expression by the likes of Drummond was not the purpose for which "the upper crust of society" congregated at clubs like Bournemouth, but rather to be entertained by dance music exclusively.

The most discriminating jazz aficionados and musicians alike appreciated Don Drummond. He was viewed as an original composer and a trombonist whose dexterity at fast tempos was of startling effect and exquisite quality. On the other hand, he was also revered as an interpreter of standards and ballads into which he inflected a heartfelt quality. Drummond's ballad performances were of such poignancy, grace and warmth that listeners were often gripped in emotion and sometimes even moved to tears. I asked Brammy to recall a story he had told me many years earlier about musician Baba Motta, who was so moved. Brammy obliged:

> The Drummond performance . . . at the Little Theatre . . . was the first outing (I believe) of Carlos Malcolm's band. They had rehearsed most of the day at Regal (Skyline Club) Theatre and I seem to remember that Don's trombone had become damaged in some way. I don't think the slide could extend fully. That didn't seem to matter to Don because he launched into some ballads and it was during one of these that Baba [Motta] started to cry at first as he accompanied Don . . . Don blew soulfully. Baba got up from the piano like a man in a trance and walked up the aisle and into the closed glass doors at the back sustaining cuts. I remember Don playing "Laura" that night. (E-mail, 5 August 2005)

Because of his outstanding performances and compositional ability, his affecting interpretations of ballads, and his dexterous handling of the trombone, Don Drummond, from all accounts, was considered a future jazz star in the making. Furthermore, the most progressive American jazz musicians he admired had established themselves as artists playing the bebop style they had developed. Drummond, a musician who certainly kept pace with those developments – the fast, complex and harmonically challenging demands bebop required – would have embraced them as much as any modern jazz artist anywhere else in the world.

Some say Don Drummond was Jamaica's greatest instrumentalist and was one of the world's top five trombone masters. That he resides at the pinnacle of our musical hierarchy is, in my mind, undisputed. For his fans the world over, he is, without question, a folk hero and a musician who touched the soul of the masses. His influence is undeniable; one only has to count the number of times his hits have been recycled into fresh new ones – the "Far East Rhythm", for example. Ska, reggae and jazz bands, including Delfeo Marsalis, internationally perform his songs, while many of their players sport stingy brim felts in the style of Drummond. His popularity is of such that many people, on hearing ska songs, automatically take it for granted that it is Drummond. They assume so in spite of the fact that the tune may not even contain a trombone. As well, songs performed by others, such as Rico Rodriquez's "Let George Do It", have been issued as Don Drummond's recordings, capitalizing on his popularity. It is, therefore, not important whether he was rated among the top five trombonists in the world. Frankly, it means nothing, except to those who wish to be continually defined by their past masters, to be measured by their yardsticks and be judged by their standards.

Drummond set his own standards. He cultivated an original attitude, concept, execution and sound. Drummond was the originator of what is today called the Far East sound, a sound carried forward by the Wailers (Bob, Peter and Bunny), the Abyssinians, the Congos, Augustus Pablo, Jackie Mittoo, Pablov Black and Earl "China" Smith, to name a few. The deceptive, almost dreamlike, ball handling of soccer star Allan "Skill" Cole clearly reflected Drummond's influence. Also, the unhurried poetry of Lawrence Rowe's batting and the gazelle-like smoothness of Michael Holding's bowling action further reveal an indebtedness to the musician by these two former West Indies cricket stars. Indeed, I dare say that the word sound of Kamau Brathwaite's and the tunefulness of Mervyn Morris's poetry are in the voice of Drummond. And while Drummond was quite endearing to some of the island's social elites, most could not embrace the originality of his music nor comprehend his eccentric personality.

Like Miles Davis, Charlie Parker and Thelonious Monk, Don Drummond was a misunderstood musical genius whose career continues to present problems for those who wish to piece his life together. Shortly after the Drummond Symposium, the remarks of the bandleader, composer, pianist and musicologist Carlos Malcolm, who happens to be a fine trombonist as well, vindicated the group of Drummond aficionados who listened as Malcolm reminisced about rehearsing with the trombonist at his Vineyard Town residence: "From the first time I rehearsed with Don, I knew I was in the presence of a genius" (personal communication, August 2000). Don was a precursor, a revealer and a liberator of an entire generation of artists. He was a bold initiator, one who, in spite of ill health, immersed himself in his efforts to fully express his art. Together, Drummond and his instrument were intertwined, the horn a mere extension of the man. It was this sense, as a trailblazer of modern Jamaican music, that won him a dedicated following among vanguard musicians and music enthusiasts alike.

Don Drummond could have followed the migratory path and experienced the dilemma faced by those other favourite sons of the soil. Wilton "Bra" Gaynair (also called "Bogey", as in bogeyman, for the magical tricks he performed on his horn), Harold "Little G" McNair, Joe Harriott, Sonny Gray and Dizzy Reese, were all outstanding musicians who chose that trajectory. By remaining at home, Drummond envisioned the possibility of maintaining his jazz sensibility by infusing it with the spiritual aura and the drum ritual that is part of Nyabinghi groundings.[7] He utilized his musical training, Africanist sensibility, nationalist ideal and his popularity to communicate with and entertain the masses, the underclass. Drummond and his coterie of musicians creatively constructed the ska sound that is today known the world over as authentically Jamaican and for which they are recognized. Of course, Jamaica had much music of note before Drummond. But ska eclipsed the calypso/mento strain, which was confined to a local audience, who understood and loved it for its topical tales and parodies, and tourists, for its patois, lilt and often scandalous lyrics (Neely 2008). As a result of remaining in Jamaica, and because he had the foresight to align himself with rhythm innovator Count Ossie, Drummond spearheaded a movement accompanied by other vanguard musicians that included members of the Skatalites, musicians who are all well known today and revered throughout the world by critics and fans alike for their ska innovation. As a consequence, Ernie Ranglin's fame as a world-class guitarist benefits more from his popularity as a reggae musician than that of a jazz virtuoso. Though the expatriate Jamaican jazz musicians are very well known, respected and aggressively collected by a minute sector of the already small jazz community, major recognition and success have eluded them. To the larger jazz community, they are either unknown or they seem a mere curiosity, being "West Indians" who played jazz.

Don Drummond, in comparison to his jazz contemporaries that migrated and most of the local Jamaican musicians of his time, today exerts a wider influence on the world music stage. This is so because, like them, he also mastered the jazz idiom, but more so, because of his central role in the transition from jazz through Nyabinghi drumming and chanting to ska, his recognition is broader. Ska, as a worldwide phenomenon and as the foundation in the ongoing evolution of popular Jamaican music, also fortifies Drummond's contributions. As a result, he is regarded as an outstanding visionary and an important innovator. Drummond's impact on the contemporary reggae community, and his towering spirit over the "conscious" narrative that roots reggae is known to propagate, endows his iconoclasm. By recognizing that music was more than entertainment or a means of diversion, and by engaging in the culture of his time (Banfield 2004, 65), Drummond produced a lasting body of music, which conveyed the history, aspirations and endurance of the Jamaican people. It encouraged confidence and personal dignity, illuminated a collective unconscious, and enabled a path to asserting a national identity. Taken together, these achievements compel recognition of Don Drummond, along with three or four others, as a Jamaican musical genius.[8]

Notes

1. In 2002, I interviewed Headley Jones, who adamantly defended the use of harmony as the linchpin of musical sophistication.
2. This period is considered the post-bop era.
3. In Eastern cultures, especially Indian, modal music was being used for thousands of years. However, Western musicians, particularly those playing jazz, started to embrace the modal form by the late 1950s.
4. Russell's ideas regarding the relationship of chords and scales and the dense textures and rhythms may have also influenced Davis's innovations that introduced the fusion of jazz and rock in the 1970s (Fraim 1996, 63).
5. Many jazz musicians, and some critics and listeners, consider jazz America's classical music.
6. Drummond was convicted for murdering his girlfriend on 2 January 1965. He was confined to the island's mental institution where he died 6 May 1969.
7. Groundations are Rastafarian camp sessions where music provides the setting for reasoning, praising Jah (God), cooking and, in general, holding group meetings.

8. I consider the jazz alto saxophonist Joe Harriott, Rastafarian drummer Count Ossie, innovative ska drummer Lloyd Knibb, reggae superstar Bob Marley, and the iconoclastic drum and bass team of Sly Dunbar and Robbie Shakespeare the other Jamaican musicians on whom I would bestow the term genius.

REFERENCES

Banfield, William C. 2004. *Black notes: Essays of a musician writing in a post-album age*. Lanhan, MD: Scarecrow Press.

Brathwaite, Kamau. 1994. *Roots*. Ann Arbor: University of Michigan Press.

Carr, Ian, Digby Fairweather and Brian Priestley. 1988. *Jazz: The essential companion*. New York: Prentice Hall Press.

Fraim, John. 1996. *Spirit catcher: The life and art of John Coltrane*. West Liberty, Ohio: Great House Company.

Hebdige, Dick. 1994. *Cut 'n' mix: Culture, identity and Caribbean music*. London: Routledge.

Kelsey, Chris. 2005. Biography of Lennie Tristano. http://lennietristano.com/biography.htm.

Neely, Daniel T. 2008. Mento, Jamaica's original music: Development, tourism and the national frame. PhD diss., New York University.

Rath, Richard Cullen. 1993. African music in seventeenth-century Jamaica: Cultural transit and transition. *William and Mary Quarterly* 50, no. 4: 700–726.

Rohlehr, Gordon. 2000. Paper presented at the conference Don Drummond: A Musical Genius. University of the West Indies, Jamaica. 6 May.

Townsend, Peter. 2001. Free jazz: Musical style and liberationist ethic, 1956–1965. In *Media, culture, and the modern African American freedom struggle*, ed. Brian Ward, 145–60. Gainesville: University Press of Florida.

10

"Blak Up! Blak Up!"
Liturgical Compositions of Barry Chevannes

ANNA KASAFI PERKINS

The importance of the Afro-Caribbean worldview in the shaping of Caribbean identity is a constant theme in the work of Barry Chevannes. A worldview is essentially "a system of beliefs and a state of consciousness", which is easy to miss because it cannot be observed directly; and in the study of religions, where it could have been gleaned, the focus has been on ritual and organization to the neglect of these underlying philosophies (Chevannes 1995). As Chevannes's work highlights, the Afro-Caribbean worldview can be demonstrated to be vividly at work in the religious traditions of Rastafari and Revivalism. This leads Chevannes to critique the established churches in Jamaica and the rest of the Caribbean for having remained essentially missionary (unlike these Afro-Christian religions), that is, basically European in doctrine and worship, and as such, having failed to indigenize themselves; they fail to give expression to the underlying Afro-Caribbean worldview of the people.

This process of indigenization would require two things, according to him: (1) a liturgy that is culturally meaningful; and (2) a theology that at least begins to reflect some of the spiritual values deeply embedded in our culture (Chevannes 1991). Ever an activist-theorist, Chevannes has made significant contributions to both these dimensions of the process of indigenization. In his exploration of an Afro-Caribbean theology, for example, he both proposes a methodology and identifies values from the worldview which are meaningful in truly indigenizing Caribbean theology (ibid.).

Not surprisingly, these values and themes are also present in his liturgical compositions, written both in Jamaican Standard English and Creole. However, perhaps due to an ignorance of their existence/value, few scholars have attempted to explore these themes as they are evidenced in his liturgical compositions. This chapter will identify and present an interpretation of elements of the Afro-Caribbean worldview as they feature in some of Chevannes's more popular liturgical compositions: "Blak Up, Blak Up", "Father Bless", "Fi Wi Gad Great", "Bless the Lord" and "Hosanna". Chevannes is a prolific songwriter, and it is not possible to do justice to his many and varying kinds of compositions. These selections simply provide a peephole into the religious dimension of his musical repertoire.

All of the songs considered in this study were composed during the relatively short period of time between 1966 and 1970–71 and so reflect some of the concerns which Chevannes wrestled with at that point: the lack of concern in the traditional churches for the cultural orientation of their message and liturgy, the need to affirm Jamaican identity via the Creole language, the relationship between the traditional church and the masses of African descent, and the place of the poor in the purview of the church. Much of his music was composed to directly address a felt need (for example, a folk or *yaad* mass), to catechize children or for use during church feasts like Pentecost and Christmas.

Chevannes's work continues to be meaningful in the larger ecumenical community, and this was demonstrated in a special way by his being commissioned to compose the theme song for the Fourth General Assembly of the Caribbean Conference of Churches in 1986. In fact, Chevannes's songs have "become an inter-denominational *lingua franca* sung by a large number of churches in as many different arrangements" (O'Gorman 1989, 41). This is perhaps a vindication of his early, bold foray into the world of Jamaican folk music and a testament to the quality of the songs and their ability to satisfy a common liturgical need.

There is no doubt that Barry Chevannes has been pivotal in the development of indigenous music in worship in the traditional churches in Jamaica:

> He was a pioneer. In his particular use of indigenous music in worship, he revealed the musical and linguistic resources of the Jamaican folk idiom as no one else had attempted to do within the Established Church; and at the time when

the beginnings of the identity crisis that was to erupt in the cultural revolution of the early 1970s were scarcely discernible; it was courageous – if not foolhardy – to dare to upset all the tenets of race and class, education and respectability to which the Church had clung for so long. (Ibid.)

BACKGROUND: MOVEMENTS IN THE ROMAN CATHOLIC CHURCH

In exploring these religious songs, it can be seen that two important currents formed the backdrop for his composing: (1) the immediate post–Vatican II developments in the Roman Catholic Church which encouraged the writing of folk music and the entry of folk forms into liturgical celebrations, and (2) the ferment of nationalism in the immediate post-independence era. The two currents intersected with and reinforced each other: the desire to indigenize the worship of the church fused with and was directly impacted by the need to promote the identity and value of the black nation of Jamaica coming to birth.

During his seven-year sojourn in the United States, Chevannes was deeply influenced by the American folk song movement that emerged in response to the teaching of the Second Vatican Council, 1962–65, which transformed Roman Catholicism. One conspicuous effect of the council was the provision of new guidelines for church liturgy, not least, church music. "The Constitution on the Sacred Liturgy", issued in 1963, charged Roman Catholic composers with the sacred task of creating new music "having the qualities proper to genuine sacred music, not confin[ed] . . . to works that can be sung only by large choirs, but providing also for the needs of small" (Flannery 1996, 155). The change was powerfully symbolized for the then liturgically conservative Jamaican church by acoustic guitars near the altar, songs in the Jamaican idiom and the priest facing the communicants. New contemporary hymnals appeared such as *The People's Mass Book*, *The Caribbean Mass* and *Praise Yahweh*.

Chevannes's own appropriation of the Jamaican folk tradition involved a rhythmic construction closely related in its melodic form to the Jamaican language and its underlying accompaniment (O'Gorman 1989). Many of his songs lend themselves to accompaniment by the mento guitar; others were conceived with other rhythmic accompaniments in mind, such as the Rastafarian, Revival or Pentecostal influenced songs. O'Gorman describes the rhythm of "Blak Up" – which is perhaps one of Chevannes's best-known songs – as being distinguished by machine-gun rapidity and accentuation of Jamaican dialect, which succeeds in conveying an unmistakeable sense of excitement (ibid.).

In a period of alienation from the church which he felt was increasingly insensitive to the poor and black, Chevannes was drawn to black political ideology. In the 1960s, in particular, Chevannes worked as musical director of Aquinas Centre, the Roman Catholic church located near the University of the West Indies campus. It served the university's students, who came from all over the Caribbean and who were young and free from many societal and parental restraints. This made Aquinas a naturally more receptive parish than the average where old habits and social customs tended to be deeply entrenched (O'Gorman 1975). This time at Aquinas was significant for both the development of Chevannes's music and the transformation of worship in the Catholic church.

> It was not long before a once-reluctant acceptance of the guitar in church had had to extend to congo drums, Rastafarian repeaters, maracas and tambourines; and, as churches began to search for more and more indigenous material that would reflect their increasing acceptance of black theology and West Indian culture, the songs of Barry Chevannes, along with a certain amount of Caribbean folk song material, began to be sought after, and used. (Ibid., 42)

ELEMENTS OF THE AFRO-CARIBBEAN WORLDVIEW

Three main elements of the Afro-Caribbean worldview can be identified as being interwoven into Chevannes's compositions: the notion of the immanence of God, a this-worldly focus, and the importance of community and interdependence.

THE IMMANENCE OF GOD

The divine is present in human reality, not above or divorced from it as an overemphasis on transcendence portrays. Chevannes finds the best expression of this value in the Rastafarian "I and I", which echoes Jesus' words in John's Gospel: "I am in the Father and the Father is in me." The common existential condition of every human being is to be "God-filled" (my words) and hence divine. The divinity of a person is not the same as the divinity of God since the person is a creature and not independent of the Creator. Nonetheless, with God present in the human person, the power of God is also present in the person and this makes great things possible. Throughout the history of Afro-Caribbean religion and politics, many leaders have either claimed or been accorded divine status and have had or displayed divine power; among these are Bedward, Howell, Prince Emmanuel, Nanny, Taki, Garvey, Bustamante and countless spiritual healers and leaders.

In addition, it is possible to nurture this inner power through communing with the source, God, by way of spirit possession or the study of the secrets of nature or magic. In "Blak Up, Blak Up", Chevannes retells, in Jamaican idiom, the events of the first Pentecost, which was the epitome of spirit possession:

> *Chorus*:
> Blak up, blak up,
> Sun a-rise an people say we blak up
> But a de spirit o' de Lord fly dong laka fire
> Grab we in de spirit like a choir
> Singing higher, higher, higher, higher
> FIRE!

Interestingly, Chevannes describes the action of the Spirit as flying and grabbing, very vivid metaphors which conjure up images of doves and holy hands. The manifestation of spirit possession is the heavenly song and fire! In the Afro-Caribbean worldview, one manifestation of the power of God in a person is the word which originates within the person, but which is capable of moving and acting upon others. "The word, once released or uttered, takes on a life of its own, independent of the utterer" (Chevannes 1991, 48). Similarly, Jesus, the truly divine man, is the Word (*Logos*) through whom all things came into being. It is no mistake, then, that the word of a human being in whom the Word dwells is also alive, creative and life-giving. It can be argued that this power of the word is at play in Chevannes's own musical compositions, which are capable of finding resonance in the being of the ordinary church goer and moving them to action and more authentic worship, worship that is more true to their Jamaicanness.

Belief in the immanence of God is evident in the verses of "Fi Wi Gad Great", a Christmas carol which Chevannes composed in reaction to the surfeit of foreign Christmas music (O'Gorman 1989). In this "urban" carol, Chevannes emphasises the baby Jesus' permanent tabernacling in the world, especially with the poor in the Jamaican ghetto. The Word became flesh and dwelt among us (in the ghetto):

> Like moonshine pon the harbour,
> Like sunshine through the day,
> So this baby love wi,
> Is stay 'im come fi stay.

The permanence of Jesus' presence is expressed using two similes that compare him to light: moonlight and sunlight. This harkens back to the Johannine Prologue, which describes the Divine Word as a light that shines in the darkness, and the darkness does not overcome it (John 1:4–5). The carol is infused with hope and joy, emotions that are often thought to be missing in squatter settlements and urban ghettos like Trench Town and Waterhouse, both places that inspired Chevannes's work.

> Early Christmas morning
> When the star dem getting t'in
> From a squatter's winder
> A hooman start fi sing:
>
> *Chorus*:
> Holy, holy, holy him name
> Fi wi Gad great fi true,
> Fi wi Gad great.

As Chevannes (2001, 131) describes them, the urban ghettoes of Kingston are enclaves whose ethnicity is their poverty. He writes: "The typical urban ghetto is a criss-crossing and interweaving of access streets, lanes and footpaths to yards separated from the outside view by zinc fences . . . Most . . . are the results of the spatial reconfiguration of the city when the affluent people moved out, taking with them their status symbols of residence and social class, and the poor people moved in, bringing with them their rural but changing worldview."

Yet, it is in such places and spaces that the Divine chooses to dwell; it is along those footpaths that the Spirit "blow laka hurricane, an' blow de fire right dong de lane". This is a clear affirmation of the masses who have contributed their worldview to the identity of the nation.

Paradoxically, the baby Jesus is both prominent political leader and divine being:

> One day soon dis likkle bwoy
> Gwine tu'un Prime Minister,
> Then Puss and Dog gwine walk an talk,
> For them tu'n breda an' sister.

The possibility of divinely inspired political leadership is never far from the surface. The effect of a low-born child was profound; his birth leads to the healing of broken relationships between natural enemies: puss and dog. Is there not hope for healing of brokenness within the nation?

> Everlasting Father,
> Shining Prince of Peace,
> Mighty God Jehovah,
> Counsellor from the East.

In this verse, Chevannes alludes to Isaiah 9:6, which is often seen as a prophetic reference to Jesus as the expected Messiah. His "additions" to the text deepen the allusion to light, for example, by adding "shining" in "Shining Prince of Peace" and "East" to "Counsellor from the East". "Shining" is self-explanatory and "East" profers a number of meanings. The sun rises in the East and it is the direction from which wisdom comes (the motto of the University of the West Indies, "*oriens ex occidente lux*", reverses this notion). Further, "East" calls to mind the coming of the wise men or the Magi, one of whom is reputed by legend to have been an African (another unconscious reference to the African worldview?). An eighth-century saint, Bede the Venerable, described the wise men this way:

> The first was called Melchior; he was an old man, with white hair and long beard; he offered gold to the Lord as to his king. The second, Gaspar by name, young, beardless, of ruddy hue, offered to Jesus his gift of incense, the homage due to Divinity. The third, of black complexion, with heavy beard, was called Baltasar; the myrrh he held in his hands prefigured the death of the Son of man. (Klein 1999, 130)

On the flip side of the record on which "Fi Wi Gad Great" was released was a second Christmas carol entitled "Hosanna" which treats of similar themes, but from within a rural setting. The original Bethlehem shades into and becomes real again in Chevannes's description of a small, close-knit rural community with the obligatory Chinese shop and cows, distant from the urban centres of power and privilege. The lifestyle of the rural folk is given some prominence. The song is suffused with the sense of the Christ child belonging to that little community; this is reinforced by a sense of the community "owning" the Christ child that refuses to allow him to be an alien to Jamaicans, especially the rural folk of African descent.

> Hosanna, Hosanna,
> Hosanna, Hosanna,
> Fi wi Jesus Christ jus' born.

The communal nature of the life of Afro-Caribbean people is emphasized by the ebb and flow of rural life that structures the song; children are divine messengers and milk, as a sign of hospitality and promise fulfilled, is shared (land of milk and honey); biblical place and imagery intertwine with local colours and happenings:

> Run go call all the pickney dem
> Fi go run go over Bethlehem,
> Carry one shet-pan o' milk
> Go gi Miss May.
> Tell her se[h] Satan reign ju' end,
> Tell her se[h] de bwoy gwine conquer deat',
> For God name im Emmanuel.

The reference to Emmanuel, "God with us", is both biblical and Afro-Caribbean, and it immediately calls to mind the Rasta's belief in God with us in the person of the late emperor of Ethiopia, Haile Selassie I. The promise of Emmanuel will bring joy and happiness now. It will cause the witnesses to express their joy in the way Jamaicans do: with movement and creativity, with enthusiasm and dance. Their joy brings to mind Chevannes's own description of the *yaad* mass which he composed with the figure of a priest in colourful robes surrounded by ordinary people dancing and singing in the closed space of a tenement. Everyone must be involved in the celebration and they must gather in the yard, which is the space of cultural identity and connection, as Chevannes develops in his later work (2001).

> Mek wi set up wi bamboo boot',
> Tap wi wo'k an go jump an dance
> Gyadder everybody inna yard,
> For the pickney bwoy promise wi
> Fi wipe way de eye water from wi eye.
> For God name him Emmanuel.

Chevannes plays on and transposes the biblical event of the transfiguration where Jesus' divinity is exposed fully to his disciples (Luke 9:28–36). In the Lucan account of the transfiguration, two ancients (Moses and Elijah) appear to "testify" to Jesus' divinity, and the disciples respond by wanting to make booths to house them while they and the Divine Word tabernacled with them. It is that same desire to offer hospitality to the divine child that Chevannes captures effectively.

A This-worldly Orientation

This valuing of divine immanence is closely tied to a second element of the Afro-Caribbean worldview: its this-worldly orientation. Belief in the immanence of God gives God a this-worldly attribute. This means that God is at all times oriented to the present world of human beings, not to the future. Again, the importance of the present time is emphasized in "Fi Wi Gad Great".

> Eena fi wi time
> God word settle dong,
> Jus like gentle dew-drop
> Pon the morning grong.

This has implications for the idea of salvation: the idea of postponing salvation to an unspecified future is alien to the Afro-Caribbean worldview. This orientation, for Chevannes, is the root of the inner compulsion of Afro-Caribbean religions to find answers and messiahs in the here and now. This makes them concerned with society and politics. Well-known examples from Jamaica's history include the Great Slave Rebellion of 1831, led by Native

Baptist leader Sam Sharpe, and the Morant Bay Rebellion of 1865, led by Paul Bogle. Again, Rastafarians brought the this-worldly orientation to new heights with their critique of the pie-in-the-sky-when-you-die being peddled to black people by the traditional religions while white men appropriated the wealth of the earth.

In Chevannes's song "Bless the Lord", what starts off like a typical pie-in-the-sky oeuvre moves rapidly into an affirmation of freedom as a present reality. The freedom provided by men is but the expression of the great love that sets human beings free. At the same time, there is a recognition that the fullness of the freedom desired is to be found in the *eschaton*, "the end times". In theological parlance, Chevannes does not reduce the tension between the "already" and the "not yet" of the *eschaton*.

Bless the Lord

Bless the Lord, the God of Israel,
Bless the Lord, he'll visit us again,
Wait for the Lord, by sunrise we'll be free.
Bless him forever.

Bless'd be our God there is freedom at hand,
No more slave!
Any day now you will see how great love can set us free,
Bless him forever.

Through Abraham every nation shall sing,
"Born again",
For God swore to be true, He'd make us all anew,
Bless him forever.

Soon we'll be free from the scourging whip,
Glory be!
No more fear little one, live the freedom of God's son,
Bless him forever.

Chevannes uses the slavery-emancipation motif to designate a promise fulfilled. Elsewhere, he refers to this as "the dream of freedom" and "the act of emancipation" (2001, 130). At the same time, he recognizes that there are aspects of human life that are unfree and may continue to remain so. It is when the Lord visits again that they will be "full free". Acknowledging human limitations can engender the hope for that day when Christ will come and all will be fulfilled in Christ.

The meaningfulness of Christ's birth is clearly this-worldly and needs to be treated as of greatest importance. It has political and social implications that must be announced to those in charge:

> Mek wi go dong a Half-Way Tree
> An go talk to de Goubener.
> Wi got bans of news fi Missis Queen
> Nat aneddr drap o' slavery, Ma',
> Cause smadi deh ya dong fi set we free,
> An God name him Emmanuel.

The focus on the present time of salvation is borne out in the last two lines of this song, where Chevannes appears to be addressing the queen about the situation of enslavement which, for all intents and purposes, was over a century past when the song was composed. But the emphasis on the experience of emancipation as already happened points to the fulfilment of the promise of Emmanuel and makes all other promises of change more credible.

Community and Interdependence

A perspective on life that pervades Jamaican society is that mutual dependence plays a key role in a life lived well. People share a mutuality of interests by being members of the same society or community. This sense of interdependence in no way implies a loss of independence. Again, the urban ghetto which is composed of yards demonstrates this perspective effectively. The urban yard is a shared space of both privacy and cooperation. Occupants cooperate by the sharing of domestic facilities and common security against strangers, the state, the police. It is a problem-solving space, particularly for women who cooperate in dealing with such matters as child rearing. Such cooperation assumes respect for other people. "People who cannot get along with others are usually forced out by protracted quarrelling, body language, singing, facial expressions that are the common legacy of the African-Caribbean people" (Chevannes 2001, 132).

As outlined, this sense of interdependence and community is alive in "Fi

Wi Gad Great". Furthermore, the larger umbilical connection between rural and urban poverty is not broken. In "Blak Up", Chevannes very cleverly evokes the communal response to perceived drunkenness: censure and ridicule.

> Dem don' got a drap a shame
> Galilee man dem is all de same;
> Dem tek dem water laka sercy tea,
> De whole a dem wan' go jail.

One could almost hear the words uttered in derision, "Jamaican man dem is all the same!" The play on "drap of shame" harkens back to the perceived drunkenness of these spirit-possessed men; water as a euphemism for alcohol echoes, for the Christian imagination, the experience of baptism, with water and with fire! Behind the response of the community to these men who are drunk with the spirit is an implied critique of the established churches that misunderstand and look askance at the spirit possession which, in the Afro-Caribbean worldview, is an intimate part of some expressions of divine immanence. The term "blak up", meaning drunk, reverberates with the darkness which requires piercing by light, the same light which came into the ghetto and the rural village and was celebrated by all:

> German, African and Indian race,
> Some musa-come from outa space,
> For dem drop dem mout' an a start fi shout
> "What a hell a-gwan roun' dis place!"
>
> Him blow laka hurricane,
> An 'blow de fire right dong de lane
> Ole Simon Pete da-cut 'im Latin an 'im Greek
> An a-reel dem off by de chain

Chevannes expresses the plurality of the Jamaican identity by referring to German, African and Indian, not the Medes and Elamites and Parthians of the Acts passage which gave birth to this religious song (Acts 2:1–13). The being and defining of Jamaicanness is a necessary and urgent task, Chevannes argues, especially in the face of globalization (Chevannes 2001).

"Father Bless This Offering" was especially composed for singing during the celebration of the Eucharist; it carries forward the regular themes of the bread and wine as sacrament which bring about what it signifies: the transformed body and blood of Christ, which is the means of salvation for fallen humanity.

> *Refrain:*
> Father, bless this offering of bread to give life
> Bless this cup of salvation evermore
> Alleluia! Come and bless this sacrament
> It's the sign that Jesus is the Christ-Messiah
> The sign mankind free.

The Eucharist has implications for the church: it makes the church truly a community, the body of Christ united in the offering of the Messiah:

> As we stand around the altar,
> Father, bless this gathering;
> One with Christ we are united,
> One with him in offering.
>
> We are now about to glory
> In the cross of Jesus Christ,
> Give the priest and people blessing,
> We share in his sacrifice.

One group which is especially deserving of care by the wider community and is more closely united/identified with the suffering of Christ is the poor. Recognizing Chevannes's deep social conscience and his care for the poor, it would therefore be disingenuous to read his references to bread and wine in this song as simply liturgical, that is, having little reference to providing for the bread and wine which the poor need to survive. Clearly, the blessing desired in order to transform ordinary bread and wine into the body and blood of Christ is also desired to transform the broken lives of those who are hungry, sick and poor. They, too, will have a share in the kingdom of God, beginning with their reality in the here and now.

> Bless the sick ones, Lord, bless the poor ones,
> Make their living more fruitful,
> Share with them your glorious kingdom,
> Bless them and be merciful.

Towards an Afro-Caribbean Ethics

There is no doubt that the traditional churches, especially the Roman Catholic Church in Jamaica, have progressed in indigenizing their liturgy and theology. This has been, in a large way, due to the work of pioneers like Barry Chevannes, especially through his contribution to music for worship. That our liturgical celebrations can more readily include forms that elevate the language and rhythm of our people – the masses – is due to the early experiments with "dialect verse, mento guitar and innate corporeality" in the "higher class churches" which, in the beginning, engendered "great consternation" among both clergy and congregation alike (O'Gorman 1975). Today, the lessened resistance and the fewer stunned silences are a direct tribute to Chevannes's efforts. Chevannes's call for an Afro-Caribbean theology that is more true to the spiritual values underlying the everyday lives of the people in the region is a call to rediscover aspects of the Christian faith that have been neglected or minimized. It recognizes the inclusive nature of what the church is about and rejects the sort of binary opposition which has been inherited from some forms of European Christianity. It is upon this foundation that the church in the Caribbean can begin formulating an Afro-Christian ethic that is faithful to and challenging of the worldview of the masses.

References

Chevannes, Barry. 1991. Toward an Afro-Caribbean theology: The principles of indigenization of Christianity in the Caribbean. *Caribbean Quarterly* 37, no. 1: 45–55.

———. 1995. Introduction to the native religions of Jamaica. In *Rastafari and other African-Caribbean worldviews*, ed. Barry Chevannes, 1–9. New Brunswick, NJ: Rutgers University Press.

———. 2001. Jamaican diasporic identity: The metaphor of yaad. In *Nation dance: Religion, identity and cultural difference in the Caribbean*, ed. Patrick Taylor, 129–37. Kingston: Ian Randle.

Flannery, Austin, ed. 1996. *The basic sixteen documents: Vatican II: Constitutions, decrees, declarations*. Northport, NY: Costello Publishing.

Klein, Peter, ed. 1999. *The Catholic sourcebook*. New York: Harcourt Religious Publishers.

O'Gorman, Pamela. 1975. The introduction of Jamaican music into the established churches. *Jamaica Journal* 9, no. 1: 40–44, 47.

———. 1989. The religious songs of Barry Chevannes. *Jamaica Journal* 22, no. 3: 39–44.

11

Creoles as Linguistic Markers of National Identity
Examples from Jamaica and Guyana

BÉATRICE BOUFOY-BASTICK

INTRODUCTION

Caribbean language development is a product of its colonial past and is guided by both current global economic forces and a search for a Caribbean identity. The current unique cross-Caribbean diglossic setting is evidenced by both the maintenance of colonial languages for global economic membership and the recognition of creolized languages for social integration. This chapter focuses on Caribbean linguistic capital construction for national identity formation in socially segregated communities, as in Jamaica, and ethnically divided communities, as in Guyana. From a sociohistorical perspective, there is a brief description of the linguistic phenomenon of creolization to shed light on the emergence of, and increasing social acceptance of, patwa (patios) in Jamaica and creolese in Guyana. This is followed by an examination of two salient factors that contributed to the acceptance and the use of patwa and creolese as nation-building socio-ethnic integrators: on the one hand, the maturing of a high Anglo-Caribbean literate culture and on the other, the assertion of an enhanced Jamaican and Guyanese linguistic identity within a global context.

Framing Creole Impregnation in Jamaica and Guyana: A Brief Sociohistorical Account

Creolized languages are rooted in the different sociohistorical contexts of eighteenth- and nineteenth-century labour migrations across the Caribbean. Creolization in the Caribbean is mainly a legacy of slavery and indentured labour and is mostly the source of the creole language diversity that is expressed in the multiplicity of indigenous creole vernaculars in the anglophone Caribbean. The degree of creole impregnation of English now varies markedly within each English-speaking Caribbean state and from one Caribbean state to another. This variation in language nativization can be explained by different sociohistorical and economic dynamics (Allen 2002). Creolists claim that the earlier slaves developed a language closer to the standard European language and explain that their mesolectal variety moved away from the standard language with the massive influx of slaves at the apogee of the plantation economy in the eighteenth century (Chaudenson 1992; Mufwene 2001). These later slaves who came to the Caribbean spoke different African vernaculars, and from the mixing of their native vernaculars and the colonial language, there emerged the creolized languages which characterized the Caribbean sugar plantation landscape. This diversity was further increased in Guyana during the nineteenth century with the arrival of indentured Indian labourers from linguistically diverse regions of India. The pressing need for intra- and inter-ethnic communication led to the merging of their Indian dialects with the language(s) of the colony in Guyana. The linguistic intricacies specific to Guyana stem from the different historical layers of various colonial languages within Guyana's creoles with their Dutch (Kouwenberg 1994; Robertson 1974, 1975, 1976), French (Alleyne 2004; Edwards 1978) and English (Holbrook and Holbrook 2002; Hosein and Mohamed 1994; Rickford 1983) lexicon. These multi-colonial influences are surprisingly tenacious. For example, the French "crapaud" is used for "toad" in Guyanese creole even though, during the Dutch English exchanges of Guyana since 1598, the French occupied a tiny part of Guyana only briefly in 1782. The diverse linguistic influences are also compounded by the relative geographical isolation of some of Guyana's communities. This accounts for the continued linguistic heterogeneity of creolized, European-based vernaculars across Guyana, not mentioning the maintenance of Guyana's nine identified Amerindian languages – Akawaio, Arawak, Arecuna, Carib, Macusi, Patamona, Wai Wai, Wapishana and Warrau. Understandably, the marked linguistic specificities of Guyana's hinterland are more blurred in Georgetown, the capital, where a non-Standard mesolectal English prevails in daily community exchanges. Noticeable speech examples are the lack of verb inflection and tense markers (for example, "*He's shoot*"), the disregard for subject-verb agreement ("*She don't teach it*") and past tense endings ("*I am please*"), and the misuse of pronouns ("*I/me see he*"). However, while Standard English is the expected linguistic code in formal interactions among the urban educated elite of Georgetown, it is not strictly followed in verbal exchanges in informal interactions. This has led some linguists to argue for a post-creole continuum, that is, the appropriation of a localized Guyanese English which incorporates non-Standard English forms (Devonish 1991; Hosein and Mohamed 1994). This intrusion of non-Standard English forms gives recognition to Guyanese English, hence clouding the diglossic divide between Standard and non-Standard English.

Jamaica, in contrast, exhibits a different historical trajectory of language creolization. Various sociolinguistic theories have been put forward to explain the diachronic emergence of patwa, such as *linguistic syncretism* with the merging of the colonial language with West African vernaculars (Alleyne 1971, 170); a *creole continuum* with the identification of phonological and lexical distortions of Standard English; a controversial *Language bioprogram hypothesis* rejecting both a substrate and superstrate influence on the emergence of new linguistic forms (Bickerton 1988); and a *post-creole continuum* focusing on the intricate merging of creole and English (Dvusten 2000). The social significance of Jamaica's language nativization was explained by Carolyn Allen (2002, 57) as "marking the point of recognition of that new type as belonging to the locale" and was recognized as an expression of an emergent Jamaican identity. This may also account for the increasing social acceptance of the most extreme nativized language forms typifying Jamaican patwa and the destigmatization of its speakers whose popular dancehall music has joined reggae as a prominent cultural artefact of Jamaicanness. Underpinning this popularity, and from a perspective of population dynamic (Nakamura, Mahimoto and Tojo 2003), is the (re-)valuing of ghetto language for shaping a localized Jamaican identity within the global, market-driven, English-speaking world.

From this cursory glance at the sociohistorical language development in Guyana and Jamaica, two seemingly divergent trends can be noted. On the one hand, there exists a noticeable trend towards the re-valuing of nativized languages as cultural identity markers and on the other, the upholding of English for participation in a globalized economy. This dichotomy is reconciled by the different functions assigned to each language: a cultural function assigned to creoles, now regarded as national languages, and an economic function assigned to English as the international language.

Endorsing an Emergent Transnational Creole Linguistic Identity

Guyanese and Jamaican societies are legacies of British colonial history. As Slocum and Thomas (2003, 557) assert, "the . . . salience, both structurally and symbolically, of colonial hierarchies that were established along the intersecting axes of race, class, ethnicity, gender and culture" persists. These hierarchies are exhibited and heightened by differentiated linguistic codes which authenticate Standard English as the language of the educated elite. This higher status ascribed to English has remained unchallenged since independence, and English continues to give an increased sense of political power and economic ascendancy to its Jamaican and Guyanese speakers. While English is regarded as the colonial linguistic capital,[1] Creoles have gained greater social recognition over the years to the extent that they are now regarded as national languages. This bilinguality highlights the ambiguous status relationship between English and the local creoles in Jamaica and Guyana which view, on one hand, the formality of English, and its utilitarian usefulness, as conferring a higher social status on its speakers (Holbrook and Holbrook 2002, 18n7.3) and, on the other, the informality of creole as an indicator of community membership. By code-switching from Standard English to creole, the educated Jamaican and Guyanese speaker can demonstrate his or her in-group membership. By contrast, his or her socially inappropriate use of Standard English, that is the use of English in informal creole-speaking social contexts, would bring him or her derision. An illustrative example is the scornful labelling of *"English duck"* for a Guyanese person's affected *"citified speech"* by creolese Guyanese speakers to show their displeasure in the inter-socially alienating use of Standard English in interpersonal interactions. There may lie the mystifying paradox of diglossic English-creole societies which are torn between promoting a prestigious English acrolect for socio-economic advancement and creolized vernacular basilects for sociocultural identity in the increasingly globalized anglophone sphere. This tension is, however, reconciled in transnational Jamaican and Guyanese communities which strive to maintain and assert their roots by using selected linguistic artefacts as an expression of their Jamaicanness or Guyaneseness. Their creolized language selection, which partly originates in the works of acclaimed transnational literary writers, has the characteristics of minimizing the original creole for transnational intelligibility. An observable example of artfully creolized speech pattern is the seemingly systematic use of stereotypical words and phrases by educated Jamaicans and Guyanese. It is this moderately creolized Jamaican and Guyanese English, with their respective patwa and creolese intrusions, which is used for transnational communication and now serves as a foundation for internationally intelligible Jamaican or Guyanese national languages.

NATIONAL LANGUAGES AS UNIFYING POSTCOLONIAL EMBLEMATIC IDENTITY MARKERS

The acceptance of creoles as linguistic markers of cultural identity can be explained from a linguistic liberalist standpoint (Dash 1999; Schwieger Hiepko 1999), which construes them as affirmations of linguistic autonomy in postcolonial Caribbean societies seeking linguistic sovereignty and appreciation for their sociocultural uniqueness – a uniqueness anchored in their people and exhibited idiosyncratically in their social diversity in Jamaica and their multi-ethnicity in Guyana. The sociocultural uniqueness of Jamaica is paradoxically expressed in the multiplicity of its social groups, each with its particular in-group linguistic code placed on a continuum ranging from the most extreme patwa speech of the Kingston ghettos to the Standard English of the Jamaican educated elite. Within this socially segregated linguistic context, the Jamaican national language emerges as an instrument of social unification, expertly merging the local patwa with the international English by functionally superimposing patwa lexical and syntactic forms onto the English substrate. Notwithstanding the outright social benefit of destigmatizing patwa speakers locally and the overt political significance of challenging English imperialism globally, the Jamaican national language creates a shared emotive medium. Likewise, the multi-ethnic make-up of Guyanese society is reflected linguistically in its phonological and lexical specificities which attest, on one hand, to its colonial demographic history which brought together Amerindians, Africans, East Indians and Europeans, each one contributing to give the exceptional richness of Guyanese English, and, on the other, to its postcolonial political history which maintained Guyanese cut off from Western influences. This isolation may be one of the factors accounting for the semantic explicitness of Guyanese sayings which define in-group experiences, such as "*she made four children*" in creolese for "*she had four children*" in Standard English, or proverbs that express contextually differentiating experiences "*when coconut fall from tree he can't fasten back*" in creolese for "*what's done cannot be undone*" in Standard English. It is this social embeddedness which is captured in Jamaican and Guyanese English and gives support to their promotion as national languages by internationally renowned literary writers, such as Louise Bennett, who forcefully pioneered patwa literature in Jamaica, or David Dabydeen, who evocatively extolled the rich poetic plasticity of Guyanese creole. Their literary skills have helped to judiciously model the atypical Jamaican and Guyanese English into unifying national languages which, on the one hand, have served to revalue entrenched creole speakers whose language was previously devalued and, on the other hand, have strengthened ties with the transnational Jamaican and Guyanese.

Conclusion

This chapter has highlighted language shifts in Jamaica and Guyana from a sociohistorical perspective. It first provided a brief overview of creolization with a view to give a diachronic insight into the differential degrees of impregnation since independence, and focused on the issue of linguistic normalization with respect to creole use for national identity formation. It examined how English and the Jamaican and Guyanese creoles have merged into transnationally shared linguistic codes in which stereotypical creole intrusions are their cultural markers. Two major factors were identified as contributing to these language shifts: on the one hand, the regard shown internationally to an emerging creole literature and, on the other, the search for national language identifiers for social integration and resistance to the imperialistic Anglo-American language hegemony. Great expectations of the role of these national languages as integrative forces able to counteract the continuing socioracial are held both in Jamaica and Guyana.

Note

1. Holbrook and Holbrook's (2002, 18n7.3) "Guyanese Creole Survey Report" found that the formality attached to English confers on its speakers a higher social status grounded in its utilitarian usefulness.

References

Allen, Carolyn. 2002. Creole. The problem of definition. In *Questioning creole: Creolization discourses in Caribbean culture – Essays in honour of Kamau Brathwaite*, ed. V. Shepherd and G. Richards, 47–60. Kingston: Ian Randle.

Alleyne, Mervyn. 1971. Acculturation and the cultural matrix of creolization. In *Pidginization and creolization of languages*, ed. D. Hymes, 169–86. Cambridge: Cambridge University Press.

———. 2004. *Indigenous languages in the Caribbean*. Society for Caribbean Linguistics, Popular Series, no. 3. St Augustine, Trinidad: Society for Caribbean Linguistics.

Bickerton, Derek. 1988. Creole languages and the bioprogram. In *Linguistics: The Cambridge survey*. Vol 2: *Linguistic Theory: Extensions and Implication*, ed. F. Newmeyer, 268–84. Cambridge: Cambridge University Press.

Chaudenson, Robert. 1992. *Des îles, des hommes, des langues: Essais sur la créolisation linguistique et culturelle*. Paris: L'Harmattan.

Dash, Michael. 1999. Anxious insularity, identity politics and creolization in the Caribbean. Keynote address at the sixth Interdisciplinary Congress of the Caribbean Research Society, Creolisation and Creole Identity, Berlin. 4–7 May.

Devonish, Hubert. 1991. Standardization in a creole continuum: The Guyana case. In *English around the world*, ed. J. Cheshire, 565–84. Cambridge: Cambridge University Press.

Dvusten, L. 2000. *Jamaican creole: A linguistic study of grammar and the post-creole continuum*. Lulea: Lulea University of Technology.

Edwards, Walter F. 1978. *Sociolinguistic models and phonological variation in Guyana*.

Society for Caribbean Linguistics, Occasional Papers Series, no. 8. St Augustine, Trinidad: Society for Caribbean Linguistics.
Holbrook, David J., and Holly A. Holbrook. 2002. Guyanese creole survey report. SIL Electronic Survey Reports 2002–011. http://www.sil.org/silesr/2002/011/.
Hosein, A., and A. Mohamed. 1994. Diglossia within the Guyanese creole continuum. Paper presented at the tenth biennial conference of the Society for Caribbean Linguistics, Georgetown, Guyana.
Kouwenberg, Sylvia. 1994. Berbice Dutch. In *Typological studies in negation*, ed. P. Kahrel and R. van den Berg, 237–66. Typological Studies in Language, no. 29. Amsterdam: Benjamins.
Mufwene, Salikoko. 2001. *The ecology of language evolution*. Cambridge: Cambridge University Press.
Nakamura, M., T. Mashimoto and S. Tojo. 2003. Creole viewed from population dynamics. In *Proceedings of language evolution and computation workshop/course at ESSLLI, Vienna*, ed. S. Kirby. 95–104. Vienna: ESSLLI.
Rickford, John. 1983. *Standard and non-standard attitudes in a creole continuum*. Society for Creole Linguistics Occasional Paper Series, no. 16. St Augustine, Trinidad: Society for Caribbean Linguistics.
Robertson, Ian. 1974. *Dutch creole in Guyana: Some missing links*. Society for Caribbean Linguistics Occasional Paper Series, no. 2. St Augustine, Trinidad: Society for Caribbean Linguistics.
———. 1975. *Dutch creole speakers and their location in Guyana in the nineteenth and early twentieth centuries*. Society for Caribbean Linguistics Occasional Paper Series, no. 4. St Augustine, Trinidad: Society for Caribbean Linguistics.
———. 1976. *A preliminary word list of Berbice Dutch*. Society for Caribbean Linguistics Occasional Paper Series, no. 5. St Augustine, Trinidad: Society for Caribbean Linguistics.
Schwieger Hiepko, A. 1999. Creolization as a poetics of culture. Edouard Glissant's "archipelic" thinking. Paper presented at the sixth Interdisciplinary Congress of the Caribbean Research Society, Creolisation and Creole Identity, Berlin, 4–7 May.
Slocum, Karla, and Deborah A. Thomas. 2003. Rethinking global and area studies: Insights from Caribbeanist Anthropology. *American Anthropologist* 105, no. 3: 553–65.

12

Understanding Sexual Behaviour in Jamaica

J. PETER FIGUEROA

The aims of this chapter are to explore sexual behaviour in relation to the HIV/AIDS epidemic in Jamaica and to reflect on how the work of Barry Chevannes has contributed to our understanding of sexual behaviour in Jamaica. I have had many conversations with him over the years with respect to sexual practices and the cultural and social factors driving the HIV epidemic in Jamaica that have helped to clarify my own thinking and given depth to my understanding.

It is well established that self-reported sexual behaviour can be notoriously misleading. For instance, Chevannes describes conducting in-depth interviews on a sub-sample of persons who had reported high-risk sexual behaviour in a cross-sectional survey (Chevannes and Mitchell-Kernan 1994). Nine of eighteen persons (50 per cent) admitted to giving misleading information. One man who reported in the survey that he had six sexual partners outside his current relationship admitted, in the interview, that he was not telling the truth at the time. One man who claimed that he had sex with prostitutes six to ten times a year turned out to have a sexual relationship with a woman whom he believed was a prostitute. Apart from her, he had never had sex with a prostitute. Another man claimed three "outside women"[1] in the survey but two in the interview. One man said he first had sex at age nineteen, but he was not really sure. One man gave 1954 as his year of birth although he did not know when he was born (Chevannes and Mitchell-

Kernan 1994). This clearly illustrates how qualitative research using in-depth interviews may add an important dimension to a cross-sectional survey. Social acceptability bias is an important concern in social surveys, particularly when dealing with sensitive personal information concerning sexual behaviour.

The Caribbean has the second highest HIV prevalence rate in the world, after sub-Saharan Africa, with an adult HIV prevalence rate of 1.6 per cent (range 1.1 per cent to 2.7 per cent) (UNAIDS/WHO 2005). An estimated three hundred thousand persons are living with HIV in the Caribbean, and AIDS is the leading cause of death among persons aged fifteen to forty-five years. AIDS cases reported to the Caribbean Epidemiology Centre continue to increase annually (CAREC/PAHO/WHO 2004). In Jamaica, there are an estimated twenty-five thousand persons living with HIV, of whom as many as fifteen thousand are not aware of their HIV status (http://www.jamaica-nap.org or http://www.nacjamaica.com). The adult HIV prevalence rate is 1.5 per cent, and reported AIDS cases continue to increase annually as shown in figure 1 below.

AIDS affects more men than women in Jamaica because the risk behaviour of men is greater than that of women. Men are more likely to have multiple sexual partners, sex with prostitutes or casual sex, which are all risk factors for HIV infection (Figueroa, Fox and Minor 1999; Figueroa et al. 1994, 1997, 2005). Crack/cocaine and alcohol use, which often lead to unprotected sex, are more common among men than women (Figueroa, Fox and Minor 1999; Figueroa et al. 2005). Same sex behaviour is a significant risk factor for HIV infection among men but not for women. In addition, the health seeking behaviour of men is far worse than that of women.

We have to ask ourselves why the HIV/AIDS epidemic continues to grow in Jamaica. Is it due to the inadequacy of the response, or is it due to the factors driving the epidemic? Perhaps it is due to a combination of both reasons. However, there are considerable social, economic and cultural factors that contribute to the continued spread of HIV in Jamaica. The strong stigma associated with HIV infection and the discrimination against persons living with AIDS make the problem worse by driving the epidemic underground (Hackett 2005). The stigma and discrimination associated with AIDS encourage denial of risk among persons, particularly those who are marginalized, and drive the HIV/AIDS epidemic underground. Persons at risk are

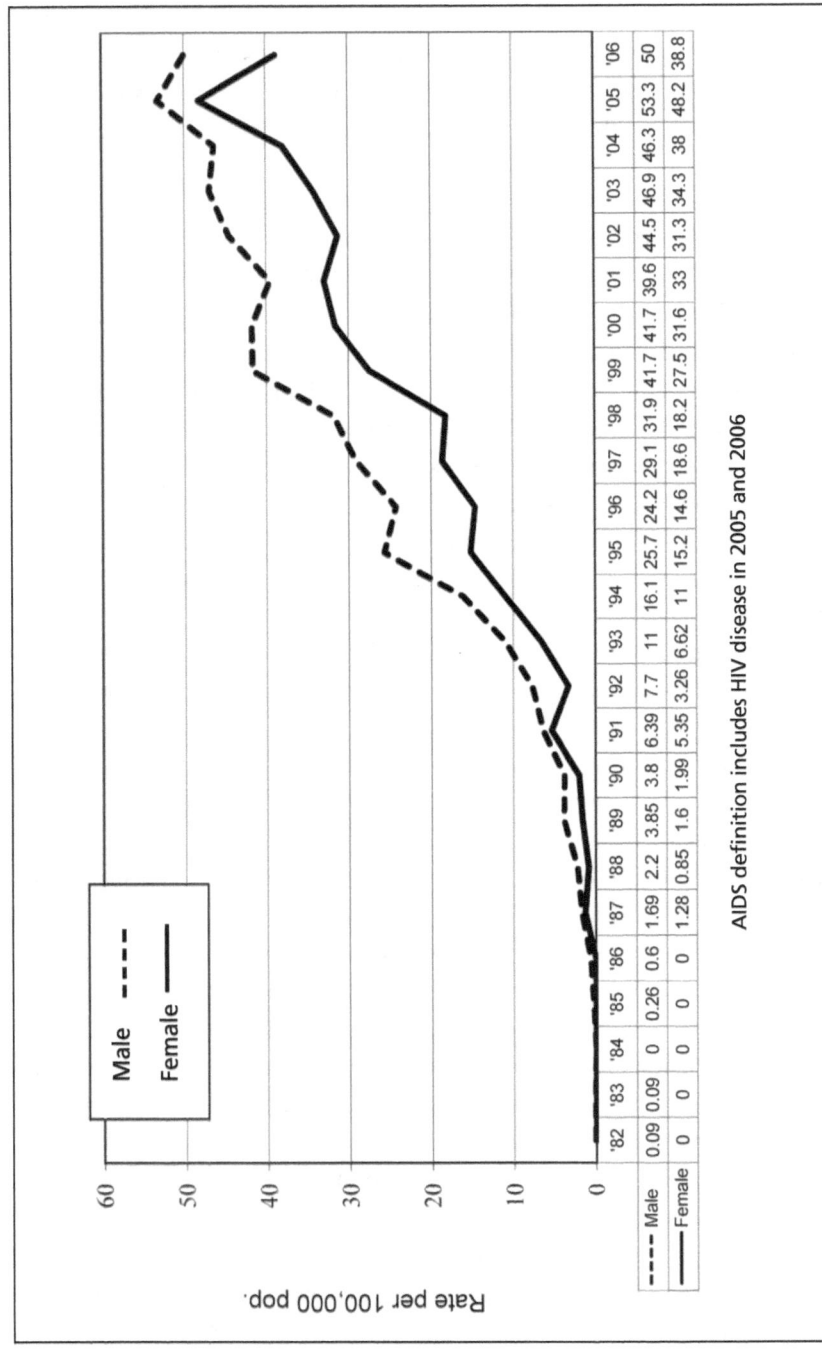

Figure 1. Jamaica: Annual AIDS Case Rates by Sex (per 100,000 population), 1982–2006

less likely to seek services for prevention or treatment and are more difficult to access by outreach workers and health providers. While the stigma has declined in recent years, it remains strong, and more needs to be done to reduce it, including measures to establish a supportive legislative framework.

The National HIV/STI (sexually transmitted infections) Control Programme has placed great emphasis over the years on educating the people, especially those more at risk, so as to change their individual risk behaviour. However, it is important to recognize that significant sectors of our population are socially vulnerable to behaviour that will put them at risk of HIV (Gayle et al. 2004). One fifth of our population is poor and another fifth is near poor. Many of these persons will participate in transactional sex for reasons of survival (Chevannes 2001a). Illiteracy and low educational levels foster ignorance, superstition and myths concerning HIV/AIDS and other STIs. In addition, the population movements of Jamaicans within the island and overseas as well as the many visitors to the island offer numerous opportunities for casual sexual liaisons, including transactional relations, that increase the risk of HIV infection.

Sexual and mating patterns in Jamaica are deeply ingrained in our culture, as are the gender roles and expectations associated with sexual practice (Chevannes 1986, 2001a, 2002). Most of these behaviours are derived socially, and emerge more spontaneously than by rational choice. Sex begins at an early age: mean age 13.2 years for males and 15.2 years for girls (Hope Enterprises 2001). Ethnographic interviews by Chevannes reveal that first sex in pre-pubescent years is regarded, both by adults and children, as a part of play and is pleasurable (Chevannes and Mitchell-Kernan 1994). This is known as "dolly house" sex, or early sexual experimentation, in which penetration may not take place. Boys are socialized into early sex, which is seen as natural and expected, and ensures that the boy is not labelled a homosexual or "mama's boy" (Chevannes 2001a; 2002). Boys are allowed to roam outside on the streets and are introduced to sex with girls by bigger boys or men or, at times, by older girls or women. On the other hand, girls are monitored closely by their mothers, or parents, and only allowed outdoors to do errands from which they must return promptly (Chevannes 2001a). This is described aptly as "tie the heifer and loose the bull" (Brown and Chevannes 1998).

Although sex begins at an early age, young people are not prepared for sex and myths remain strong. Only 38 per cent of persons aged fifteen to twenty-four years can correctly identify three ways of preventing sexual transmission of HIV and reject major misconceptions (Duncan and Figueroa 2006; Hope Enterprises 2004). Adults twenty-five to forty-five years are not much better off, as only 46 per cent respond correctly to this indicator. Teenage pregnancies have decreased over the years but remain common, as do STIs. Family life and health education in schools is not mandatory or examinable. In any case, most teachers are not comfortable with sex education or HIV education, and the content is less than satisfactory. Nor are most parents comfortable talking with their children on these matters. While condoms are readily accessible to the general population, it is not always easy for young persons to get condoms because of the negative attitudes of many adults to adolescents having sex and the embarrassment faced by the youth (Gayle et al. 2004). Hence, adolescents have a relatively high rate of unprotected sex (Hope Enterprises 2001).

Multiple sexual partnerships are common in Jamaica, especially among men. The proportion of men reporting more than one sexual partner in the past twelve months ranges between 49 per cent and 59 per cent in various surveys since 1985 (Figueroa, Fox and Minor 1999; Figueroa et al. 2005; Hope Enterprises 1992, 1994, 1996b, 2000, 2004). Despite repeated educational campaigns that include a message to "stick to one faithful partner", there appears to be little change in this sexual practice among men, although a significant decline was noticed in multiple partnerships among men in national surveys conducted between 1992/1993 and 2000 (Figueroa, Fox and Minor 1999; Figueroa et al. 2005; Hope Enterprises 1992, 1994, 1996b, 2000). Masculinity is often viewed by men in terms of how many women or baby mothers they have. It is clear that the practice of men having an outside woman is a deeply ingrained cultural practice (Chevannes 1986, 2002).

It is much more difficult to assess the proportion of women who have multiple sexual relationships, because admitting to this is not viewed as socially acceptable and is likely to be under-reported in surveys. In national surveys with face-to-face interviews, 11.4 per cent to 15 per cent of women aged fifteen to forty-five years reported having more than one sexual partner in the past twelve months (Figueroa, Fox and Minor 1999; Figueroa et al. 2005; Hope Enterprises 1992, 1994, 1996b, 2000). However, when women at sites in Kingston, Jamaica were allowed to write down their answer without speaking and placed the questionnaire in a separate envelope, 48 per cent reported a new sex partner in the past twelve months compared with 35 per cent of women interviewed face-to-face (unpublished data from the 2005 baseline survey of a randomized controlled trial of the PLACE method [Priorities for Local AIDS Control Efforts]). Carefully conducted focus groups also suggest that 30 per cent to 40 per cent of women may have had multiple sexual partners in the past year (Chambers and Chevannes 1994). This is a much more realistic estimate given the high rate of men reporting multiple sexual partnerships. This practice is more common among younger than older women. In the popular culture, it is a source of amusement when a woman gives a man "bun" (has sex with another man behind his back), and it is a source of great embarrassment to the man. The phenomenon of "jacket" is also well established, whereby a woman is pregnant for one man but passes the baby off as being the child of another man who she favours as the father (Chevannes 2001b, 2002). Where paternity is disputed and a paternity test is done, as many as 34 per cent of results show that the reputed father is not the biological father (Chevannes 2001b).

Women may enter into transactional sexual relations with a man other than their main partner for economic reasons (Chambers and Chevannes 1994; Chevannes 2001a, 2001b). Many Jamaican women, especially among the poor, expect to be supported financially by their male partner. Hence the popular saying "no money, no love". Men who are not able to contribute financially to their babymother or girlfriend are at a serious disadvantage, and their relationship may be undermined. High rates of unemployment among the youth make the formation of stable unions more difficult for both males and females. Men who have money have an advantage in forming sexual liaisons or winning sexual favours. Some women will target a man with money and grant him sexual favours as long as he supports her financially and gives her gifts. Such a man is seen as a "boops". At the same time, some men define their manhood in terms of the number of women that they have sex with, and they will seek to have several women and babymothers to show that they are virile.

Some women may have an outside man for sexual satisfaction while in a stable relationship, as do many men (Chambers and Chevannes 1994; Chevannes 2001b). As more women have become economically and socially independent, it appears that some of these women have also become sexually independent and adopted practices usually associated with males. A number of these women have a man who is financially dependent on his woman for whom he must grant sexual and other favours. This is the phenomenon of the "toy boy". Generally, women must be very discreet in having sexual partners outside of their main relationship in order to avoid verbal and physical abuse or being labelled a whore. On the other hand, it is not unusual to hear men boasting of having several women without the social sanction faced by women for the same behaviour.

Over 80 per cent of persons living with AIDS in Jamaica report having multiple sexual contacts (http://www.jamaica-nap.org or http://www.nacjamaica.com). It is not unusual for the names of some of these sexual contacts to be unknown, indicating the casual nature of the sexual encounter. More than half of persons with AIDS give a history of having another STI. This is both an indicator of risky sexual behaviour and the fact that persons with an STI are likely to have more than one STI. It is also well established that other STIs facilitate HIV transmission (Wasserheit 1992). Nearly one third of all persons with AIDS have participated in commercial sex, which is one of the strongest risk factors for HIV infection (http://www.jamaica-nap.org or http://www.nacjamaica.com). Approximately 10 per cent of AIDS cases have used crack/cocaine, which is also a known risk factor for HIV infection. However, a significant minority of persons with AIDS in Jamaica (less than 20 per cent) has no obvious risk factor for HIV infection. Most of these persons are women who are at risk of HIV because of the risk behaviour of their male partner. In fact, we are aware of women who have had only one lifetime sexual partner and have become HIV infected and developed AIDS. Once a person is sexually active, he or she is at risk of HIV/AIDS.

Although the adult HIV prevalence rate in the general population is estimated to be 1.5 per cent, there are certain vulnerable populations in which HIV rates are significantly higher. Among persons attending public STI clinics and substance abusers (primarily crack/cocaine), HIV rates approximate 6 per cent (Brown and Chevannes 1998). Surveys of inmates of correctional institutions indicate that HIV rates may be as high as 12 per cent; among male homosexuals and bisexuals, rates could be twice as high. A recent survey of female prostitutes on the streets of Kingston, Ocho Rios and Montego Bay found HIV rates of 9 per cent (Brown and Chevannes 1998). Several years ago, a similar survey in Montego Bay found HIV rates of 20 per cent (Figueroa et al. 1998). The critical lesson here is that these vulnerable populations are at significantly higher risk of HIV infection than the general population. However, these vulnerable populations are interwoven with and not separate from the general population. The extent to which these vulnerable populations are stigmatized and marginalized is the extent to which the epidemic is driven underground, placing the general population at greater risk. A person who is stigmatized is far less likely to disclose their risk behaviour or HIV status to a sexual partner. Nor can you tell by looking. Hence, our advice to use a condom every time you have sex. Moreover, the potential for the HIV/AIDS epidemic to continue to grow in Jamaica is real.

In the past two decades, commercial sex appears to have grown and become more diverse in Jamaica. There are now nightclubs with exotic dancers throughout Jamaica, including in rural areas. Live sex on stage, known as "freaky" shows, is not unusual. Massage parlours offering sexual massages and escort services are now commonplace and are advertised in the daily newspapers. Many girls and young ladies see their good looks and ability to dance as an asset to be marketed, and commercial sex, exotic dancing or sexual massage are all job options, especially where economic needs cannot be met through other conventional means. Unemployed boys, especially those on the street, also see sex with men who pick them up as an option for survival.

There is a considerable demand, primarily from men, for commercial sex. We need to consider why there is such a demand for commercial sex. Many men can satisfy a sexual desire or need through commercial sex without the emotional and economic ties or commitment usually associated with regular relationships. Sexual negotiation is straightforward once you have the money to pay. Commercial sex also offers the possibility of oral sex or other sexual practices as well as sexual variety that may not be available from one's regular partner. Moreover, there is a pool of unemployed women (and boys) who can make good money from it. Many female sex workers report that they do not like the trade, but it pays better than most other employment that they can do, such as domestic work, and they need the money to look after their children. Only 4 per cent of persons fifteen to forty-five years admit to commercial sex in national surveys (Hope Enterprises 2004). However, as many as 20 per cent report giving or receiving money or a gift for sex when a self-administered questionnaire is used, indicating that transactional sexual relationships are widespread in Jamaica. Such relationships place significant numbers of people at risk of HIV infection and help sustain the HIV/AIDS epidemic.

Jamaica has had a comprehensive National HIV/AIDS/STI Control Programme for many years that has slowed the epidemic and averted over one hundred thousand new HIV infections. A variety of behaviour change messages has been promoted over the years. The primary messages have been for young persons to abstain from sex and for adults to stick to one faithful partner and use a condom every time. Although we have promoted the idea that there are 101 ways to say no to sex, there is little evidence that young people are abstaining more from sex, though abstinence among adult women may have increased marginally. We have encouraged young persons to "reclaim their virginity" in order to get them to recognize that they do not need to continue having sex. We have also promoted "double protection" or dual method use, namely, using the condom as well as a more effective method to prevent pregnancy, such as the contraceptive pill or injection. Chevannes points out that many persons have reinterpreted these messages to mean "skin-to-skin sex with every partner in whom you have faith or in whom you want to have faith, and condom sex with those in whom you don't" (Chevannes and Mitchell-Kernan 1994). This remains an outstanding challenge in promoting safe sex in Jamaica.

The National HIV/AIDS/STI Control Programme has been successful in increasing condom sales and distribution fourfold, from 2.5 million condoms in 1985 to approximately 10 million condoms annually since 1996 (Hope Enterprises 1993, 1996a, 2003). In fact, the proportion sold increased from 20 per cent in 1985 to 70 per cent since 1996. The proportion of men reporting condom use at last sex with a non-regular partner has been approximately 75 per cent since 1992. Among women, the proportion reporting last time condom use with a non-regular partner increased from 37 per cent in 1992 to approximately 60 to 65 per cent since 1994 (Brown and Chevannes 1998; Hope Enterprises 1992, 1994, 1996b, 2000, 2004). However, this level of condom use is still not high enough to prevent continued HIV spread, given sexual patterns of behaviour in Jamaica.

In order to reach more persons at risk of HIV, the national programme is targeting prevention interventions at sites where people go to meet new sex partners. This is known as the PLACE method (University of North Carolina 2005). In phase one, we identify sites by asking people to name places where persons go to meet new sex partners. In phase two, interviewers visit these sites and talk to a knowledgeable person at the site. In phase three, customers at the sites are interviewed to get baseline information concerning sexual behaviour. Targeted interventions are developed based on the data collected. After a period of intervention, a follow-up survey can be conducted to assess whether there has been any behaviour change among the customers.

When the PLACE method was applied in Montego Bay in 2003, as many as 421 sites were identified (University of North Carolina 2003; Figueroa et al. forthcoming). Approximately 35 per cent of women and 50 to 58 per cent of men interviewed at a sample of these sites reported having one or more new sex partners in the past twelve months, with 20 per cent of the men having four or more sex partners during this period. Among people who had a new sex partner in the past year, most men (76 to 80 per cent) reported using a condom the last time they had sex with one of those partners. Between 39 and 49 per cent of respondents reported using a condom at last sex with a regular partner in the last year. However, fewer than 10 per cent of respondents had a condom with them at the time of the interview. There was a significant gap between opportunities onsite for prevention and actual prevention activities. According to site representatives, 81 per cent of sites were willing to have prevention programmes and 41 per cent of sites were willing to sell condoms (University of North Carolina 2003; Figueroa et al. forthcoming). Measures have been put in place to address these needs for prevention.

In recent years, we have increasingly emphasized the need for all sexually active adults to have an HIV test in order to know their HIV status. This is particularly important because so many persons are unaware that they or their sexual partner are HIV infected. In fact, we estimate that as many as fifteen thousand persons, or 60 per cent of all HIV infected persons in Jamaica (twenty-five thousand), are not aware that they are HIV infected. Most of these persons look and feel quite healthy and are often surprised to learn that they have been living with HIV when they do find out their HIV positive status. Although we repeatedly stress that you cannot tell who is HIV infected by appearance, this remains an abstract concept for most people. It is estimated that approximately one-third of the adult population has never had an HIV test. Our aim is to have all sexually active persons do an annual HIV test.

In order to control the HIV/AIDS epidemic in Jamaica, we need to better understand the sexual behaviour of the people. This requires more research of similar quality to that conducted by Chevannes, whose work was primarily qualitative and anthropological. We also need to recognize that sexual patterns and gender roles are deeply rooted in the culture and will not change readily. The coverage, scope, cultural dimension and quality of prevention programmes, including through the education system, need to be increased greatly. Structural programmes in society that increase employment, education and opportunities for advancement among the poor and marginalized, as well as achieve a reorientation of gender roles and greater gender equity, will reduce social vulnerability of the population to HIV/AIDS.

NOTE

1. An outside woman is a sexual partner other than one's spouse or main partner.

REFERENCES

Brown, Janet, and Barry Chevannes. 1998. *"Why man stay so?" An examination of gender socialization in the Caribbean.* Kingston: University of the West Indies/UNICEF.

Caribbean Epidemiology Centre (CAREC)/Pan-American Health Organization (PAHO)/WHO. 2004. Status and trends, analysis of the Caribbean HIV/AIDS epidemic 1982–2002. CAREC. http://www.carec.org/pdf/20-years-aids-caribbean.pdf.

Chambers, Claudette, and Barry Chevannes. 1994. *Report on six focus group discussions: Sexual decision-making project, ISER-UCLA.* Kingston: Institute of Social and Economic Research.

Chevannes, Barry. 1986. Jamaican male sexual beliefs and attitudes. Report to the National Family Planning Board, Kingston, Jamaica.

———. 2001a. *Learning to be a man: Culture, socialization and gender identity in five Caribbean communities*. Kingston: University of the West Indies Press.

———. 2001b. Fatherhood in the African-Caribbean landscape: An exploration in meaning and context. In *Children's rights: Caribbean realities*, ed. Christine Barrow, 214–26. Kingston: Ian Randle.

———. 2002. Gender and adult sexuality. In *Gendered realities: Essays in Caribbean feminist thought*, ed. Patricia Mohammed, 486–94. Kingston: University of the West Indies Press.

Chevannes, Barry, and C. Mitchell-Kernan. 1994. *How we were grown: Cultural aspects of high risk behaviour in Jamaica*. Sexual Decision-making Project, ISER-UCLA. Kingston: Institute of Social and Economic Research.

Duncan, J., and J.P. Figueroa. 2006. *Jamaica UNGASS report January 2003–December 2005 declaration of commitment on HIV/AIDS*. Kingston: Ministry of Health.

Figueroa, J.P., A. Brathwaite, J. Morris et al. 1994. Rising HIV-I prevalence among sexually transmitted disease clinic attenders in Jamaica: Traumatic sex and genital ulcers as risk factors. *Acquired Immune Deficiency Syndrome* 7: 310–16.

Figueroa, J.P., A. Brathwaite, M. Wedderburn et al. 1998. Is HIV/AIDS control in Jamaica making a difference? *AIDS 1998* 12: 589–98.

Figueroa, J.P., C. Brewer, D. Dale and S. Hileman Bassett. Forthcoming. Weir. An assessment of sexual networks in St James, Jamaica, using the PLACE method.

Figueroa, J.P., K. Fox, and K. Minor. 1999. A behaviour risk factor survey in Jamaica. *West Indian Medical Journal* 48, no. 1: 9–15.

Figueroa, J.P., E. Ward, J. Morris et al. 1997. Incidence of HIV and HTLV-I infection among sexually transmitted disease clinic attenders in Jamaica. *AIDS and HR* 15: 232–37.

Figueroa, J.P., E. Ward, C. Walters, D.E. Ashley, R.J. Wilks. 2005. High risk health behaviours among adult Jamaicans. *West Indian Medical Journal* 54, no. 1: 70–76.

Gayle, H., A. Grant, L. Bryan, M. Yee Shui, C. Taylor. 2004. *The adolescents of urban St Catherine: A study of their reproductive health and survivability*. Spanish Town, Jamaica: Children First Agency.

Hackett, Volderine, ed. 2005. *Champions for change: Reducing HIV/AIDS stigma and discrimination in the Caribbean*. Georgetown: CARICOM Secretariat.

Hope Enterprises. 1992. *National KAP survey 1992*. Kingston: Hope Enterprises.

———. 1993. *Condom market surveys 1993*. Kingston: Hope Enterprises

———. 1994. *National KAP survey 1994*. Kingston: Hope Enterprises.

———. 1996a. *Condom market surveys 1996*. Kingston: Hope Enterprises.

———. 1996b. *National KAP survey 1996*. Kingston: Hope Enterprises.

———. 2000. *National KAP survey 2000*. Kingston: Hope Enterprises.

———. 2001. *Adolescent condom survey Jamaica*. Kingston: Hope Enterprises.
———. 2003. *Condom market surveys 2003*. Kingston: Hope Enterprises.
———. 2004. *National KAP survey 2004*. Kingston: Hope Enterprises.
United Nations Programme on HIV/AIDS (UNAIDS)/World Health Organization (WHO). 2005. *AIDS epidemic update*. Geneva.
University of North Carolina, MEASURE *Evaluation*. 2003. PLACE in Jamaica: Monitoring AIDS prevention at the parish level, St James 2003. MEASURE *Evaluation*, University of North Carolina at Chapel Hill, Carolina Population Center. http://www.cpc.unc.edu/measure
———. 2005. The priorities for local AIDS control programs (PLACE) manual, 2005. http://www.cpc.unc.edu/measure.
Wasserheit, J.N. 1992. Epidemiological synergy: Interrelationships between human immunodeficiency virus infection and other sexually transmitted diseases. *Sexually Transmitted Diseases* 9: 61–77.

13

The Third Crisis
Jamaica in the Neoliberal Era

DON ROBOTHAM

Since emancipation from slavery in 1838, Jamaican society has passed through three major crises. The first was the disillusionment with emancipation which culminated in the Morant Bay Rebellion of 1865. The second was the crisis of the free trade period which led directly to the 1938 revolts out of which the modern political system of Jamaica sprang. Since 1989 and the liberalization of the Jamaican economy, we have entered our third major crisis: the crisis of neoliberalism.

HISTORICAL BACKGROUND

The 1938 crisis had its roots in the second half of the nineteenth century. During that period, the British free trade regime drove down the price of sugar and created havoc in the Jamaican countryside. At the same time, the passage of land monopoly legislation from 1871 onwards sharply reduced the quantity of land available for settlement by Jamaican small farmers (Satchell 1990). The upshot was acute rural impoverishment and mass migration to Central America, Cuba and the United States, as well as to Kingston. This is the background to the rise of what I have elsewhere called "the colonial ghettos" of western Kingston – the impoverished inner-city areas which form the core of "garrison communities" and political violence in Jamaica. This was also the beginning of the formation of the "downtown" side of the Uptown/Downtown axis which frames urban living in Kingston – the cultural context out of which Rastafarianism, reggae and dancehall emerged and flourished, as Barry Chevannes has documented at length in his many works.

As with today, the state responded to the nineteenth- and twentieth-century crises by offering incentives to attract foreign investment and by embarking on a major programme of infrastructural development to support these investments. The key pieces of contemporary policy and legislation which echo nineteenth- and twentieth-century development efforts are the Tourism Master Plan for Sustainable Development, 2000–2010; the Northern Coastal Highway Improvement Project and the Highway 2000 Project. These are all the contemporary equivalents of the Aliens Amendment Acts and the Railway Extension Law (Commonwealth Secretariat 2002).

Even the financialization of the Jamaican economy, which we think is entirely new, actually began during that late nineteenth century when the British government floated loans on the London money market in order to finance Jamaican infrastructure. The funds were used, among other things, to finance the extension of the railway to Ewarton and Porus as well as to pay for the Rio Cobre Irrigation Canal which was critical for the restoration of the southern St Catherine–Clarendon sugar lands. The finances of the railway were particularly complex and burdensome, with the government guaranteeing an initial loan of £1.5 million at 4 per cent and holding an additional second mortgage of £700,000. Both of these debts the colonial government ultimately had to take over.

Just as today, global economic changes exacerbated the already deep social inequalities and the crisis which ensued led to one Commission of Inquiry after another. There was the Commission of Inquiry into the Conditions of the Juvenile Population of Jamaica of 1877, followed in 1884 by the Royal Commission to Investigate the Finances of Jamaica and other British West Indies Colonies with special reference to the incidence of taxation. Finally, there was the comprehensive Royal West Indies Commission of 1897, in which the Colonial Office made one final attempt to grapple with the social and economic distress which free trade had created in the Caribbean. As a result of all these combined efforts, major (but contradictory) transformations did take place in Jamaican society. In the banana sector (out of which early tourism arose), the restructured sugar industry and the expanded small export crops, the foundations were laid for the formation of the post-emancipation Jamaican middle class as well as the working and business classes. However, neither the investment incentives nor the various inquiries proved able to devise a stable solution to the poverty of the masses of the people, now beginning to huddle in Kingston. It was not until the abandonment of free trade and the restoration of protectionism and imperial preference in 1932, following the Ottawa Conference and the creation of a Sterling Area, and especially the post-war period of import substitution development, that some relative stability and substantial economic growth resumed in the Caribbean. Even then, the results were very uneven, as the have-and-have-nots debate which erupted between 1958 and 1959 proved.

THE NEW INTERNATIONAL CONTEXT

This broad historical perspective is particularly important at this juncture in Jamaica, for we tend to see our current problems in purely local terms. But the crisis of today is also a crisis which results from a fundamental change in the global regime. The collapse of both state socialism and social democracy and the restoration, in the 1980s, of a nineteenth-century-style free trade regime at the international level have had a determining effect on Jamaican social, economic, political and cultural life in the last twenty years.

After 1932, when protectionism was restored and the Sterling Area, of which we were a tiny part, was established, the international context in which society developed in Jamaica was fundamentally different from what went before. Especially in the period after the Second World War until the collapse of the Bretton Woods agreements in 1973 and 1979 – *les trente glorieuses*, "the thirty glorious ones", as the French call them – a very specific social, economic and political regime prevailed internationally. Our development as a society proceeded in this framework, and all our institutions – our political parties, our trade unions, our civic associations, our educational systems, our economy, our values and culture, our social and personal expectations and ambitions: the entire edifice of our existence – were built on this foundation. The anti-colonial movement – the struggle for political independence and for economic development – unfolded entirely within this framework. Caribbean societies have historically been and currently are among the most open in world history. So, changes in the global environment have a direct and enduring impact on us in a manner which may not be the case for larger and less open societies. There is not a single aspect of our public and, even in a sense, our private life which was not shaped in a formative manner by the global social democratic characteristics of those thirty glorious years. But these years came to an end after 1989.

A good example of the problems which we have faced as a result is the state of our political parties and the two-party system as a whole. Contrary to what some have written, it is a travesty to regard this simply as a clientelistic system of scarce benefits and spoils. Of course clientelism exists in every political system, including those of developed countries. And, if one regards social democracy as inherently clientelistic, then, of course, clientelism prevailed in Jamaica. But that would simply be tautological: all it would mean is that anywhere that there was social democracy – Britain, Germany, France, Scandinavia and so on – would be, by definition, clientelistic. But such usage is basically useless and not what is meant when the charge of clientelism is laid against the Jamaican political system.

The issue is not whether clientelism has existed in the Jamaican political system but whether this was the substance of the system. In my view, clientelism was far from being the substance of our situation. On the contrary, with all their limitations, both parties arose out of deep historical aspirations of different strata of Jamaican society and embodied their most cherished ideals. Failure to understand this basic point prevents some from grasping the most elementary truths about Jamaican society. Had the parties not been deeply rooted, how could they have survived for so long? How could they not only survive but retain the sympathy of large sections of the population to this day, even when such people become alienated, withdraw from politics and refuse to lend their support? The Jamaican political parties were not at their core clientelistic, although parasitic elements certainly existed within and around them, as they do around all parties all over the world. These Jamaican parties embodied and, to some extent, continue to embody some of the deepest historical aspirations of the Jamaican people.

Nonetheless, today the parties are a shadow of their former selves. What has reduced them to this state? At first glance, the answer that comes to mind is the proliferation of garrison politics and of political violence. But what has produced such phenomena? A closer look will reveal some clues. I would suggest that the chief reasons for their decline are twofold: first, there is the vast growth of the informal sector of the Jamaican economy, now estimated to be about 40 per cent of the employed labour force. Second, there is the withdrawal of the organized social classes – the organized working class in trade unions, the organized middle class in professional and other associations and the organized business community – from active participation in national political life. Individuals from these groups remain, but the organized presence of these critical social strata in the Jamaican political process has been temporarily suspended almost to the point of boycott. As this withdrawal has proceeded, there has been a corresponding engagement of the informal sectors more and more in our civic and political life, with predictable results.

As in other countries, the basis for democracy, the two-party system and the legitimacy of the state in Jamaica derived from the active participation of the relatively stable social groups in the political process. The organized middle class formed the People's National Party (PNP) in 1938. The organized working class formed the Bustamante Industrial Trade Union and then the Jamaica Labour Party (JLP) in 1942. The capitalists, after a disastrous foray into independent politics with the Jamaica Democratic Party in 1946, by and large entered the JLP, especially after 1948. Later, sections of the working class joined the PNP, and sections of the capitalist class, especially the fledgling manufacturing sector, became critical supporters of the PNP. In the 1960s in particular, important sections of the middle class, especially the light-skinned pro-colonial elements, defected to the JLP, a process accelerated in the 1970s under Michael Manley. Wherever they stood, these organized and stable social strata provided the ballast for the Jamaican ship of state.

But now that ballast is gone, with predictable results. A rambunctious lumpen is pervasive in both parties. What has caused this political retreat which is, in fact, a national catastrophe? The process of "lumpenization" started in the 1970s, accelerated in the 1980s with the huge growth in the so-called informal commercial importers, but in its political (as distinct from economic) impact, it is a 1990s and twenty-first-century phenomenon. It was consolidated primarily after 1989, during the second Manley regime and the period thereafter, led by former prime minister P.J. Patterson.

In Jamaica, as elsewhere, the participation in politics of all stable social groups rested on an expectation that the state and the political parties would be able to deliver economic and social progress for the majority of Jamaicans. If one reads the founding documents of the PNP, this rationale is put forward quite explicitly. Put us in political power, boot out the British, and together we shall achieve economic development and social progress for all. The very reason for political independence was framed in such terms: the rationale was that because we were a colony we remained poor and underdeveloped. Boot out the British and support our efforts and together we would build a better Jamaica. That was the claim. This was to be achieved more or less by social democratic means – whether explicitly enunciated by the PNP or pragmatically implemented by the JLP. The aim was to develop a strong welfare state which would regulate and protect the local market, foster import substitution manufacturing, and redistribute revenues in the form of a social wage in health, housing, education and other benefits. Throughout the entire postwar political history of Jamaica up until 1989, whether through PNP or JLP regimes, this was the social contract with the population; these were the accepted political expectations and this was the foundation of the legitimacy of the state and the two political parties.

The problem was that the fulfilment of this vision depended on a set of favourable global economic and political circumstances which began to cease to exist from the 1970s. These conditions had lasted so long and seemed so durable that we had come to take them for granted. Who could have imagined that the Soviet Union would collapse? Who would have foreseen that social democracy too would wither away, first in Britain and then even in Scandinavia? Who could have foreseen the collapse of Bretton Woods, the death of deficit financing and the triumph of monetarism? Who would have thought that the entire world would return to a nineteenth-century free trade regime which had deeply discredited itself in the First World War, with the Great Depression of 1929 and the rise of Fascism? Who could have imagined that not only Marx and Lenin would be abandoned but Keynes as well, and that the world would return to Adam Smith, David Ricardo and John Stuart Mill as the inspirations for public policy? But that is exactly what came to pass.

The result of this transformation at the international level meant that the old import substitution model, which both Jamaican political parties had pursued, was dead. The requirement of low inflation meant that deficit financing of significant social benefits – health, education and housing – was also dead. Likewise, large state budgets with huge numbers of government employees became a thing of the past. Thus, the state and the political parties were forced to break the historic social contract with the Jamaican people, which had been the very basis for their initial formation and continued existence. What was the point of political independence if one was worse off? What was the point of political parties if they were, in fact, not in control of real life events but were powerless and ineffective in the face of them?

Moreover, the downsizing of the state in the 1980s and the privatizations and liberalization meant that we have an economy which is much more of a market economy than ever before. The early years of this transformation have been documented by Professor Patricia Anderson in a well-known study (Anderson and Witter 1994; Anderson 2001). Any acquaintance with the data will show that there has been a remarkable expansion of private business activity at the small and medium levels during and after the 1980s (Robotham 1998). Therefore, the reality is that the vast majority of the Jamaican population is not dependent on the Jamaican state for their bread and butter. Those who remain dependent on the state – the civil service, nurses, teachers and security services – find that the state does not have the resources to satisfy their traditional claims. So they, too, rapidly become disenchanted with this fiscally challenged state. The only groups who remain are those – from the bottom and the top – who parasitically depend on contracts from the state for their well-being. In a word, the downtown lumpen and the uptown lumpen.

The state and the political parties, like many other such states and political parties in Latin America (Venezuela is the classic case), built on an import-substitution social democratic platform, proved incapable of meeting their historic responsibilities to the Jamaican people: neither crime, nor economic development nor social equality could be addressed effectively during the eighteen deflationary years of the Patterson regime. This had the effect of deeply undermining the legitimacy of the state and the political parties. But the basic cause derived neither from the political parties nor from the state. Nor, it should be noted, did it derive from a cabal of scheming international financiers. The changes had a deeper root and were objective in their nature. The root failure derived from the collapse of the global economic premise upon which the entire social and political compact rested. Where the politicians and parties have failed is in their tardy, and even ignorant, response to this transformation. Even now, many are in denial and simply repeat populist phrases learned by heart in the 1960s and 1970s.

Because of the structural stagflation and huge monetary imbalances in the leading Western economies, the development-friendly social democratic Bretton Woods regime could not, and did not, last for more than thirty glorious post-war years. Following the collapse of the gold standard in 1971 and the stagflationary crisis in Western economies, especially in the United States in the 1970s, a sharp shift in global economic conditions took place in the 1980s. It was this drastic anti-inflationary high-interest-rate regime adopted by the United States in the 1980s – unavoidable in the circumstances, it should be clearly understood – which did in the Seaga regime. Despite unprecedentedly high levels of balance of payments support and comprehensive social and economic assistance, amounting to over US$1 billion, the Seaga efforts at reform were overwhelmed by the global anti-inflation policies of the United States in particular.

The basic reason for our deep economic, social, political and cultural disorientation is to be found here. The shift to a liberal global regime *sans* foreign aid, *sans* development cooperation, and *sans* concessionary balance-of- payments support, without capital controls, fiercely competitive and intolerant of inflation has completely shattered the very foundations of our political and social existence. The basic premises of our social, economic and political order – the expectations of upward social mobility, the welfare role of the state and, thus, the legitimacy of our political institutions – have been dealt a body blow. But it was not only the fact of this drastic change which produced our crisis but the manner of it. Given the realities of globalization by 1989, the Jamaican economy simply could not have continued in the old way – especially with the sidelining of the Caribbean Basin Initiative by the rise of the North American Free Trade Association. The Jamaican economy had to face these realities – we had to liberalize.

But in our case, Manley proceeded by shock therapy after 1989 and immediately liberalized the economy without preparation. The fact that the Jamaican budget had huge deficits, that our current account position was deeply in the red, and that we had few reserves and an extremely vulnerable currency – all these profound structural imbalances – were regarded as secondary. A mission was sent to study the liberalization process in the Dominican Republic. It concluded that rapid liberalization was the better course to take. The very predictable upshot was not only the stream of devaluations, the 80 per cent inflation of 1991 and the subsequent banking crisis. Those were the immediate economic impacts for which, incidentally, we are still paying and for which our children and grandchildren will continue to pay dearly.

More importantly, the Manley shock not only disoriented the economy, it also deeply disoriented the society and the political system. The basic premise of the anti-colonial movement, the fundamental rationale for political independence, at least in the form which had been presented to the people, went by the wayside. With these actions, Manley also removed the cornerstone of the legitimacy of the Jamaican state. If the parties were no longer there to advance a popular social and economic agenda through the state; if the state was now to become simply a liberal nightwatchman state; if the population was now told to seek its own salvation and to sink or swim in the market, then what was the point of politics? Moreover, if all these truly drastic changes were not to be phased in over a five-year or even a one-year period but in the very budget year of 1990, then the situation was dire and urgent in the extreme.

As was the case in Cuba during the so-called Special Period after the collapse of Soviet support, political disorientation and decay was inevitable. A mass scramble of each social stratum immediately began, each seeking to fend for itself, desperate to protect its standard of living. Higglering, hitherto the "coping strategy" of the poor, spread quickly into the middle classes. Teachers hawked cosmetics and jewellery, and nurses became important sources of clothes and shoes. "Occupational multiplicity" ran rampant. As we shall see, literally hundreds of thousands were plunged below the poverty line by the way that this swerve in public policy was executed.

Democracy in any country depends on the active participation of stable social groups in the political life of the country. But what if no social group is stable? What happens if public policy has the effect of shaking the basis of the existence of such groups at their very foundations? This is precisely what the Manley shock of 1989–91 achieved, with lasting political and social consequences. The organized social groups were deeply destabilized: the unionized working class was threatened with mass layoffs, the professional middle classes were plunged into higglering and the business community was driven to the most crooked financial speculations. Demoralized and shattered, they withdrew from public life of all kinds (including volunteerism) out of sheer self-defence and the necessities of economic survival. As these groups withdrew, the lumpen advanced. This is also the period when Jamaican involvement in international drug trafficking really got going, and the dons began to assert a relative independence from the fiscally wounded political apparatus. The Patterson political leadership, which succeeded Manley, ignored this deterioration and stood idly by as the influence of the lumpen increased enormously. They took no organizational or ideological steps to combat it politically.

For reasons which can be understood, this is not how the crisis in Jamaica is understood or analysed locally. Many argue as if they believe that the problems of Jamaica are unique and that they have to do with some peculiar local failing. A deep insularity combined with the language barrier makes for a general public and intelligentsia uninformed about similar social crises in Latin America (Argentina, Bolivia, Ecuador, Peru, Nicaragua, Uruguay and Brazil). Local failings are certainly in abundance – one has a vast menu from which to choose. But the greatest failure is our failure to understand the roots of our crisis. The roots are international, and what our failure consists of is the failure to adapt flexibly, intelligently and in a timely manner to the new international context in which we find ourselves.

Countries incomparably larger and stronger than Jamaica – one thinks of Sweden or Denmark or Finland (all with populations well under 10 million) – have no choice but to adapt to the international economic environment in which they find themselves. Society and the political leaders in these countries are clear about the fact that they are too weak to make the international environment. This environment is a given to which they must adapt if they are to prosper. Yet, this does not mean that the struggle for a more just international order is to be abandoned. In Jamaica in particular, for various "rebel" reasons, we find this obvious truth unpalatable. Unpalatable it undoubtedly is, but that makes it nonetheless true. Let me repeat it: Jamaica or the entire Caribbean, including Cuba and now Venezuela, is too weak to shape the international environment – whether this environment is moving to the Right or to the Left politically. Because of size, openness and history, we are environment takers, not environment makers. This does not mean we must roll over and die. It does not mean that we abandon our historic struggle for economic, social and political justice at the international level. But it certainly means greater realism, grasp of our condition and understanding of the balance of power in the world today. The task before us is to exploit the many opportunities created by this environment and to abate the impact of the many negatives. But we cannot approach that task wilfully, doing as we wish. We will only be effective if we study this environment carefully, understand it and our position within it deeply, and act both skilfully and in the public interest.

This is particularly important at this point in time because, as in Latin America, a deep alienation from neoliberal policies is also welling up from below in Jamaican political and cultural life. It is not that market relations in themselves are culturally alien to Jamaicans. On the contrary, Jamaica historically was formed entirely within the framework of the expansion of the global market from the fifteenth century onwards. Jamaicans, with our strong peasant traditions, have a strong attachment to private property, especially land. However, it is this very same small property economy which has produced a deeply rooted moral economy, expressed above all in ideas of self-reliance, most fully captured in Rastafarian philosophy.

This outlook is hostile to sharp differences in wealth and to the commoditization of public goods such as education and health. In that sense, Jamaica, culturally speaking, is a social democratic nation. This is the meaning of the "cultural" turn in the music and the return of "conscious" lyrics – "Serious Times" indeed! This is the meaning of the riots in Brown's Town and elsewhere or, for that matter, the spontaneous mass protest in Mandeville, of all places, around the SuperPlus affair in 2006. It is also the meaning for the mass enthusiasm which greeted the rise of Portia Simpson Miller to become Jamaica's first female prime minister – "from the bowels of the people" – in 2007. This reality also explains the photo-finish of the recent Jamaican general elections. Despite having access to vast campaign resources and facing a weakened and divided opponent, the business-friendly JLP was only able to defeat the PNP by a margin of 0.4 per cent.

Inequality and Poverty

Against the background of understanding our political crisis, I wish to address two of the economic impacts of neoliberal globalization on Jamaican society in recent years: the growth of inequality and the reduction of poverty. Financial deregulation in Jamaica and the strategy of using high interest rates to reduce inflation and support the exchange rate have resulted in an unprecedented transfer of wealth from the middle and lower levels of the society to the richest social strata. In an article titled "Turning the Corner", I have referred to this process of silent enrichment as "the cynical political secret of the day in Jamaica" (*Sunday Gleaner*, 1 May 2005). It is, in fact, the economic glue which has largely kept the upper strata of the society sympathetic to government financial policies, despite the very grave reservations which they have with respect to the crime situation.

The abrupt financial liberalization of a poorly regulated financial sector led to a near collapse of the banks, which then had to be rescued at huge cost to the national budget in the form of a domestic and foreign debt of US$13.4 billion by 2006. The bulk of the debt is owed not to the international community but to local lenders, with a significant portion held by the upper echelons of Jamaican society, the traditional light-skinned creole elites and the black bourgeoisie. An annual payment of US$500 million to domestic debt holders during this neoliberal adjustment period would mean that Jamaican society has received about US$5 billion dollars in the decade from debt service repayments. While the major part of these repayments has gone to institutions (National Housing Trust, National Investment Fund, private pension funds and so on), upper-echelon private investors would have garnered from US-denominated debt alone, on a conservative estimate, about US$200 to US$400 million in debt-service income over the decade.

For signs of enrichment at the top, one can point to the very visible proliferation of local investment houses, the emergence of a new stratum of wealthy persons, and the rise to national prominence of a remarkable group of young Jamaican entrepreneurs, both male and female. Further evidence is the sharp inflation in the real estate market and the continued construction of luxury houses and condominiums in bourgeois neighbourhoods of Kingston as well as of country homes in the tourist areas.

The annual survey of living conditions, done regularly in Jamaica since

1988, and which provides reliable data to measure poverty, does not collect or present data on the growth of inequality. They are expenditure surveys which capture gross movements in expenditure especially of food, housing, transportation and consumer durables. They present the analysis at a gross level, dividing the population into quintiles, whereas the wealth differentials are probably occurring at the level of the top 5 per cent of income earners. The kind of increase in inequality we are discussing – inequality flowing from increased ownership of financial assets – is not likely to be captured by such a survey.

The rise of violent crime and the high homicide rate are inextricably connected to this growth of economic and social inequality in Jamaica between 1991 and 2006 as well as to the devil-take-the-hindmost liberalization of the economy. In a small society such as Jamaica, it is hardly possible for all strata of the society to fail to appreciate the fact that an unprecedented enrichment of a tiny minority has been elevated to a principle of public policy in a Jamaica led by a black nationalist regime. Historically speaking, what is new in this process is that, unlike in the past, enrichment is not confined to the old light-skinned creole elite. This enrichment of an expanding black elite has drawn them further away from their mass base in economic, social and spatial terms. These realities lie behind the relative ineffectiveness of the cultural nationalist policies of former prime minister P.J. Patterson (Emancipation Park and the like). While these have huge popular appeal, they are accompanied by mass cynicism as a result of the enrichment of a black bourgeoisie.

Just as important, the social result of this shock therapy was a sharp increase in poverty levels from 30.5 per cent to 44.6 per cent in 1991, although this subsequently declined to 15.9 per cent by 1998. By 2004, this had increased somewhat to about 16.9 per cent below the poverty line which is more or less where it remains today. It is worth reminding ourselves that the bulk of the poverty in Jamaica is to be found in the countryside, among the rural poor, hidden away from the tourist resorts. Poverty rates among rural households – mainly small farmers – are about double the national rate. At the same time, unemployment in rural areas also averaged 20 per cent for 2004, in contrast to the rate in Kingston of 9 per cent and an overall national unemployment rate of about 12 per cent. If one wants a sure ticket to poverty in Jamaica, then one should become a small farmer. One should also be young (unemployment rate 30 per cent) or, worse yet, female. The surest guarantor of the harshest poverty is, of course, to be all three: a small farmer who is young and female. This reality is connected to the quite striking spread of violent criminality and gang banditry to some of our rural areas in recent years and to the role that women play in giving at least passive support and succour to criminals.

The fact that inequality has soared to some extent helps to obscure the reduction in poverty, but only partially. As Handa and others have pointed out, the sharp reduction in inflation since 1991, the growth of the informal (and illegal) sector, and the huge increase in remittances, coupled with the way poverty is measured, adequately explain the real movements in and out of poverty captured by the survey of living conditions. This is because a large number of households cluster just above and below the poverty line: lower-middle-strata persons in the fourth quintile teeter upon the poverty line. A slight shift upwards or downwards can result in significant real movements. Handa has proved that this is precisely what has happened in Jamaica throughout the 1990s, and there is no reason to doubt that this continues to be the case (Handa 2004). What the poverty data, therefore, is reflecting is this churning around the line. Those who now are barely above the poverty line were below it only yesterday and have a powerful sense of insecurity about where they stand.

But there is a critical point being obscured here which needs to be discussed fully. The really significant point is that the effects of liberalization and deregulation have been far from totally negative for the masses of the population, even in the marginal terms referred to previously. The proliferation of cheap imports of clothing and electronic goods due to trade liberalization, the import activities of higglers and others bringing goods in from China, have resulted in an important increase in the real consumption levels of hundreds of thousands of poor and middle-income Jamaicans. The reduction in inflation and the results consistently captured in the survey of living conditions can sustain no other interpretation. All one has to do is to use one's eyes and observe the consumer durables, cellphones and electronic goods now taken for granted in many working-class Jamaican households, the quality of shoes and clothing owned and worn, the number of cars on the road, the growth of the megamarts, the insignificance of malnutrition and the low maternal mortality rate (not to mention the rapidly collapsing birth rate), and it becomes clear that important, positive, real changes have indeed occurred in reducing poverty levels in Jamaica. The claim that the former prime minister Patterson became increasingly fond of trumpeting to an incredulous population, that in the last fourteen years his government had reduced poverty levels from 44.6 per cent to 16.9 per cent between 1991 and 2004 and that this represents 675,600 persons, cannot be simply dismissed. Even if there is some manipulation at work here due to the base year conveniently selected, the claim is not totally without substance.

Nonetheless, whatever base year one chooses, this still is a substantial poverty reduction figure of 13.6 percentage points between 1989 and 2004. It represents a net lifting out of poverty of about 331,700 persons, assuming a coefficient of 24,390 person-reductions for every per cent point reduction in poverty levels.

But there is a larger point to be made. What both the increases and decreases in poverty in recent years in Jamaica prove is that the major force reducing poverty in Jamaica is not poverty reduction programmes. Nor is it social programmes, such as food stamps or school feeding programmes, for example. It has not been the result of raising the minimum wage nor of increases in the social wage. Nor has it been the result of wage increases negotiated by trade unions or, least likely of all, wage increases unilaterally awarded by kind-hearted employers. It has not been the result of any memoranda of understanding or social contract, although these certainly are important for the fiscal side of the equation. Nor, sad to say, has it been the result of an improvement in the notoriously low levels of Jamaican productivity.

Poverty reduction has been the result of macroeconomic policy. It is the achievement of the Ministry of Finance and the Bank of Jamaica – the minister of finance, the financial secretary and the governor of the Central Bank should take the bows. Monetary policy has been its father and remittances from overseas its mother. With all the reservations stated above, the substantial reduction in poverty recorded in Jamaica is indisputably a result of the extremely high real interest rate regime and trade liberalization pursued over the past fourteen years. It is the reduction in inflation largely by monetary means which has been decisive and the influx of cheap imports from Asia which are responsible. Remittances are also an important part of this success, as remittances are now running at US$153 million per month. Without doubt, this is a victory for neoliberalism, a victory which, incidentally, Hirsch

(2005) has also noted for South Africa, where liberalization has achieved similar outcomes in poverty reduction but with a (somewhat) more balanced deployment of monetary and fiscal policy. But it is a victory won solely on the easier consumption side of the equation and, in practical terms, it is not as significant as the figures would suggest. Moreover, as pointed out earlier, it has been accompanied by substantial increases in asset inequality which we need to attempt to measure and study. But where we have failed is on the production side – especially in our archaic educational system. We must focus our energies on that more difficult side now. That is the key to our future.

Conclusion

When one reviews the difficult period through which Jamaican society has passed and is still passing, one is struck by the extent to which the larger picture of which we are a part has been neglected. As the data on poverty reduction indicates, and other studies such as Edelman's recent review of the experience in Costa Rica, Mauritius and Chile argue, the consequences of globalization for Jamaica have not been all negative, but they are far from being primarily positive either. The limited benefits gained have been won at a huge cost and, in any event, are tenuous and wholly on the consumption side. Nothing has been consolidated, and little has been achieved on the production side which is where the real benefits reside and where the far more difficult challenges lie. To address that enormous challenge is hardly a question of resurrecting idle slogans about "balancing people's lives", or of "private-sector–led, government-facilitated development" or any such cliché. A far more profound understanding of the requirements of the market, especially of the global market, and of the severe weaknesses in our human resource and production systems is called for, which is where the research comes in.

Given the reality of neoliberal globalization, Jamaica had no choice but to deflate its economy over the last ten years. Now that that painful experience has been completed, serious challenges lie ahead. The fact is that the political leadership to achieve our economic and social goals – in the current state of our two-party system – does not exist, although it could emerge. This depends on the degree to which both major political parties can subordinate the lumpen and renew the Jamaican political process on a less tribalistic basis.

Nor does the research knowledge currently exist on which to base sound public policy, although this too could emerge. If this chapter establishes one point, it is that the entire basis of our institutions (including the political parties, the state apparatus and the educational system) is in need of a comprehensive makeover and a fundamental reform. We should not deceive ourselves into imagining that the current reshuffling of parties and personalities constitutes such a renewal. Renewal is hardly the relatively simple matter of replacing this leader with that. Renewal is actually in the hands of civil society and civil society only. It cannot be achieved without the stable groups in civil society stepping out of the shadows of privacy into the full glare of political life. It requires the re-insertion of these stable groups into an active role in the political arena. Only these groups and their representatives can themselves bring this about by means of their own autonomous, independent civic activity.

In principle, it is not too difficult to see how this could be achieved, if one takes a leaf out of our political past. In the 1930s, before political parties and trade unions were formed, various citizens' associations, voluntary groups and artistic movements proliferated in civil society. It was these groups that provided the inspiration, the analysis, the organization and the leadership which established our formative political institutions. A process of a broadly similar nature, adapted of course to the very different global and domestic conditions of the present, is needed and, indeed, to some extent, is already underway. With some determination, clear-headedness and luck, we may actually be able to emancipate ourselves from the unbearable mental slavery of talk-show tyranny and begin to make some progress on our real problems. By pursuing this course, the challenge to which Barry Chevannes has devoted his entire life – the advancement of the well-being of the mass of the Jamaican people – can be met.

References

Anderson, Patricia. 2001. Poverty in Jamaica: Social target or social crisis. *Souls: A Critical Journal of Black Politics, Culture, and Society* 3, no. 4: 39–55.

Anderson, Patricia, and Michael Witter. 1994. Crisis, adjustment and social change: A case study of Jamaica. In *Consequences of structural adjustment: A review of the Jamaican experience*, ed. Elsie Le Franc, 1–55. Kingston: Canoe Press.

Commonwealth Secretariat. 2002. *Master plan for sustainable tourism development, Jamaica*. London: Commonwealth Secretariat.

Handa, Sudhanshu. 2004. Poverty paradox: Social-sector strategy. In *Revitalizing the Jamaican economy: Policies for sustained growth*, 237–92. Washington DC: Inter-American Development Bank.

Hirsch, Alan. 2005. *Season of hope*. Scottsville, South Africa and Ottawa: University of KwaZulu-Natal Press and IDRC.

Robotham, Don. 1998. Transnationalism in the Caribbean: Formal and informal. *American Ethnologist* 25, no. 3: 307–21.

Satchell, Veront M. 1990. *From plots to plantations: Land transactions in Jamaica, 1866–1900*. Kingston: Institute of Social and Economic Research.

An Autobiographical Note

BARRY CHEVANNES

> We enter this world naked, alone
> Naked, alone we must go
> But what we do in between,
> What fruits we bear –
> We bear with help from the Crew
> – *Barry Chevannes, "The Crew"*

I came to anthropology quite by accident. In training at the time as a Jesuit, I prepared myself with a master's degree in Classics from Boston College to return to Jamaica to teach Latin. I had been in love with Latin since high school, had spent my last summer at the seminary in the Berkshire mountains of New England reading all of Virgil – the *Aeneid, Georgics* and *Bucolics* – and written my thesis on the Roman poet Catullus. But things were a-changing – Martin Luther King had come to Boston; Bob Dylan, Joan Baez and Pete Seeger were singing; Nina Simone had visited the Tanglewood music festival; John XXIII had thrown the windows of a musty church open and Latin America was being set on fire with the theory and practice of liberation theology. So even before returning to my homeland in 1966, I knew Latin was doomed. But if not Latin, what? I had no clue. I knew no other love.

Two things, however, had happened. With the civil rights movement in full flow and me drawn into it, a Jesuit more advanced than I in the long training, who had taken a master's in anthropology, handed me a copy of a book that I should read – Melville Herskovits's *Myth of the Negro Past*. No other piece of literature, scientific or fictional, meant more to me. Herskovits's *Myth* made me into a new man. It gave me a peace of mind and a confidence in being black that I never knew was possible in a white, racialized world, and it opened up my mind and my heart to something called *culture*. "We have a culture!" I felt like shouting out and I took delight in being the only one around who could balance a load on his head, a skill every peasant boy and girl in my native Jamaica learned as a matter of course.

But I was still the Latin scholar, reading Tacitus, Seneca, Ovid, Plautus. With the winds of change sweeping through the church, the entire Society of Jesus seemed to me infected with the idea of "relevance". So one day when my classmate Doug McDonald told me he was going to study sociology, a feeling of panic suddenly overcame me. It had never bothered me before that I was the only member of my class taking a master's in Latin, but now it did. Sociology seemed just the right thing – it had something to do with society, right? And so, following a year of teaching Latin at the newly established Campion College in Kingston, our dean of studies encouraged me to enrol at the University of the West Indies. Sociology was a mix of the discipline as then taught in Britain and social anthropology. I read Parsons and C. Wright Mills, but under the tutelage of the late Robin MacKenzie, who had studied under Radcliffe-Brown, I also read Malinowski, Lévi-Strauss and Durkheim. Durkheim, as one of the celebrated founding fathers of both sociology and anthropology, was in the late 1960s the most frequently heard name in the department. His *Rules of the Sociological Method* and *Suicide* were as fascinating as his *Elementary Forms of Religious Life*.

Meanwhile, I was undergoing a personal two-dimensional crisis that had begun during my years in the seminary. The more I understood the civil rights movement, the more disturbed I became at the distance of the church in general and of the Society of Jesus in particular, from what clearly was the most important social issue of the day. Except in the case of Father Robert Drinan, the Boston College Law School head, who went on to serve as a member of the United States Congress and a Father Kenealy, who once had to disguise himself in order to escape being lynched in the South, the civil rights issue was a distant and alien struggle among New England Jesuits. Nationally, the Jesuit brothers Daniel and Philip Berrigan were the only Catholic voices creating a necessary disturbance in the immoral social order – no bishop, no archbishop, no cardinal, no leader of the church. The indifference was changing fast, but that was how it seemed to me. I returned home in 1966 to find a similar indifference. There was Campion College, where children of the rich went, and across the street Sts Peter and Paul where their parents went, and next door to the church was Chambers Lane, a limestone bluff on which lived a community of poor Jamaicans. Not one priest from Sts Peter and Paul or Campion had ever set foot there. Shockingly, the church erected a wall to shut out Chambers Lane. We were outraged, Jim Schecher and I. Jim had just completed his fifteen years of training as a Jesuit priest. Together we started an outreach programme in Chambers Lane.

This disappointment with the church was, however, secondary to my unsustainable position as a celibate. I had been so committed to the priestly vocation that I was willing, as a young idealist, to remain celibate. The scrupulous observances of religious life – modesty of eyes and touch, purity of thought, for example – worked for a time, but increasingly, with every passing year, the vow of celibacy was becoming an impossible imposition. When, during my first year at the University of the West Indies, I made the decision to leave the society, it all seemed so logical and simple that I was gripped with a new concern: how could I not have seen the futility of celibacy? What is the source of the power of religion that it could have blinded me for all of nine years? Elevating this personal problematic into a broader intellectual challenge, I resolved to make religion the focus of my master's thesis. And what better group to research than the Rastafari, who had been creating such a stir throughout the 1960s?

I spent the whole summer of 1969 among the Claudius Henry group of Rastas in Clarendon, observing their ceremonies and interviewing the membership, including the leader himself, and proudly reported to my supervisor, Robin MacKenzie, what I had done. He listened keenly and taking a big gulp, as was his wont before speaking, told me that what I had done was fine, but now I should go find and study another group. My research funds exhausted, I had little choice but to confine myself to Kingston, where I soon found a Revival group in the Waterhouse area, and spent the next several months among them, uncertain of what I would find or how I would put everything together. Thus was my introduction into ethnography and the comparative method of social anthropology. The experience was most rewarding. It may not have done much to assuage my intellectual concern, but by bringing me into intense and direct contact with black Jamaicans and the religions they created, it imbued me with respect for their cultural creativity and made me their partisan. It forced me to think. No two religions could appear more different from each other than Revival and Rasta, yet by probing the historical sequencing, I was able to come up with the original thesis that Revival was a dying religion that had passed the baton to Rasta and Pentecostalism. That I was later to revise this position as a result of being challenged by one of my own students did not matter.[1] What mattered was I had found my *métier* – anthropology.

My dream was to study under Sir E.E. Evans-Pritchard, whose BBC lectures and work among the Nuer somehow made me feel that I had found my mentor. But not knowing how I would pay my way through Oxford, I applied instead for a Commonwealth Scholarship to enter the University of East Africa, whose Makerere campus had a social anthropology programme. I did not get it, but I met Vera Rubin and Lambros Comitas. The founder and director of the Research Institute for the Study of Man, Vera's was a name all students of the Caribbean were familiar with. Lambros, a great friend and admirer of M.G. Smith, was chair of the applied anthropology programme in Teachers' College at Columbia University. I was recommended to join their research team studying the long-term effects of chronic ganja use, my task being to assist in locating thirty chronic ganja smokers, find controls for them, administer life history interviews to all sixty and convince each of them to spend a week at the University Hospital undergoing tests (see Rubin and Comitas 1975). I was well into the research when, on one of his visits, Lambros in his usual, casual way, suggested that I join him at Columbia. It was as simple as that. Assisted by a generous fellowship from the Research Institute for the Study of Man, I spent two years there in an intensely intellectual atmosphere, in daily encounters with scholars and intellectuals like Marvin Harris, Conrad Arensberg, Robert Murphy, Chuck Harrington, Joan Vincent and George Bond.

I enjoyed my years at Columbia immensely, supported by my wife and our two very young daughters. Looking back, I might have profited from spending more time, but I was anxious to return home and contribute to the deepening of our understanding of the Jamaican people. The University of the West Indies found me anthropology, Columbia certified me.

The usual model of success is of a man who, by dint of hard work and ingenuity, achieves his goal – a self-made man. Not me. I can make no such claim. What I became and the varied contributions I have made to Caribbean anthropology have been the results of encounters, mostly unplanned, and accidents. So, I

> Give thanks to the tens who've touched and loved,
> Give thanks to the hundreds who've cared
> Give thanks to the thousands who've passed my way –
> All have made my day,
> All have made my day.
> *Barry Chevannes, "The Crew"*

Note

1. Revival was not dying but transforming itself. See my paper with Jean Besson (1996).

References

Besson, Jean, and Barry Chevannes. 1996. The continuity-creativity debate: The case of Revival. *New West Indian Guide* 70, nos. 3 and 4: 209–28.

Rubin, V., and L. Comitas. 1975. *Ganja in Jamaica*. The Hague: Mouton.

Contributors

HORACE LEVY is Research Fellow in the Centre for Public Safety and Justice at the University of the West Indies, Mona, Jamaica. He has published on community violence and compiled *They Cry "Respect": Urban Violence and Poverty in Jamaica*.

DIANE AUSTIN-BROOS is Professor Emeritus of Anthropology, University of Sydney. She has published articles and books on Jamaica, including *Urban Life in Kingston, Jamaica*, and on Pentecostalism, *Jamaica Genesis: Religion and the Politics of Moral Order*. Her research in Australia includes *Arrernte Present, Arrernte Past: Invasion, Violence and Imagination in Indigenous Central Australia*.

JEAN BESSON is Reader in Anthropology at Goldsmiths College, University of London. In addition to several articles, she is author of *Martha Brae's Two Histories: European Expansion and Caribbean Culture-building in Jamaica* and co-editor of *Caribbean Narratives of Belonging* and *Caribbean Land and Development Revisited*.

BÉATRICE BOUFOY-BASTICK lectures in French at the University of the West Indies, St Augustine, Trinidad. She has wide cross-cultural experience and is the author of numerous publications in the area of language and culture. Her research has led to the development of culturometrics, a new field in culture research.

BARRY CHEVANNES is Professor of Social Anthropology, former Head of the Department of Sociology, Social Work and Psychology, and former Dean of the Faculty of Social Sciences at the University of the West Indies, Mona, Jamaica. His many publications include *Rastafari: Roots and Ideology* and *Learning to Be a Man: Culture, Socialization and Gender Identity in Five Caribbean Communities*.

CHRISTINE CHIVALLON is an anthropologist and geographer, employed by the National Center of Scientific Research in France. She is the author of *La diaspora noire des Amériques, expériences et théories à partir de la Caraïbe*.

J. PETER FIGUEROA is Chief, Epidemiology and AIDS, Ministry of Health, Jamaica; Director of the National HIV/STI Control Programme in Jamaica; and Honorary Professor, University of the West Indies, Mona, Jamaica. He is the author of numerous papers and co-editor of three books.

KIM JOHNSON is Senior Research Fellow at the University of Trinidad and Tobago. He is the author of *The Fragrance of Gold: Trinidad in the Age of Discovery*; *Renegades*; *Descendants of the Dragon*; *If Yuh Iron Good You Is King* and *The Soul in Iron*.

HERBIE MILLER is Director/Curator Designate of Jamaica's National Music Museum. The curator of exhibitions with musical and social themes, he is also the author of several articles including *Brown Girl in the Ring: Margarita and Mulungu* and *Syncopating Rhythm: Jazz and Caribbean Culture*. His three-decade involvement with the music industry informs his insider perspective on Jamaican popular culture.

JAHLANI NIAAH is a researcher in the Office of the Deputy Principal, and coordinator of the Rastafari Studies Archive and Programme in the Institute of Caribbean Studies, University of the West Indies, Mona, Jamaica.

SONJAH STANLEY NIAAH is Lecturer in Cultural Studies, University of the West Indies, Mona, Jamaica. She is the author of numerous articles on Jamaican popular culture and the forthcoming book *One Dancehall: Performance Geographies from Slave Ship to Ghetto*. She is associate editor of *Wadabagei* and serves on the editorial board of *Cultural Studies*.

ANNIE PAUL is Publications Officer, Sir Arthur Lewis Institute of Social and Economic Studies, University of the West Indies, Mona, Jamaica. She is a writer and critic, currently working on her book *Suitable Subjects: Visual Art and Popular Culture in Postcolonial Jamaica*, and associate editor of *Small Axe*.

ANNA KASAFI PERKINS lectures at St Michael's Theological College, an affiliate of the University of the West Indies. She has published articles in her area of research on justice and equality.

KHITANYA PETGRAVE is a doctoral candidate in Modern History at the University of Oxford. Her main research interests involve questions of culture and identity construction in the British West Indies during the period of political decolonisation.

DON ROBOTHAM is Professor of Anthropology, the Graduate Center, City University of New York. He has written extensively on issues of race and class in the Caribbean, and his most recent book is *Culture, Society and Economy: Bringing Production Back In*.

VERONT M. SATCHELL is Senior Lecturer in the Department of History, University of the West Indies, Mona, Jamaica. He is the author of *From Plots to Plantations: Land Transactions in Jamaica 1866–1900* as well as numerous scholarly articles.